LET US PRAY

Studies for the
Prayer Meeting

FRANCIS LYALL

For Heather, my strength and support through these many years.

ISBN 978-1-78222-920-9

Book design, layout and production management by Into Print
www.intoprint.net, +44 (0)1604 832140

Cover design: Heather Lyall

CONTENTS

Preface

The Gilcomston congregation in Aberdeen, Scotland, has existed in one form or another for over two hundred and fifty years.[1] With the exception of the period c. 1930 to 1944, it has held a regular meeting for prayer, which, since the time of the ministry of William Still (1945–1997), has been held on Saturday evenings. Each meeting begins with a short study by a member of the congregation of a passage from the Bible, and for many years now we have been progressing successively through the Psalms. How many iterations there have been, *nescio*. This book collects the contributions I have stored in my computer. I begin with Acts. 4: 23–31 because that account demonstrates the power of prayer.

Each psalm is usually first read out loud. Psalms were composed to be read, to be read to an audience, or to be sung. In church services we are often instructed to 'hear the word of the Lord', but in private mostly we just read the text silently. 'Hearing' can make a difference, particularly if the delivery is done well.

These are my texts as written. Written as scripts they were delivered orally more or less as is. Occasionally I did depart a little from the text, but that has not been taken into account in these pages. Inflection, pace, pause and gesture are needed to put a script across. The texts are not articles, essays or academic disquisitions. They have not been revised to be read as successive chapters, and may be read in any order. There is occasional repetition, and, thanks to the computer, some 'cut and paste'. However, as the dating shows, individually they were spread over many years. Only I have been present at the delivery of all of them. Six psalms have been treated twice, and I have chosen included both versions. Make what you wish of that.

Finally, as I have written elsewhere: 'remember Baruch' (Jeremiah 45).

Francis Lyall, June 2022.

---

1   F. Lyall, *Gilcomston: An Aberdeen Congregation*, (Paragon Publishing, 2020).

Acts 4: 23–31/2

I like Luke. He was a physician – a medical doctor (Col. 4: 14). Probably he was a Gentile, not a Jew, for Paul names him separate from the Jewish colleagues in the greetings list in Col. 4: 10–14. One tradition is that Luke hailed from Antioch, which allows us to speculate that Luke, a Gentile, may have been one of the first to be called Christians (Acts 11: 26). There were Gentiles in the church there. Nicolas, a Gentile convert from Antioch, was one of the first seven deacons (Acts 6: 5). How had the gospel got there? After the death of Stephen there was great persecution – amongst others by one Saul (Acts 8: 3). Some had fled to Phoenicia, Cyprus and Antioch and had spoken to the Jews about Jesus. But there was also a great success in Antioch when some of the fugitives began to speak to the Gentiles (Acts 11: 19–21). The church in Jerusalem heard about it and sent Barnabas to report. Barnabas, rejoicing at what he found, went to find Paul in Tarsus, recognising that Paul had the skill to teach these new non-Jewish converts. Indeed Barnabas and Paul were to spend a year teaching the Antiochian church (Acts 11: 26). Ironic, isn't it. Paul teaching a church that he had inadvertently caused to exist. No matter. My point is that perhaps Luke first met Paul when Barnabas brought him there back from Tarsus (Acts 11: 26).

Another tradition, possibly more credible, is that Luke came from Troas, and the famous change in Acts from an objective account of Paul's journeys to the 'we', which appears and disappears in the rest of Acts, shows that that may indeed be where Luke and Paul linked up (Acts 16: 10). But that leaves a question. If they met in Troas, was Luke already a Christian, or was he one of Paul's converts?

But enough of that. Luke was an observer, a historian. He was not around during Jesus' ministry. He found things out and set them down for others to read. He did his homework. He wrote the third of our four gospels, but got his data from others. He was not a participant during the life of Christ. The beginning of his Gospel makes that clear. Luke says he had looked into what others had taught and had 'carefully investigated everything from the beginning' so that Theophilus would know for certain what to believe (Luke 1: 1–4). Indeed that desire to get things right may be why Luke's account of the birth of Jesus is the most complex and detailed that we have. He may have had the data from Mary herself.

Our passage tonight is unlike others we have considered these past few weeks. The others were prayers by a named individual. This one is different. Peter and John have just been released by the Sanhedrin (v. 15). The previous day they had gone to the Temple, and on their way in had healed the cripple. Then within the Temple precinct itself they had preached about Jesus and the resurrection from the dead. About five thousand had believed (Acts 3 and 4: 1–4). As a result they had been arrested and kept in jail overnight (it brings to mind that handy Scots crime, 'breach of the peace'). Next day they were interrogated by the Sanhedrin (v. 15) which, for the purpose, included Annas the High Priest, and Caiaphas, John, Alexander and others of Annas's family. Annas and Caiaphas: remember those names from the 'Trial' of Jesus? (John 18: 12–14. Cf. Matt. 26: 3, 27: 3; Mark 14: 53–65; Luke 22: 66–71). I wonder whether their guts curdled as 'Jesus' came onto their agenda once again.

The Sanhedrin was a very respectable and intellectually able body. Peter and John confounded it by their reply. By what power or on what authority were they doing this healing? (v. 7). Peter replied that though the question was just about the healing of the cripple, the matter of their authority really went beyond that. Their authority was Jesus. It was 'by the name of Jesus Christ of Nazareth, whom you crucified but whom God raised from the dead, that this man stands before you healed. He is the stone you builders rejected, which has become the capstone. Salvation is found in no one else, for there is no other name under heaven given to men by which we must be saved' (Acts 4: 8–10). The healed cripple was standing there – presumably he had been arrested as well. In a sense he was 'best evidence': Luke notes he was over 40, a mature reliable age. Peter's reply and the presence of the cripple discombobulated the Sanhedrin. So it had them removed while they debated. The summary is in vv. 15–7. The miracle could not be denied. The best the high-heid-yins could think of was to tell Peter and John to go away and say nothing more about Jesus (v. 17).

So Peter and John went back to at least some of the five thousand to tell them what had gone on – I imagine a goodly number had been milling about waiting to find out what had happened. So Peter and John report. And then we have a problem. Do Peter and John combine in this marvellous prayer of thanksgiving? Or is this Luke summarising what was prayed by the gathering? That view has some force. The prayer is introduced by the words 'when they heard this', and in v. 29 it looks as though the gathering is indeed praying for Peter and John. But there is a third possibility. Maybe a single individual started to pray, in the terms we have, and the rest joined with him – just as later in this room various will pray and we will join with the prayer. Maybe that individual found the experience so uplifting that years later he remembered it and told Luke. That would explain the precision of Luke's account. Another thing, the pray-er was clearly biblically well-informed, as we should be. He knew his Old Testament and was able to link it with what Peter and John had said. Is that surprising? Something I was reading recently quoted CS Lewis in his *Letters to Malcolm* as saying that 'in prayer God speaks to God'. [Michael Ward's *Planet Narnia* (Oxford: OUP, 2008) at 250]. Now there's a thought.

Whatever. This prayer summarises what Peter and John had been preaching, coupled with a prayer for their continued faithfulness and strength.

Read vv. 24–31: 'When they heard this [the report] they raised their voices together in prayer to God. "Sovereign Lord," they said, "you made the heaven and the earth and the sea, and everything in them. You spoke by the Holy Spirit through the mouth of your servant, our father David: " 'Why do the nations rage and the peoples plot in vain? The kings of the earth take their stand and the rulers gather together against the Lord and against his Anointed One. Indeed Herod and Pontius Pilate met together with the Gentiles and the people of Israel in this city to conspire against your holy servant Jesus, whom you anointed. They did what your power and will had decided beforehand should happen. Now, Lord, consider their threats and enable your servants to speak your word with great boldness. Stretch out your hand to heal and perform miraculous signs and wonders through the name of your holy servant Jesus.' And the place was shaken, v. 31.

God is sovereign, the maker of heaven and earth. That sets things in their right perspective. Our God made the Universe, and yet listens to our prayers. The Holy Spirit has spoken through David foreseeing it all. Why do people plot, taking their stand against the Lord and his Anointed One? The folk in charge and the people in general had conspired against Jesus. Both the rulers and the people had called for his death. But see precisely what is said here. The pray-er, and the group, new converts all it would seem, recognise that the Herod/Pilate conspiracy took place because that was what God had determined would happen. God had decreed that salvation would come through the death of his Son.

It is an astonishing brief summary of truth. But history is to go on. The good news about Jesus was to be spread. The prayer runs on to ask that Peter and John would be strengthened for their task. They at least are to go on to do miracles, signs, wonders. Their authority is Christ. Maybe none of us can do signs and wonders in the physical sense, but through prayer much can be accomplished. Surely we have seen that here. So we are to pray. See what happened as a result of the prayers of Acts 4 (v. 31) and that request for power for Peter and John. After the episode of Ananias and Sapphira, Acts 5: 12–16 tells of miracles, signs and wonders performed by the apostles. So I wonder whether the prayer of Acts 4: 24ff was indeed the voice of one individual, with whom others agreed, and whether he himself remembered his words later to repeat them to Luke. How otherwise do you explain the precision of the prayer we have?

The immediate result of the prayer was that they were all filled with the Holy Spirit and spoke the word of God boldly. And – and this is why I extended the passage to Acts 4: 32 – they were all of one mind. May we speak boldly of Jesus when opportunity is given, and may we all be of one mind.

Now go back to our beginning, Acts 4: 23. The scene is that Peter and John have come from the Sanhedrin back to what Luke calls 'their own people'. That little phrase is important. In the next part of this evening we will praise God. That is good and right. Later we will pray for people and situations. The data is in the Prayer News, or what we ourselves know about, or which people here will mention at an appropriate point. Folk out there write, email and phone to report – telling us about what is going on so we can pray about it. As far as they are concerned **we** are 'their own people'. So our praying is not some ritual – a telling of beads or a sterile listing of names. It is a welling-up of concern, real concern, not so that we feel good because we have gone through a list or recited traditional phrases. We take up our voices just as did the group that heard from Peter and John. We pray for our own people that God will strengthen them, and give them power to speak the word with great boldness, and maybe even to do wonders.

Let us pray.

Gilcomston Prayer Meeting, 11 September 2010.

Psalm 2

It has been a long time since I was at this end of the Hall for a Prayer Meeting. Indeed, there were long stretches when I was not here at all. As you know my back had to be unzipped to fix an acute neural problem. So, first, before launching into the Psalm, I want to say thank you to those who prayed for me during the sciatic period, and for the operation and subsequent recuperation.

But what a psalm to come back to! With apologies to those for whom the name means nothing, I feel like Leonard Sachs of the 'Good Old Days'. I wish I had on a gaudy waistcoat and had huge purple handkerchief to wave! Psalm 2 is a coruscating cornucopia, a panorama of surpassing richness, a plethora of astonishing insights, a deluge of delicacies. At the same time it is a succinct survey of history. Like a Faberge creation, it unfolds beauty by the juxta-position of gems.

What triggered these magnificent verses? Is there any point in asking the question? Should we not simply dive into it, and see Christ and his Kingdom, as any Christian would see even on a superficial skim? Well, as to that, a function of our brief study of a biblical passage at the start of our meeting is to encourage us to prayer. Obviously, these glimpses of Almighty God and his Christ tempts most of us immediately to praise, but to real praise or to well-worn syllables?? Let me digress for a little on the trigger track.

Perhaps this Psalm, probably the work of David, was produced as he sat quietly in the sun, munching a date or two, and brooding, mulling over the glory of God, and as he did so, God led him mistily to see through the centuries to the coming of David's greater Son, and to his Kingdom. There is something to be learned here. Not all of us have spent any time quietly this week. Maybe we should have. But my point is that some scholars see triggers for this Psalm in David's career, and that can help those of us who are sore pressed at work, with infirmity, with stress, and who are struggling and apt to forget who is in charge.

Two possible triggers for this Psalm lie in 2 Samuel. Note that in v. 6 David says that the Lord terrifies his opponents saying 'I have installed my

King on Zion, my holy hill'. In 2 Sam. 10: 6-19 there is the story of how the Ammonites with Aramaean mercenaries came up against David for reasons we need not go into. Joab, David's Commander in Chief, defeated them and David reigned on. But a more satisfactory possible trigger is in 2 Sam. 5: 17-25. As soon as the Philistines heard that David had been made king, they came with a strong army against him. There were two battles. In both David sought the counsel of the Lord, and relied on it —the second battle being the occasion when he was told to circle round the Philistine army and wait for the sound of the wind in the balsam trees. In both battles David defeated the Philistines.

So what? Why do that detour into triggers for a magnificent Psalm? Well, if either of these occasions did prompt this Psalm, it makes the point that when we are hard pressed or in trouble, we should seek the Lord and do as he shows us. David did not always go to the Lord as swiftly as he should. But when he did, see what happened. It may well have been out of those experiences that he forged Psalm 2. We need to seek the Lord early, and mull over what he does with us – and perhaps write our own Psalm 2. Yes, seek the Lord – that is a truism of our faith. But do we do it in practice – or do we just say we do, so as to say the right thing when a solicitous friend asks? Is it part of our culture, or is it part of our essential being? We all need training here – I certainly do. Was my back going to get better, or was it to continue to be a matter of 50 yards and then sit down? We need to consider what God has done with us. That will lead us to praise, maybe not immediately, but it will.

Now, look at the Psalm. There are, of course, other Psalms where David and others call on God to repel attacks on them, but this one stands out in its clear grasp of the cosmic dimension of the battle between good and evil. It is like one of those Italian church frescoes where at the bottom you see what is going on earth, and above you see what is going on in heaven, as God on his throne surveys all.

'The One enthroned in heaven' (v. 4) is the pivot round which the whole Psalm turns. This is not some doddery old fogey, barely in touch with what is going on – the kindly old man with a beard, of so many caricatures. This is not the God of Peanuts' Lucy van Pelt, a God who will forgive anything, because 'it's his job to forgive'. This is the Lord God who laughs (v. 4) at those who oppose him. He scoffs (v. 4b). So there is a real question at the start of the Psalm. Why _do_ the nations conspire and the peoples plot in vain

(v. 1)? Some of the commentators see this as a rhetorical question – one just to start the Psalm off, without requiring or expecting an answer. But _why do_ the nations conspire and peoples plot? It's hopeless, but the thing is they do not realise it: they do not accept it. The Devil still hopes to win. But 'conspire' and 'plot' are perhaps too anodyne a way of putting it. To revert to the AV: 'Why do the heathen rage and the peoples imagine a vain thing'. Have you noticed how the most urbane can turn nasty when matters religious come up? Contempt and anger suddenly surface. These last few months it has been intriguing to see in _The Times_, how commentators who are steady and balanced on matters political, froth at the mouth when it is suggested that there is such a thing as evil or sin. That is what lies behind these first verses of our Psalm. The kings and rulers of v. 2 get together against the Lord and his Anointed One, and '"Let us break their chains", they say, "and throw off their tethers"' (v. 3). Throw off the rule of the Holy God – that is the underlying intent of so much of our culture.

The response of the One enthroned in heaven is to laugh and scoff, or 'have them in derision' as the AV has it (v. 4). I can find those words troubling. If God is God, surely it is not right for him to scoff at those who in fact hopelessly have no chance. How cruel! And God rebukes them in his anger and terrifies them in his wrath (v. 5), when, as he is God, they have no option? Is this the sadistic God, the one CS Lewis wrote of in _A Grief Observed_? My way out is to say that here there is an outcrop of theological geology with a mixed conglomerate showing. Here free will and predestination collide, and I do but note it. To skip through to Revelation, we know that even in the face of the Last Things those who oppose God will not turn (Rev. 9: 20-21; Rev. 16: 1-11). They will hide from the wrath of him who sits on the throne, and from the wrath of the Lamb (Rev. 6: 16). That is their free will, operating in a creation, which is controlled by the predestination of God. The integration of these concepts, Free Will and Predestination, is something we may know more of hereafter – in the hereafter. Here, I see it, and pass on to the main course in the feast of this Psalm.

See how the Lord terrifies those who rise against him: he says, 'I have installed my King on Zion, my holy hill' (v. 6). David doubtless saw some application of that to himself. If the triggers are right, he saw that since his army had been successful, he, as king in Jerusalem, had been set there by God. But then he goes beyond himself. His reign is but a pale shadow of the reign of the Son of God to come. And we see the phrases of this Psalm echoing down through the ages, into the New Testament and beyond. Paul is invited to speak in the synagogue in Psidian Antioch – just below about the middle of our Turkey. He summarises the history of the Jews (Acts. 13: 16ff), and gets to the point in v. 32. 'We tell you the good news: What God promised our fathers he has fulfilled for us, their children, by raising Jesus. As it is written in the second Psalm: "You are my Son; today I have become your Father"', thus quoting the decree of the Lord that David recounts in our v. 7b 'You are my Son, this day I have become your Father – this day have I begotten thee', as the more robust AV has it. (Acts 13: 33). This fulfilment is the whole point of history.

Hebrews uses the verse twice. In Heb. 1: 5 the writer disposes of the suggestion that Christ was an angel: 'To which of the angels did God ever say "You are my Son, this day I have become your Father"'. And in Heb. 5: 6 the writer uses the verse to show that Jesus was made our High Priest, and did not take that office upon himself.

But note something else here. Paul's use of v. 7b of our Psalm is to a Jewish audience, the synagogue in Psidian Antioch, and it is also cited to the recipients of the Epistle to the Hebrews. To some extent that makes sense, doesn't it? Only a Jewish audience would cotton on to the quotation. I apologised already for referring to Leonard Sachs. You don't quote something that does not connect with your audience – not if you are wise.

But to us non-Jews, and with the whole Bible to help us, the quotation also makes sense. For here we can move on through the rest of the Psalm. David indicates that the King, installed by the One that sits in heaven, will have the nations as his inheritance and possess the ends of the earth, even to the edge of Europe, and beyond. He can rule with an iron sceptre, or dash in pieces like pottery. Therefore, says the Psalmist, those of v. 1 who conspire and plot should think again, and be wise and be warned (v. 10). Rather than rebel and seek to cast off his 'chains and fetters' they should 'Serve the Lord with fear and rejoice with trembling; and kiss the Son, lest he be angry' and they be destroyed as his anger flares (vv. 11-12).

But there is a better way. It is in the last sentence of v. 12. Fear and trembling may be real enough; kisses to avoid flaring wrath may be insincere. But to take refuge in this King is far better. To take refuge is to trust, and that is the basis of a relationship that will last forever. I think David knew that.

So I still have this picture of him, sitting under an awning in the sun, with a handful of dates, musing on what the Lord has done for him, and through that seeing, hazily but for real, the coming Saviour, his Saviour, and as a result this poem coming together in his mind. Let us do the same. Let us pray.

Gilcomston Prayer Meeting, 17 July 2004.

Psalm 3

Have you come across the concept of the dehydrated Psalm? If so, please let me know. But in a way I hope you have not, because it may be a contribution to biblical scholarship that came to me when I was thinking about tonight. It's the matter of the rubric to the Psalm, of course. 'A Psalm of David. When he fled from his son, Absalom'. Drop that into a glass of water and stand back.

This is the first Psalm that has a title. It gives us the context. We are in 2 Sam. 13–19. Absalom was the third son of David. His mother, Maacah, was the daughter of Talmai, King of Geshur (2 Sam. 3: 3: cf. Josh. 12: 5 and 13: 2). The Geshurites were one of the original inhabitants of the Land, whom the Israelites did not drive out (Josh 13: 13). Absalom means either 'Father is Peace' or 'Leader of Peace' – rather ironic given his history. He is erratic. He seems to have been a brooder. His sister Tamar was raped by his brother Amnon (2 Sam. 13: 1–19), who was David's oldest son (2 Sam. 3: 2). He gave her refuge. Two years later in revenge he arranged Amnon's assassination, but maybe also to promote himself in the succession stakes. He fled to Geshur – where his maternal grandfather was still in charge (2 Sam. 13: 37). Absalom stayed three years in Geshur, though maybe David might have allowed him back sooner (2 Sam. 13: 35). Eventually Joab arranged for his return, but by then David would not receive him (2 Sam. 14: 24). Absalom then remained two years in Jerusalem. During that time he fathered three sons (who may not have lived long) and a daughter (2 Sam. 14: 17). He was handsome (2 Sam. 14: 25–6), and conceited. He erected a pillar to himself because he said he had no son (2 Sam. 18: 18). He drove about in a chariot with fifty men to run ahead of him – the equivalent today of police outriders (2 Sam. 15: 1). Not unaffected by his father's refusal to see him for years, he started to foment dissatisfaction. He would meet those who came to Jerusalem seeking justice, ask them about their dispute, told them they had a good case, and then regretted that the King had no time to arrange to have cases heard, whereas he – well, he would do things differently (2 Sam. 15: 5). The old man up the hill was past it – and to an extent David was – or maybe spending too much time with his concubines (2 Sam. 16: 21–2) – for David did not see what was coming. In short Absalom 'stole the hearts of the men of Israel' (2 Sam. 15: 6). The next step was actual rebellion, and David had to flee. The rebellion did not succeed – we won't distract ourselves by going into that detail – the machinations as well as the struggle. Suffice it to say his army defeated, Absalom was killed. David returned to Jerusalem.

Absalom's death struck David deeply (2 Sam. 18: 33), but we are thinking of days before that. The context of this Psalm is David in flight from his likely heir – for Absalom was by now David's eldest surviving son.

The Psalm has four elements – each of two verses. In the first section, David acknowledges that many are against him. This is not a matter of a dip in the Opinion Polls. This is The People against David. Amongst them were many who had been his supporters. They included Ahithophel, formerly a trusted adviser – though given our knowledge, Ahithophel was a practitioner of *real politique* rather than of principled government (2 Sam. 15: 31; cf. 2 Sam. 16: 15 – 17:23). When David flees (2 Sam. 16: 16–18) it is mostly non-Israelites, Kerethites, Pelethites and Gittites that go with him. Where were all the supporters of yester-year? David had lost them. A messenger reports 'The hearts of the Israelites are with Absalom' (2 Sam. 15: 13).

Note the ambiguity of our v. 2. Are the people saying that God *cannot* help David? No. They are saying that God *will not* deliver him. What could spark off that opinion? Well, we know of David's chequered life – Uriah the Hittite and all that (2 Sam. 11: 1–16). Remember Shimei's curses as David went down from Jerusalem (2 Sam. 16: 5–13). Shimei says David deserves all he is getting – David is a man of blood, and God has torn the kingdom from him. David even thinks it possible that Shimei is right, which is why he stops Abishai from going over to cut Shimei's head off for cursing the Lord's anointed (2 Sam. 16: 10–12).

In all this David turns, as so often, to his God. But see what the Psalm says. Here we have David in flight from a son, who, it seems, would have killed him (2 Sam. 16: 11) – a son who, remember, had already killed his own brother. Earlier, during the flight itself, David had said to leave Shimei alone, in the hope that God would see David's distress and repay him with good for the cursing he was getting (2 Sam. 16: 12). 'Help me, Lord. I am in deep trouble' is the sort of phrase we might expect in our Psalms. You get it in other Psalms. What we get here is different. Many foes have risen against David – vv. 1–2 – 'But you are a shield around me, O Lord, my Glorious One, who lifts up my head. To the Lord I cry aloud, and he answers me from his holy hill' (vv. 3 – 4). No appeals for help here – instead a blazing statement of confidence – 'you are a shield around me' – coupled with an assurance of answer received. Is this post hoc exhilaration? No. I think it is pure reportage. This is how David felt at the time.

And so? Well, when David and his entourage got to their destination they were exhausted (2 Sam. 16: 14). On the way David had been active. He arranged for Hushai, for example, to go back to Jerusalem to thwart the advice Ahithophel might give Absalom. You might think David's head would be spinning. But no. We have vv. 5–6. 'I lie down and sleep; I wake again because the Lord sustains me. I will not fear the tens of thousands drawn up against me on every side.' There is a time to wrestle in prayer like Jacob (Gen. 28: 10–22). There is also a time to trust. Ah: the ability to turn things over to God, and switch off. It's difficult enough for us in modern Aberdeen. How many don't get full, proper sleep because the mind whirrs on? I was Dean of Law twice and saw many problems. But we're not organising a retreat from a murderous son and faithless friends. David trusts his Lord.

What about the last two verses? When were they written? Well, when was the poem written? 'Arise, O Lord! Deliver me, O my God' – that looks like things are still going on. Yet immediately v. 7b indicates that God has been at work. 'For you have struck all my enemies on the jaw; you have broken the teeth of the wicked'. Certainly the end of the Absalom rebellion – and of Ahithophel – fits with that. But I think David had that assurance earlier than that.

How does all that apply to us, here tonight to pray. Well, we should pray in similar vein. With confidence, not in a whining smarmy way trying to flatter God into doing what we ask. We seek him to tell us what to pray for, and then we pray for it with confidence. And there's something else, buried back in v. 4 – which rebuked me. 'To the Lord I cry aloud'. Silent prayer is one thing. Praying aloud makes you think what you are saying. Spurgeon said somewhere – I lift the quote from a website: 'Surely, silent prayers are heard. Yes, but good men often find that, even in secret, they pray better aloud than they do when they utter no vocal sound.'

In that vein, let us pray to this same God that David trusted. Then for the folk we know throughout the world. And in due course for our own. As David tells us in v. 8, the last verse – 'From the Lord comes deliverance. May your blessing be on your people.'

Gilcomston Prayer Meeting, 28 July 2007.

Psalm 4

There are variant translations of this psalm. The KJV is reflected in our Psalter, but for tonight I will go with the NIV, but the NIV of my iPad, which is a bit different from the one we use in church.

A few words across the tops of several psalms – the rubrics – clearly show that they have been composed in reaction to an event. Some, indeed, can be traced to one identifiable happening. Some are clearly devotional. And some are designed to teach. This is one of these last. David sends it to the Director of Music and tells him that it was to be accompanied by a string band. It was probably not for the congregation to sing, at least at that time. More likely it would be sung to or at them. The players and the singers would be some of those David had designated in 1 Chron. 25 to lead the worship of God. In some ways it is curiously like the role of choirs in Episcopal ceremonials. You could imagine it being sung during a church service. Settings by John Rutter, Ralph Vaughan Williams, or Charles Villiers Stanford can be inspiring. As I say, as almost a sermon this psalm was directed at the congregation to teach them. It also targets us tonight.

So, what is this Psalm saying? Verse 1 introduces the matter. Despite what I just said about singers, it may have been intended for a soloist, or for two passing the argument to and fro between them. The first soloist starts by asking God to answer him. Note that he is addressing *his* righteous God. The 'his' is important. Several elements here. First, 'his' implies a choice. There are many gods, but the God he addresses is the one he has chosen. However, second, have I got that that the right way round? You could also think that the choice was *by* 'his' God. But finally, note this is not a grovelling approach by someone uncertain of the reception he is going to get. There is no flattering rehearsal of the glories of God, and the profuse gratitude of an obsequious petitioner. This man knows his God as a friend. A righteous God, yes: but a friend. What is a friend? Someone you are comfortable with. Someone you can speak with without first planning what you are going to say. Centuries later Paul catches that point when he tells the Ephesians that in Christ and through faith in him we can approach God with freedom and confidence (Eph. 3: 12). Just so the psalmist asks God to respond (v. 1a).

Verse 1 goes on to ask for help. 'Give me relief from my distress; have mercy on me and hear my prayer.' What distress? For some David distressed means enemies and they place the writing of this psalm to David's time of troubles with Saul, or perhaps the difficulties with Absalom. But that is not necessary. One rule of statutory interpretation is that you stick to the plain meaning of words and phrases unless there is good and clear reason not to. So look at v. 2: 'How long will you people turn my glory into shame? How long will you love delusions and seek false gods?' David is distressed, both for himself and on behalf of God. His people, those under his charge, who as a godly people would be his glory, are not living as they should. They are shaming David as they go their own way. Their delusions and false gods are not specified, but they don't need to be. Just think of what you can see filling contemporary minds. Think what their goals are, if any. Or think of the way they blank out their minds. Go to v. 6: 'Many, Lord, are asking, "Who will bring us prosperity?"' Have my numbers come up? – Not will my number be up? The inference of v. 7 is that they are looking for grain and wine to abound.

David's distress is over the spiritual condition of his people, their many self-centred concerns. Our distress should be the condition of Aberdeen, not to go any further afield. And David's distress was particularised. It was the condition of his people. It shames him. Yes, he stands a little apart from them in this psalm. In v. 2a he speaks of 'you people'. There is a detachment there, but a necessary detachment. To help someone from a bog you need to stand on firm ground yourself; otherwise you too might be overwhelmed. But see also that it is his particular people that he is worried about. He is not spraying about a woolly concern for the world in general.

David calls on the people to tremble. He calls on them not to sin, to examine themselves and be silent (v. 4). For the man the Lord has set aside as his servant will be heard when he calls on God, as he is doing in this psalm (v. 3). They are to offer the sacrifices of the righteous and trust in the Lord (v. 5). Offering the sacrifices of the righteous has nothing superficial about it. It's not a matter of going through the approved rituals, bringing a lamb to be sacrificed or making some other large donation, and, that done, going back into the old normal rut. They have to trust in the Lord, not just tip their hat to Him. Trusting in the Lord goes through the whole of life. That is where their true prosperity will reside, for then the light of God's face will shine on them. Then, their grain and their wine will abound (v. 7).

So, the prayer of David in v. 1 is for the reformation of his people. Ours should be the same.

We could stop there, but the psalm has one thing more to teach us. David does look forward to the people being reconciled to God. He does think they could see grain and new wine abounding, whatever that may mean for each particular individual (v. 7). But, however that may turn out, David turns the whole over to God. Yes, he remains distressed as per v. 1, but he is going to sleep easy. On my iPad NIV reading, if the people do as he has instructed, prosperity will come, the grain and the new wine will appear, and David will rejoice. But I was intrigued to note that the KJV and the church NIV version of v. 7 take things differently. By them, with the Lord's gladness in his heart, David is happier with his God than the people ever were when they were prosperous, wallowing in grain and wine.

No matter, David himself just has to wait, and not worry. David has done what he has to do. Now it is over to God. David will remain distressed until reformation comes, but he will not fret.

David is detached. Ultimately what happens does not rest on his shoulders. His words, sung to a congregation gathered to worship, instruct them. That was his purpose in this psalm. If they did not pay attention, if they did not change their ways, he would not be to blame for the consequences. He would not have failed to do his duty. He would not be at fault. He had met his duty of care for them, to use the modern jargon. It is up to them whether they pay heed. Verse 8: David can sleep easy. His Lord makes him dwell in safety. There's a lesson there for us as well.

Gilcomston Prayer Meeting, 13 July 2019.

Psalm 8

This is an important Psalm. The Writer to the Hebrews quotes from it (Heb. 2: 6–8). It is a simple psalm. It is a profound psalm. It is a theological analogue of $E = MC^2$ —energy is equivalent to mass multiplied by the square of the speed of light.

This psalm cleanses. When you are feeling care-worn, when you could do with a good shower to take away the dusty grubbiness of the day, this psalm does the job. But see how it does it. It doesn't fuss over you. It doesn't pat your hand. It doesn't comfort. It doesn't reassure. You are not the focus. God is. God, and what he thinks of Man. That perspective cleanses and heals. But rather than rushing into comment I want us first to think about its making. Sometimes knowing what triggered a psalm helps to understand it. We have seen that often in these Saturday meetings. Tonight we have no such clues. So I have invented a possible background for the psalm. I hope that that will help us understand its message. I could be wrong, but let's think about how this psalm could have been conceived.

*

Close your eyes and imagine. We travel in time and space. Time? Three thousand years back will do. Space? We are in Jerusalem. It's the gloaming. Dusk is on us. It's uncomfortably warm. To get some air you come up onto your flat roof, carrying a candle to light your way up. Put it down on that table, that one over there in the corner. Blow it out. There is a couch over there, to the right. Lie down. Look up, and let your mind loose. It has been a troubling day, maybe a hard week, maybe longer. Your mind drifts, and is caught by God.

Listen. There's kids still playing in the street down below. Screams of excitement drift upwards. Unintelligible, but the bairns are enjoying themselves. Now a mother is calling her brood in. It's bedtime. They're straggling off, complaining.

Night comes swiftly here. Now it's quite dark – no street lights back then. No Moon tonight. Above are the stars. See Sirius, sparkling. To the right and up a bit, the blue-white one is Rigel. Up to its left is the reddish Betelgeuse.

Between them those three are Orion's belt. Is that over there Saturn, or Jupiter? Watch the Milky Way wheel slowly westwards.

Isn't God wonderful! Keeping all that going.

Where do we fit in?

You burp slightly. That meal tonight was good. Lovely bit of lamb. And there's enough left for tomorrow. Drowsiness is creeping up. Fight it.

Where were we? Oh yes. Stars. Wonderful stars. There's other wonderful things as well. There's the Earth itself.

That lamb was from one of your flocks. Maybe goat later in the week? Or some fish? They say the fishing's been good down in Galilee.

You drift off. The mind's still free-wheeling. But you are not needed. Sleep now. God is looking after it all. Where do we fit in? Stars, flocks, herds. Do you snore?

The dawn chorus begins. Wake now. You've had a good sleep.

Your mind retrieves last night's musings. And, as so often happens, a poem begins to form. You work at it.

You work at it, and tonight we have it here in Gilcomston.

*

We have it. So let's look at it.

Note first the book-ends. 'Lord, our Lord, how majestic is thy name in all the earth!' The fanfare of v. 1 is repeated in v. 9. We'll get back to that shortly.

Second, I spend no time on v. 2. Calvin and Augustine expatiate on its possible layers. It is enough to remember those kids in the street below. There is a childhood innocence that confounds.

What about those glories of creation? Those stars. We know so much more than Calvin or Augustine, to say nothing of our psalmist. Did you ever wonder whether David thought the earth was flat? Did Augustine think the sun went round the earth? For twenty-five years we have had those marvellous pictures from the Hubble Space Telescope, imaging the infra-red and ultra-violet as well as the light our eyes can see. The Deep Field picture of 1995 was a Hubble scan of a tiny area. Think of the diameter of a tennis-ball seen from 300 feet away – that was the area of the Deep Field. Yet within it Hubble disclosed 3000 galaxies. In 2012 the eXtreme Deep Field Project (XDF) imaged a small part of the Deep Field, and found 5500 more galaxies. Galaxies, 13.5 billion light years away! Galaxies all over the place! We now know we are but in a peripheral bit of our home galaxy, and it is a minor one compared with those we have detected. No longer are we the centre of all. What is Man that thou art mindful of him? (v. 4a)

Go the other way, from the vastness of the Universe to the atomic level. We now know of three classes of fundamental particles – quarks, leptons and bosons. No, I don't understand them either. But it tickles me to know that the quarks come in six types – the scientists call them flavours – up, down, strange, charm, top and bottom. If you want to know more try Wikipedia.

Then there is the creation that we know rather better, the flocks and herds, the seas and all that swim in them. Whales, like Heather and I saw recently in Alaska.

Creation is full of wonders. Do you wonder at it? Piet Hein in one of his Grooks points out: 'We glibly speak of Nature's Laws, but do things have a natural cause? Black earth into yellow crocus is undiluted hocus-pocus.' Daisies and pansies. Orchids and roses. Pines and oaks. Birds. Let Art and Music lubricate your wonder gland. Do not do without artistic rejoicing in creation! So many canvasses do that, Dutch landscapes such as Ruisdael's, Constable's Norfolk, the North American landscapes of Thomas Cole, Albert Bierstadt or F.E. Church. In music think of the various Bachs. They seem to have known as much about creation as Higgs of the boson. What of Mozart? Nearer our own time there's Bruckner, Vaughan Williams, even the bird-song man Olivier Messiaen and his Turangalila Symphony, all rejoicing in creation.

Rejoice in creation. Then see where Man's place is among it all. God has made Man a little lower than the Angels and given him dominion over the works of his hand (vv. 5–6). Look at that statement again, and put it alongside industrial pollution and climate change. Shame on our stewardship of his creation.

But why has God done this, as the psalmist affirms? The fact is God loves creation – he loves creating. And within his creation he loves men. He loves you and me. God cares (v. 4).

That explains those bookends that I dodged round. Yes, the Lord's name is majestic in all the earth (vv. 1 and 9). But there is more to it than that. Our psalmist does not summon his energies to praise a remote deity. He does not address a chunk of wood, or some beautifully carved block of stone like those you can see in the Louvre. His phrasing of vv. 1 and 9 is 'Lord, *our*

Lord'. This is the living God, the Creator-God who cares for us, and who has given us a high position in his creation. So, like David let us pray to the Lord, *our* Lord.

Gilcomston Prayer Meeting, 3 September 2016.

Psalm 13

This is a short psalm. Notwithstanding, I am going to offer two interpretations. Franz Liszt set it for a tenor, choir and orchestra. The agnostic Johannes Brahms set it for a female chorus, organ and strings. I have not come across either. It would be interesting to hear what they made of it.

If you tackle it as free-standing, single, alone, the psalm can read as a plangent complaint, but one that ends with a twist as David affirms faith notwithstanding. What of a context? Is he overstressed? After all being king was a high-powered job in those days. Is he sick? Some Jews recite this psalm at the bedside of an invalid. Maybe it was triggered by some event or other, but we don't know. Is this yet another case of David and his enemies? Is David dodging Saul, or are we in the middle of the Absalom affair? David sees at least one enemy potentially triumphing over him (v. 2b). Unless God does something David will die. An enemy will rejoice in his fall, and brag that he has brought David down (v. 4). And God is silent. The quadruple 'How long's of vv. 1–2 toll like a mourning bell, even a knell bell. They put me in mind of Edvard Munch's *The Scream*. Spurgeon called it the 'Howling Psalm'. God is silent. David is depressed, and his enemies are writing his obituary. Despite it all David still has his faith. That has a message that we can need. He clings on. David is not protesting devotion to that silent god just in the hope that he will respond. He is relying on him. David will trust in God's unfailing love and rejoice in his salvation, for the Lord has been good to him (vv. 5–6). Is 'good to him' not put in question by the previous verses? No. The times when God was good may be in the past, treasured memories. But sometimes, recalling God's previous acts of grace can strengthen the finger-nails.

That's pretty bleak, isn't it? A message almost of desperation. But, if so, what is it doing in Scripture? Is it there to show that even those of the strongest faith can have severe wobbles and hang on notwithstanding? Certainly that is the impression that I get from Calvin. C.S. Lewis' *A Grief Observed* of 1961 is a modern meditation on similar lines. Bleak, but latterly inspiring. Well worth reading. We need to pray for those who are in similar circumstances.

There is another way to look at this psalm. Maybe David is not as self-oriented as it seems. The NIV is vehement in its rendition of the 'how long's. Other versions are more measured, and if you go along those lines David is less anxious. Indeed they make the ending an affirmation of deep-rooted faith, not a twist. Think of its audience, not just its author. Remember it is not just a psalm of David; it is a psalm that David composed and sent to the Director of Music for public consumption. A few lines ago I characterised the four-fold 'how long's as the tolling of a mourning bell. Instead, they may be a tocsin – a warning bell, an alarm call, an urgent summons to confront imminent reality. I got this notion while wallowing in the Proms and thinking about this psalm. A favourite of mine was played, Shostakovitch's Eleventh Symphony, 'The Year 1905'. 'Tocsin' is the title of its last movement. It is a defiance of autocracy. Towards the end, as the orchestra charges onward to its final bars, in that final two minutes, a loud bell sounds, and sounds, and others clang, one semi-tone below the key the orchestra is playing in. Startling, even if you are expecting it. It undercuts the orchestral exuberance. Telling, even if you don't know the history of St Petersburg in 1905, foreshadowing 1917. Perhaps our psalm serves as a warning, undercutting complacency. Maybe it's not as bleak as it looks. If so, the last verses, the assertion of faith, fit well.

Nine weeks ago we saw Ps. 4 as a rebuke and a warning to the congregation that it was sung to. David was distressed by the spiritual condition of his people, and the psalm was warning them. But it was up to them whether or not to change their behaviour and turn back to God.

Look again at Ps. 13, v. 2. David says he is wrestling with his thoughts. Daily his heart is full of sorrow. What thoughts? What sorrow? Yes, there is that threatening enemy, but what thoughts, what sorrow?

In accordance with the principles of numerology Ps. 12 comes just before Ps. 13. There also David is asking his Lord for help. He complains. No-one is faithful any more (v. 1a). There is no loyalty. People lie, flatter, deceive and boast (v. 1b–4) as they plunder the poor (v. 5). The wicked strut about and honour what is vile (vv. 7–8). They are in an evil state. You get the same litany in the first half of Ps. 10. Perhaps in Ps. 13 it is that – the state of the people – that occupies David's thoughts, and causes him such deep sorrow. As king he bears a responsibility for them. Yes, he is distressed, and this time he is certainly not as detached as in Ps. 4. He is impatient. God has not reacted to the unfaithfulness of the people. God has not responded even to

David. David realises that indeed his enemies may, as they think, triumph. Vv. 3–4 may not be a cry of despair. Instead they could be a realisation of potential fact. If God does not act, David may indeed die and that enemy will triumph, in his own eyes at least. Perhaps David is warning his people that he is concerned, and is urgently taking his concern to God. But perhaps he is also calling on them to share his disquiet, and his prayers. Whichever. Despite vv. 3–4, in vv. 5–6 David affirms his trust in God. The God, who is his salvation. Why?

Here I go back to the idea of the tocsin. What does the tocsin-ringer do when he has clanged out his message? He gets himself into the safest place he can find. And that is what David does. He shelters in his God – the one he knows loves him – even if apparently unresponsive. These are words of confidence, not of hanging-on despite everything. His God will respond. Meantime he is safe.

So David ends this poem singing the praise of God, who has been good to him. And he sends these words to the Director of Music to be set to music, to be sung to the congregation. The 'how long's warn those in the congregation that will hear, maybe even sing, the words. They ask the congregation to join with him. David has called on God. Perhaps God will delay, but perhaps not. It makes no difference to David. He is secure with his God. The end of this psalm is confidence based on knowledge, which goes far beyond hope.

So where does this leave us? We too can be depressed as we view our civilisation. We should seek God about it. But when we do not see much difference – when God seems silent – having prayed, we should rest in confidence with our Saviour.

Gilcomston Prayer Meeting, 14 September 2019.

Psalm 19

I like God's sense of humour. Mike asked me to tackle Psalm 19. I turned it up, and laughed. Currently I am writing on the law dealing with the Moon and other celestial bodies.

The Psalm has two elements: the glories of the celestial bodies and the Law of the Lord. Let me start a little way away from all that. The root is a matter of our perception or understanding. We know so much more of the heavens than David did. We know the solar system. We have the wonders disclosed by the Hubble and Spizter space telescopes. The Hubble Wide-Field photo was taken of what was thought to be a very narrow and empty segment of space, and yet the long exposure – thirty days – showed hundreds, not hundreds of stars, but hundreds of galaxies. Is it a cold unfeeling universe in which we are an accident?

It's curious how occasionally popular culture illuminates a theological truth. We're getting towards Christmas, and I hope that ITV will again show 'Hogfather' – a film version of the Terry Pratchett novel (London: Gollancz, 1996). The Auditors of Reality have arranged for someone to kill the Hogfather – the Discworld equivalent of Santa Claus. The Assassin Tea-time almost manages to do it by crushing belief – in this case belief in the Hogfather. Towards the end, Susan Sto-Helit, has to rescue the Hogfather. She asks what happens if she doesn't succeed. Her grandfather, Death, tells her that if she doesn't, the next day the sun will not rise. Oh, it won't be dark, but what will rise will be merely a blazing fiery ball of gas. The point is that belief calls for the **sun** to be, not just a ball of flaming gas.

Now see David's rejoicing in the sun in vv. 4b–6. 'In them he has set a tent for the sun, which is like a bridegroom coming forth from his pavilion, like a champion rejoicing in his course. It rises at one end of the heavens and makes its circuit to the other; nothing is hidden from its heat.' We see the physicality, and yet we see beyond it – from ball of flaming gas to sun. We see past the physics to the glories. We rejoice in the heavens, in the nebulae, in the star nurseries in the Lagoon Nebula. In them we see the glories of their Creator.

Others have done the same. 'The heavens are telling the glory of God' is one of the marvellous sections of Joseph Haydn's 'The Creation' (1796–8). The joy that bubbles up through the intertwined voices is thoroughly infectious. Indeed Haydn (1732–1809) himself reminds me of the irrepressible fecundity of the created Universe. His output was immense – some 750 works (Hoboken catalogue) – 10 a year over his 77 years – including 108 symphonies – 2 or 3 a year over his most productive years. It is not irrelevant that Haydn's output was underpinned by a strong faith. Before he began a composition Haydn normally wrote across the top of each manuscript 'In nomine Domini' ('In the name of the Lord') and at the end when he had finished he put 'Laus Deo' ('Praise be to God'). Frail, he was carried in to a performance of 'The Creation' just a year before his death. The audience broke into spontaneous applause when he appeared. But 'Papa Haydn', as he was affectionately known, pointed upwards and said: "Not from me – everything comes from up there!"

Of course, it can be difficult. That emptiness of space, the immensities of distance, the aeons of time, can appal when considered in relation to your five feet plus and perhaps a few decades of life. But we need to get out and really consider the heavens, not just think about them abstractedly. Modern street lighting is a curse that David did not experience. Most of us don't see a starry sky for years on end. But if not the stars, think of the sun. At least we can still see it. And by it we can see what I just called 'the irrepressible fecundity of the created Universe'. GK Chesterton suggests we consider God's delight in daisies – God made one, loved it and then said 'do it again, and again, and again'. When did you last have a good look at a daisy? Look at the nature and the astronomy programmes on the TV. I am tempted to cite music as well, but we might get into argument as to the likes of Shostakovich or Mahler. In any event I would not wish to get into the miasmic morass of Intelligent Design, but would only comment that, confronted with creation, 'there's nane say blin' as them as winna see': 'there's no one so blind as he that refuses to see'. Compare Death's comment to Susan, also in *Hogfather*. He cannot understand humans. How, living in such a marvellous Universe have they invented 'boredom'?

But none of that tells us how to live. That takes us to the second part of the Psalm, vv. 7–13. Back to *Hogfather* again. Near the end of the story Death points out to Susan that you can grind up the whole Universe, and sieve it oh so thoroughly, analyse it oh so carefully, and you will never find a single atom of truth, or justice, or mercy, of beauty or loveliness. These are things of the mind – for Pratchett the human mind, but surely for us the mind of God. How to live is not prescribed by the laws of physics – the collision of what Piet Hein called 'milliards and milliards of particles, playing billiards and billiards and billiards' (Piet Hein, 'Atomyriades'). It is the Law of the Lord that is perfect, refreshing the soul, the statutes of the Lord that make wise the simple (v. 7). They tell us how to live right.

David knew all about that. He values God's precepts 'more than gold, than much fine gold' (v. 10). To David God's precepts are sweeter than the purest honey (v. 10). They warn us: keeping them brings great reward (v. 11).

And yet they can also make us afraid. They warn. David is *very* conscious that he may not meet the standard they set. He had cause. Remember David's life. That was certainly not sin-free. David knows that he may sin wilfully and prays to be kept from such (v. 13). And, apart from wilful sin, who among us may know his errors and hidden faults? (v. 12).

That is why at the end of the Psalm David turns to his God in the way he does. He does so want to be blameless and innocent of great transgression (v. 13). So at the end he presents his Psalm as a kind of offering, and prays that the word of his mouth and the meditation of his heart will be acceptable in the sight of God (v. 14).

Well, actually he does not. David sees more clearly than that. His is not a formal, clinical request that some preachers make at the start of a vacuous sermon – piety without love, maybe also without conviction.[2] David sees further through – past the legislator of those precepts, to the love of God. He knows God as a tender friend. At the very end of the Psalm he addresses God directly and prays that the word of his mouth and the meditation of his heart will be 'acceptable in your sight O Lord, my Rock and my Redeemer' (v. 14). The giver of law, those statutes, precepts and commands, is David's Redeemer. He is also ours. Let us thank him.

Gilcomston Prayer Meeting, 17 November 2007.

---

2 Cf. Edward Lear, quoted in V. Noakes, *Edward Lear: The Life of a Wanderer* (Collins: 1968: pb. 2004) 158, from *Letters of Edward Lear* (1907), 276-7.

Psalm 20

This psalm has to do with leaders and rulers. It is intriguing that we have got here now just as 2016 has seen major changes: Brexit, the departure of Cameron, the arrival of May, Trump elected President of the United States. France, Germany and others have elections coming up next year. So??

Psalm 20 is another for which we get no help from knowing what caused it to be composed. Was it a one-off? Does it split at v. 6, the first bit being a response to an impending crisis, and the rest thanks for surviving it. Or did David compose it as a model to be used as and when needed? Augustine saw it simply as David speaking to Christ, foretelling things to come, but I am not sure that is immediately helpful. Indeed Augustine's comments struck me as perfunctory – perhaps he was not wholly convinced that that was the right way to take the psalm. Matthew Henry is equivocal. For him it could be a one-off, or it could be a prayer for general use. Either way he thinks there is much to instruct in it. Calvin is quite clear that it is a model, not a one-off. It could have arisen from some particular event, but he thinks that the Holy Spirit intended to give the Church a common form of prayer, to be used whenever any danger threatens. That is not to say that Calvin thought that that was its limit. On the contrary, he thought that beyond the prayer for help there is something further. For him, under the figure of the temporal kingdom, David also describes a far more excellent government, on which the whole joy and happiness of the Church depended. David wants the children of God to have such a concern about the kingdom of Christ that they will be stirred up to continual prayer. And that, of course, is what we will do later this evening.

Back to basics. The people are to pray for the welfare and success of the King, the anointed of v. 6. Verse 9 makes that clear. These verses give a pattern, a form to thought. Now is that not a piece of cheek, self-serving – self-centred indeed? I am King. Pray for me. Here's what to say. Calvin nails the point. The King embodies the people. This is a model prayer for leaders in general. David was not self-absorbed. Ultimately, though the words relate to the King, the prayer has to do with the welfare of the community, its distresses, its crises, its security and its successes. It applies to the secular world down to the smallest aspect, from Westminster to Holyrood, to the local Council, even down to your boss. It applies to all sorts of communities, including congregations. It applies to secular politicians as well as to the religious. In them all so much hinges on the leaders.

We are to pray for our rulers whether or not they are Christian. Remember Jeremiah's instruction to serve the King of Babylon and live (Jer. 27. 17). Recall Daniel's career, or Pharaoh's deputy, Joseph. Paul urges Timothy that petitions, prayers, intercessions and thanksgiving be made for all people, for kings and all those in authority, so that we may lead peaceful and quiet lives in all godliness and holiness (1 Tim. 2:1–3).

As to Christian leaders, secular or religious – clearly we will pray that the Lord will answer when the leader is in distress, and that he will protect him (v. 1). We will ask that the Lord will send help and support (v. 2). We will ask the Lord to grant his requests and we will shout for joy and lift our banners in the name of the Lord when victory comes (v. 5, rearranged).

But what about vv. 3–4, the plans and desires of the king, v. 4, the sacrifices and the burnt-offerings, v. 3? To pray thus properly we must have confidence in those for whom we pray. That is a matter of their integrity, and ours. Elsewhere in the Old Testament God rejects offerings and sacrifices, feasts and assemblies. There are condemnations of burnt offerings, sacrifices and feast days in Isaiah. Isaiah 1: 10–15 part of a long denunciation – almost a diatribe – as God indicts the people for their faithlessness. Psalm 51: 16 – God does not delight in sacrifices and takes no pleasure in burnt-offerings: he looks for a contrite heart. Amos 5: 21–23 – God despises the festivals and assemblies, the noisy songs, and the offerings made during them.

What's the problem? Simply the festivals, those sacrifices and offerings were no longer centred on God. Had the leader gotten too prominent? Maybe the focus had changed. The purpose of the festivals, the sacrifices and the offerings had become the pleasure of men. That is possible. The occasion becomes more important than the substance. It's Christmas without Christ. The Catechism has been distorted. 'Man's chief end is to glorify God, and enjoy him forever' is the answer to its first question. Too easily we change our priorities. It becomes that our chief end is to enjoy ourselves, and, secondarily, to enjoy God. No! God must be our centre. There are many examples. Hosea 6: 6ff, God desires mercy, not sacrifice. Samuel tells Saul that the Lord prefers obedience to sacrifice (1 Sam. 15: 22–23). Sacrifices and burnt-offerings, feasts and festivals are meaningless when the heart has gone astray.[3]

Sacrifices and burnt-offerings; the plans and desires of leaders. Religious leaders are to be prayed for with care. Recall Matt. 7: 23. At the Second Coming many will claim they have done wonderful things in Jesus' name. His reply is 'I never knew you. Depart from me you evildoers'. See also Luke 13: 24–30. Frightening!

We must pray with discernment. The Devil is adept at corrupting religious leaders. We must shield them with prayer. Take the Calvin line – pray this psalm when danger threatens the Church. Look through history. Would you have prayed Ps. 20 for Ananias and Caiaphas? Doubtless they were rigorous in their observance of the calendar of feasts. Look around. Major denominations tolerate agnostic ministers: atheist ministers are not unknown. Providing religion has always attracted hucksters and shysters. Sinclair Lewis' *Elmer Gantry*, published in 1926, ninety years ago, remains relevant. Religious charities are a minefield with many explosions. There have been so many abuses. You get the controlling cults. I had an aunt who joined the Cooneyites, orthodox in form, but their leaders were so manipulative. The doctrinally orthodox can go astray. The lures are many. The ego searches for a platform, status, popularity fame, acclamation. There is the lure of money – the Gehazi syndrome (2 Kgs 5: 19–27). Businesses appear, even religious franchises often held by dynasties. Practitioners of the art claim to speak for God as they organise the sacrifices, burn the offerings, and tell people how to live, what to think. They are often strong on the duty of at least tithing, if not more. That emphasis can run on into the 'prosperity gospel'. Power and influence are other lures, whether small or grand-scale. Look at the procession of religious leaders that lined up to endorse or denounce candidates in the US elections. Trump courted the self-styling evangelicals and many evangelical entrepreneurs backed him. Were they not seeking power and influence? Filling the Scalia seat on the US Supreme Court does not adequately explain their attitude. Beyond that, consider the TV and radio evangelists. We need to be aware of the religious area in broad terms, for what goes on in it can affect how our witness is approached by those to whom we speak. So while we pray for our religious leaders, be careful. Scrutinise them. Detect flaws. Pray accordingly.

---

3 Cf. the many references in https://www.openbible.info/labs/cross-references/search?q=1+Samuel+15%3A22.

That said, there are true leaders, true kings, for whom we should pray the earlier verses of the psalm. We know some. We know that for them there will be victories to be celebrated. So, pray that our leaders do trust in the Lord and not in futile accoutrements – the chariots and horses of v. 7, the sacrifices and burnt-offerings of v. 3, the feasts and assemblies, whatever form they take in the modern world. Those who do not trust in the Lord, those whose efforts are not centred on Him, will fail (v. 8). Those who trust in the Lord will stand firm. Their prayers will bring the blessing (vv. 8–9). And finally, maybe Augustine got it right. Calvin did. Beyond our current leaders and would-be leaders, we pray for Jesus and his church.

So, let us ask the Lord to give victory to our King. As v. 9 says, Lord, answer us when we call.

Gilcomston Prayer Meeting, 27 November 2016.

Psalm 21

You may have noticed that Psalm 21 comes after Psalm 20. That's fairly obvious, isn't it? It does so numerically. But it does so in another way as well. It follows on from the prayers of Psalm 20. In that one the writer/composer seeks help (vv. 1–5). Yes, in its latter half there is assertion of the saving power of the Lord, but to me there is a strain of whistling to keep your spirits up. We trust in the Lord, not in chariots and horses (Ps. 20: 7). We stand and they fall (Ps. 20: 8). Yes, these are right things to sing. Yet Psalm 20 finishes 'O Lord, save the king! Answer us when we call' (Ps. 20: 9). It hopes.

Go on to tonight's psalm. It is first an explosion of relief, of thankfulness for victory won, and only then goes on to the future. But note that, while it is headed as a Psalm of David – he wrote it – it is the people who sing. This is not a solitary meditation. It is for the general chorus. David provides the words, but the people perform or join in it. Indeed, perhaps the word is that they declaim it. They really get into it.

I have found this a difficult psalm. When Mike suggested it to me for tonight I looked it up, checked tonight's date, and, without further consideration, thought I could tackle it. After a few days and some thought I nearly pulled out, but by then it was too late. My problem is this. Although I can relate to the psalm in its essence, I do so with difficulty as to the costs of the victories of which it speaks. We can forget the costs of victories.

I was angry at our Remembrance Service last November. My father, a Master Mariner in our Merchant Navy, was killed, bombed, drowned – we don't know – on Atlantic convoy in 1941. My mother was thirty-two. I was one year old. I never knew him. The annual Remembrance service has its resonances. After the Silence, dismissively and abruptly the person conducting the service moved us on to other things. And yet, as I mulled things over I found that that experience helped my thinking about this Psalm.

The Psalm has two parts. The first section, vv. 1–7, is addressed by the king to the Lord. Then in the second the people speak of what their king, through the Lord, will do, vv. 8–13a. The psalm ends with the people affirming that they will sing and praise the Lord, v. 13b.

In 2013 there are two ways to read this Psalm. We can surely apply it to its writer, David, and his time. Beyond him we can apply it to Christ. I first thought to take these ways of looking at it separately. But I soon realised that that would mean repeating the material, probably tediously.

In Part One the writer addresses God the Lord, thanking the Lord for what he has done for him. Remember that Psalm 20 was asking for help. This psalm starts by rejoicing in victory won through the gift of the Lord. That has dual aspects. In the immediate situation it must have been inspired by a particular victory. We don't know exactly what, or when. But there were victories for the king in David's reign. There is also the victory of the Resurrection, as our Saviour conquered death. Look at the middle, vv. 3–6. There is the welcome and the crown, v. 3. The king asked for life, and was given more than mere life. Yes, the king would have asked for life just before the battle. But can you see the agony in the garden, and the crucifixion, there? The king asks for life. He is given an abundance of life, a length of days – and note it is length of days, for ever and ever, v.4. That surely cannot be David, unless you dismiss it as hyperbole. Maybe it was hyperbole when David wrote those words. But we know that David sometimes wrote more than he knew. Through victory the glory of the king is great – again with a double application. Eternal blessings, and the joy of the presence of the Lord, v. 6. He trusts the Lord. Through the unfailing love of the Lord, the king will not be shaken, v. 7. David?? Jesus, as we know him?

Then the Psalm shifts. In Part Two, vv. 8–13, the people speak of the triumphs that are to come through their king, and through the Lord. Note that clearly, whatever the king does is also done by the Lord. We could, directly, refer these verses to the Second Coming, but I will stick to the Davidic era. The king will seize his enemies, v. 8. The Lord will burn them up, v. 9. Their posterity will be eliminated, v. 10. Enemies will plot evil but their wicked schemes will not succeed. They will be struck down as they flee, v. 12. The Lord will be exalted in his strength, v. 13a.

All well and good. We can rejoice as the king and his Lord succeeds. But it was just there that I balked. Battles have casualties. Battle is not unilateral. Both sides have losses. Look at the many TV programmes about the world wars. The Somme. Normandy. The serried ranks of headstones in the war graveyards. There are terrible injuries. Remember we are thinking of David's times. Swords, spears, axes.

And here I go back to that Remembrance Service, and indeed to all Remembrance Services. In our psalm there is nothing about the costs of victory. Was David, poet and commander, indifferent as to the cost to his troops? I cannot think so. But he knew that the people would sing the words he wrote. I think the people just accept that the victories to come will require sacrifice. Victory will not otherwise come. Christ's victory came at a cost we really cannot imagine. Separation from God: 'Eli, Eli lama sabacthani: My God, my God, why hast thou forsaken me?' (Matt. 27: 46).

We are here to pray. Among those we pray for are those who battle for the Lord, those who have made sacrifices that the Word may be spread, as Jesus commanded, in many different foreign fields and different situations. And it's not just the missionaries, professional and semi-professional. Here in Aberdeen analogously we make our sacrifices in effort, time and money, as we are called so to do. Does that feel good? Maybe. But what is in my mind is this. Think of the casualty rate among missionaries. Physical problems. Mental problems.

But there are things beyond. Almost every day I get a posting from two websites. One is 'Human Rights without Frontiers'; the other is called 'Law and Religion Headlines', which links to other websites. Many in Gilcomston get updates from Barnabas. Such sources chronicle persecutions, church burnings, mob riots, the deaths of our Christian brethren – India and Pakistan, Indonesia and Burma, China, the 'stan' remnants of the former Soviet Union, North Korea. These, our brethren, hang on – for Christ's victory. They pay fuller costs for Christ's victory than we do. They are the ones who properly, fully, hymn, chant and sing the second section of our Psalm, praising the King. Consider, then, what they sing. Verse 8ff.

Let us join their voices. Verse 13: we will 'praise your might'.

Gilcomston Prayer Meeting, 28 December 2013.

Psalm 23

Tonight we look at Psalm 23. It has associations for me. When I was small my mother used to tell me the story of the Lost Sheep, and link it with Psalm 23. Another association is that on 30 March 1969, – 35 years ago – this Psalm was the content of the first sermon I preached from the Gilcomston pulpit. But let's sing it first – to Crimond.

I asked for Crimond because it is so familiar. At funerals it has an elegiac quality, a poignancy. And yet that can reduce its effect, dissipating it in generalised mushy feelings and we don't connect properly with the words.

Let me ask a couple of questions. What is on the back of a two-pence piece? Whose face is on a twenty-pound Clydesdale or Bank of Scotland note? We take these things for granted, but never really see them. This Psalm can be the same. The Twenty-third Psalm has gone into the Christianness of the church. We take its images for granted. Exactly because of that familiarity this Psalm's elements get blurred. We can slide over its details too easily. But there's a lot in the detail.

We can take it in various ways. Apply it to Jesus – in two aspects. First consider his relation with his Father, and pick up 'The Lord is my Shepherd', 'He leads me', 'The shadow of death', and the final consummation of the feast in the presence of enemies.

Second, link 'The Lord is my Shepherd' with Jesus' own words. 'I am the Good Shepherd'. I will come back to that.

And, of course, we can apply it to ourselves.

Where do all these wonderful ideas and images come from? They were in the mind of David as he contemplated God. But they were not conjured through some romantic appreciation of country life, some pastoral idyll. They draw from reality, from living with grubby, flatulent, self-willed beasts. They root right back to David's own experience as a young boy. He was a shepherd lad. Remember he was not around when Samuel came looking for 'the King-to-be' among the sons of Jesse. He was away looking after the sheep and had to be sent for from a faraway field. Jesse parades his other seven sons before Samuel. "[B]ut Samuel said to him, 'the Lord has not chosen these.' So he asked Jesse, 'Are these all the sons that you have?' 'There is still the youngest' Jesse replied, 'but he is feeding the sheep'. Samuel said, 'Send for him; we will not sit down until he arrives' (1 Sam. 11: 10–11). And when he comes? – v. 11c – 'Then the Lord said, 'Rise and anoint him: he is the one.'

'The Lord is my shepherd' – David's Psalm is grounded in experience.

That leads him into that pithy set of verses, which expand with meaning the more you think about them in the light of David's experience, and which we can each apply to ourselves.

'I shall not be in want' (v. 1) cannot mean I will never be in want. Think of the Holy Land. There the shepherd leads his flock. Note, by the way, that the shepherd leads. Here our shepherd usually drives the flock, and has dogs to help control the errant mob. That is not the picture in Ps. 23. There the shepherd goes before and guides the flock from pasture to pasture. But on the way there will be barren areas to be negotiated, otherwise why move?

The want we experience in such areas is temporary. Then there are the green pastures and the quiet waters, and the shepherd leads to them. He protects. The rod and staff comfort these sheep, for they know they are not instruments to harry the flock. They are the weapons the Good Shepherd uses to defend, to beat off the wolves and other predators. 'I will fear no evil for you are with me: your rod and your staff, they comfort me.' Verse 4b has a broad application.

There are other things here. Green pastures and quiet waters sound wonderful (v. 2). They are. Quite idyllic – a Rubens landscape. But they can be dangerous as well. Quiet waters? Still waters run deep! Lush green pastures? So you go down to those enticing waters to have a drink, and your narrow hooves slip on the well-watered river-bank. Your fleece, suddenly wet, becomes heavy and pulls you further. Do sheep swim? I think not. But your shepherd has that staff to pull you out. The shepherd's crook is very practical, you know. And, though it is not explicitly in the Psalm, I am sure David had experience of hearing a sheep bleat in alarm, and heading off to rescue it. The parable of the Lost Sheep was told by Jesus. We get a wee kick out of seeing ourselves as the bedraggled, but cute, little animal being rescued. David would have filled it with real meaning.

'He restores my soul' (v. 3). We think of that in terms of rest and refreshment in the quiet waters. But I rather think that here there may also be an element of correction. Remember Paul had that thorn in the flesh to keep him from getting above himself (2 Cor. 12: 7). David was a King, and elsewhere in the Old Testament kings are spoken of as shepherds of their people. Later the religious rulers were to be spoken of in that way as well. But kings and religious leaders can get above themselves and fail to do their duty. They are excoriated by some prophets (cf. Zech. 12–13). Consider the terrible verses applied to the false shepherds by Jesus (Matt. 23: 13). But this King had learned dutifulness and humbleness before his shepherd, no doubt through some of the dunts that he had received from the shepherd's rod and staff. And even the dunts comfort this sheep. They show that the shepherd cares. We are restored in refreshment and in correction through the Word and otherwise.

The Shepherd leads. 'He guides me in paths of righteousness (v. 3). The guidance is personal. There is not '*The* path of righteousness'. Each sheep is guided on its own path. They may travel as a flock, but they don't travel in line astern. We here tonight are a flock. Is this not our experience too? Have we not been led, each on our different path?

David trusts his shepherd. Even into the valley of the shadow of death (v. 4a). Even into the valley of the shadow of death? That's not what it says. It says 'Even *through* the valley of the shadow of death.' Yes, there is the alternative reading in the footnote of 'the darkest valley', but what else is that? It is also important to say again that this shepherd leads. Jesus has been through death. Somehow or other David sees, perhaps dimly, a shepherd who goes into death before his flock. From our place in time, we can see the man who spoke of himself as the Good Shepherd who lays down his life for his sheep (John 10: 1–6).

Then the imagery changes. Unless you use FX or computer graphics and can see yourself as a sheep sitting at a table, using a cup, being anointed the imagery becomes ludicrous. Better now to change the imagery.

The shepherd prepares a table for David in the presence of David's enemies. He anoints David's head with oil, and David's cup overflows.

This must be a late Psalm, composed out of a full life. Want, green pastures, quiet waters, paths of righteousness, led through the darkest valleys, the comfort of the protecting rod and staff – all these elements are based on life as a hero who killed Goliath, was a fugitive from Saul, a refugee among the Philistines, as a king – but a king with all those plotters and enemies we read of in so many other Psalms, someone one of whose sons killed another (Absalom and Amnon, 2 Sam. 13: 12–31)), someone hounded out of his capital by his arrogant son (2 Sam. 15–18), and yet was so often protected. It is also rooted in the life of one who was errant, (Bathsheba and Uriah, 2 Sam. 11).

This is the man who knows that what he writes at the end of this Psalm is true and will be true. This is something we can all say. Come back to the first verse. As you know, I have spent time setting exam questions. But this is not 'The Lord is a Shepherd. Discuss'. This Psalm begins not 'The Lord is a shepherd'. It begins not 'The Lord is David's shepherd'. It begins 'The Lord is *my* Shepherd'. Now come to the last verse of the Psalm. But I quote it in the AV because of one word. This was written by a man who needed love to follow him, sure, as you have in the NIV. But within love there is mercy, and, like David, we all need that. So David finishes this wonderful Psalm:

'Surely goodness and mercy (love) will follow me all the days of my life, and I will dwell in the house of the Lord for ever' (v. 6).

Gilcomston Prayer Meeting, 11 December 2004.

Psalm 24

'Of David, a psalm.' A familiar psalm. Now and again we sing the whole, with hallelujahs. Many have set it to music. The second half, 'the gates' bit is in Part 2 of Handel's Messiah. It is the Psalm of the Day for Sundays for both Sephardic and Ashkenazi Jews. They also sing it as the Torah scroll is put back in its place at the end of a synagogue service. And that is an important clue for us tonight, for the enclosure – I could say 'cupboard' – where the scrolls are kept is called 'the Torah Ark'. We'll get back to that.

'Of David, a Psalm'. The superscription is different from the usual 'A Psalm of David'. Apparently that is important. One rabbi's commentary on the psalm told me that 'A Psalm of David' tells us that this is when David sang and as a result God's spirit came to him. 'Of David, a Psalm' means that the spirit of God came on David causing him to sing – an intriguing difference.

The psalm has that word 'selah' at the end of v. 6. Whatever you think 'selah' indicates, this psalm has two major sections, vv. 1–6 and vv. 7–10. It is also right to see, as Handel does, that there are antiphonies in it, different parts responding to each other, as questions are asked and answered.

We have no sure knowledge of when it was written, but Jewish tradition is that David wrote it for when the Temple was to be consecrated. David had dearly wanted to build a Temple, but God had told him that it was his son, not he, who would build it (1 Kgs. 5: 3–5; 2 Chron. 6: 7–9). So David wrote this psalm for when that would happen. When the Temple was consecrated the Ark of the Covenant was brought and placed in the inner sanctuary, the Most Holy Place. The suggestion is that this psalm was sung to command the opening of the Temple gates for the entry of the Ark (1 Kgs. 8; 2 Chron. 5). And, to go back, if you think of 'Of David, a Psalm' as being in some way composed by God and given to David, that surely adds to its lustre.

We can speculate how the psalm was performed on the day. That has gone round my mind in the weeks since I agreed to tackle it tonight. Years before the Jews had developed the superstitious habit of taking the Ark with them on campaign, and the Philistines captured it. However, that did not go well. Dagon, their god had been smashed, and wherever the Ark was taken the people were afflicted with boils. So they sent the Ark back, with gifts (1 Sam. 5 and 6). Back in Jewish territory it remained at the house of Abinadab. Later David wanted to bring the Ark on up to Jerusalem. But on its way there was the episode of the death of Uzzah, and the Ark was parked with Obed-Edom for three months (2 Sam. 6: 1–11). Then David finally got it up to Jerusalem and had it placed in a special tent (2 Sam. 6: 12–23). That final stage was quite an occasion, a parade, a scene of joy. David was a good organiser. There were sacrifices (2 Sam. 6: 17–19). There were shouts of celebration. There were rams' horns and cymbals, lyres and harps, and singing. 1 Chronicles 15: 3–23 tells us who was blowing what, who was banging the cymbals, who was playing the strings and who were just singing. David himself danced in front of the procession (2 Sam. 6: 14–15; 1 Chron. 15: 28–29), which led to the rupture with his wife Michal, who, Victoria-like, was not amused (2 Sam. 6: 20–23). But I don't envisage that that sort of thing as happening when the Ark was finally brought to the Temple by Solomon. This psalm is solemn and dignified. That is the point of the 'selah' in v. 6. We are to take the occasion, and the psalm, seriously, dignifiedly.

What about the text? The earth is the Lord's and everything in it, the world, and all who live in it. Why? Because he made it (v. 1). That has two elements. First, the world. Second, the people. The world. The psalms have much about the glories of creation, the sun and the stars, the richness of the Earth. We have modern astronomy and the space telescopes. 'The heavens declare the glory of God; the skies proclaim the work of his hands' (Ps. 19: 10). We have those wonderful TV programmes, including Attenborough's Planet Earth series now in a third iteration. But do we really see it as His? If we don't, if we take it for granted, if we are too busy, too hashed properly to appreciate flowers, trees, bushes, birds, landscapes, rivers, clouds, sunrises and sunsets, the progress of the seasons, we are out-of-kilter. As W.H. Davies, the professional hobo, put it in his poem 'Leisure' (1911):

What is this life if, full of care, we have no time to stand and stare,
no time to stand beneath the boughs and stare as long as sheep or cows.
No time to see, when woods we pass, where squirrels hide their nuts in grass.
No time to see, in broad daylight, streams full of stars, like skies at night.
No time to turn at Beauty's glance, and watch her feet, how they can dance.
No time to wait till her mouth can enrich that smile her eyes began.
A poor life this if, full of care, we have no time to stand and stare.

Stare and marvel, it is all God's.

But, what of climate change, of global warming? That takes us on to the people. Are we treating, have we treated, his world as the stewards we were commissioned to be back in Gen. 2: 15, even if you take Gen. 3: 17–19 into account? However you stand on that, v. 1 of Ps. 24 is clear that, whatever the people may think, as a matter of fact they too belong to the Lord. Other bible passages show that at the end all shall bow to the Lord. But v. 6 makes it clear that those who seek the Lord are the ones that he prizes. Who are they? Those with clean hands and a pure heart, those who do not trust in idols or swear by false gods, they are the ones who will ascend the mountain of the Lord and stand in his holy place (v. 4). Take that too fast and superficially that could lead you to think that a rigid programme of self-discipline will get you up the mountain. Calvin and others torpedo that notion. Clean hands, avoiding idols and false gods are fruits, not precautionary rituals. They are results, not causes. The next verse proves that, for it speaks of the Lord, the Saviour (v. 5) and v. 6 makes it clear that those standing in the holy place of the Lord are those who seek him. The Lord (NIV) vindicates them, or as the KJV puts it, they will 'receive righteousness from the God of his salvation'. In contrast recall Jesus' disavowal of some in Matt. 7: 22–23. Despite their claims to have done so much in his name, he never knew them.

Think about all of that. Have a 'selah'. Then call for the gates to be opened for the solemn procession. But see, this is not now the Ark alone that is being processed. The King of glory is entering. And as we read in 1 Kgs. 8: 10–11 and 2 Chron. 5: 13c–14, when the Ark, the symbol of the King, was set in its place, God's glory filled the Temple to the extent that the priests could not perform their service and had to retire, perhaps in confusion.

We cannot leave this psalm there. But I will leave you, as already knowledgeable, and therefore able yourselves to expand the following thoughts. Down through the centuries Christian commentators have linked this psalm to Christ, our Saviour. There are three aspects. First, for many the psalm adumbrates Christ entering heaven at the last things. He certainly meets the criteria of vv. 3–4. And some taking that view also see him as accompanied by those he has saved through his sacrifice – they singing this psalm.

Second, something I had not appreciated until we were looking into Hebrews these past few weeks. Written for those with a Jewish background,

Hebrews uses just what we have been considering. Remember that the Ark was brought into the Temple and installed in the Most Holy Place. Hebrews 6: 19–20: our hope is anchored, firm and secure. Why? Because it links us to that inner sanctuary behind the curtain where our forerunner, Jesus, has gone 'on our behalf'. Hebrews 8: 1–2: we have a high priest who 'serves in the sanctuary, the true tabernacle set up by the Lord'. Hebrews 9: 11–14 and 28: Jesus is a high priest entering the Most Holy Place, but he enters carrying his own blood as the once and for all sacrifice and offering. And then Hebrews 10: 1–10 speaks again of the finality of that sacrifice, ending any need for further repetitive offerings.

Third: a rather different set of images. This psalm can, maybe should, speak to us of Jesus entering our hearts as we trust in him. He becomes for us the indwelling Christ. To use the Aberdonian, Jesus said: 'Anyone who loves me will obey my teaching. My Father will love them and we will come to them and we will bide with them' [sc. make our home with them] (Jn. 14: 23). But such ideas require contemplation, not disquisition.

I end with a memory. When William Still was laid in the ground in Springfield Cemetery, the coffin had been lowered into the grave, those present, I think led by Malcolm Duff, spontaneously broke into song – 'Ye gates lift up your heads; Ye doors that last for aye be lifted up . . .' (Ps. 24: 7–10, Psalter version).

Gilcomston Prayer Meeting, 30 November 2019.

Psalm 29

Last week Tom Scott noted that Ps. 28: 5 speaks of those who have no regard for the works of the Lord. Psalm 29 commands them to pay attention.

Ten psalms before this one we are invited to think of the glories of creation, the sun and the stars, the richness of the Earth. 'The heavens declare the glory of God; the skies proclaim the work of his hands': Ps. 19: 1. Remember it? For its first six verses you think of the wonders of creation, and then you are led on to celebrate his Law. 'The law of the LORD is perfect, refreshing the soul': Ps. 19: 7. Calvin rightly contrasts Ps. 19 and this one. He notes that while Ps. 19 is contemplative – quiet in tone – Ps. 29 shouts. The instruction of both is that glory and strength be ascribed to the Lord, to give him the glory due to his name, to worship the Lord in the splendour of his holiness (vv. 1–2). But they are very different.

Why the difference between contemplative Ps. 19 and rambunctious Ps. 29? Calvin reckons the explanation lies in the audience. What audience? Here we get into the translation problem. Some translations, for example the NIV version on my iPad, see the call as being addressed to 'heavenly beings', presumably angelic beings like those in Job 1 and 2. That makes little sense. Do 'heavenly beings' need to be instructed thus? Would the heavenly beings, who chronoclastically from our point of view, see God juggling with galaxies, be impressed by God's accuracy in splitting a cedar with a thunderbolt (Ps. 29: 7 with 5).

Some translations refer to the 'Sons of God', and commentators cross-refer to the sons of god that married the daughters of men (Gen. 6: 2). How that fits escapes me. It adds nothing to the thought. I prefer the views of others including Calvin that it is the 'sons of the mighty' who are being addressed. These are the rich and powerful, humanly speaking, the nobles and rulers. This is a call to the 'sons of the mighty' – and the phrase may used in irony. It is a call to the self-reliant. As I said, Calvin contrasts Pss. 19 and 29. Ps. 19 is addressed to believers. In Ps. 29 God, addresses the mighty of the Earth, who often have little or no time for Him. But this is not a polite cough and an 'excuse me '. . .'. As Calvin says, God is shouting at them to get their attention. And remember that this is Jehovah doing the shouting.

This is God, the Almighty. Ignore Him at your peril!

Look at it. Look at it in many translations to savour the imagery. This is the King James Version:

> [3] The voice of the LORD is upon the waters: the God of glory thundereth: the LORD is upon many waters. [4] The voice of the LORD is powerful; the voice of the LORD is full of majesty. [5] The voice of the LORD breaketh the cedars; yea, the LORD breaketh the cedars of Lebanon. [6] He maketh them also to skip like a calf; Lebanon and Sirion like a young unicorn. [7] The voice of the LORD divideth the flames of fire. [8] The voice of the LORD shaketh the wilderness; the LORD shaketh the wilderness of Kadesh. [9] The voice of the LORD maketh the hinds to calve, and discovereth the forests: and in his temple doth every one speak of his glory. [10] The LORD sitteth upon the flood; yea, the LORD sitteth King for ever.

Words are so secure, fixed on paper before our eyes. It is easy to glide over them, and not really feel what they say. Get away from the words to the actuality. Free your imagination. What about this version from *The Message Bible*, Eugene Peterson's attempt to capture the tone of the bible language.

> [3] GOD thunders across the waters. Brilliant, his voice and his face, streaming brightness — GOD, across the flood waters. [4] GOD's thunder tympanic, GOD's thunder symphonic. [5] GOD's thunder smashes cedars, GOD topples the northern cedars. [6] The mountain ranges skip like spring colts, The high ridges jump like wild kid goats. [7-8] GOD's thunder spits fire. GOD thunders, the wilderness quakes; He makes the desert of Kadesh shake. [9] GOD's thunder sets the oak trees dancing. A wild dance, whirling; the pelting rain strips their branches. [[We fall to our knees—we call out, "Glory!" [10] Above the floodwaters is GOD's throne from which his power flows, from which he rules the world.]]

Yes, we better understand the technicalities of weather now, but as Piet Hein says in his Grook on 'The Miracle of Spring': 'We glibly talk of nature's laws. But do things have a natural cause? Black earth into yellow crocus is undiluted hocus-pocus.'

God over the waters. The turmoil of Aberdeen Bay in storm. Niagara. Iguassu. Last year the deluge of Storm Frank came close to collapsing

Abergeldie Castle near Crathie as the Dee flooded, and look what the river did just a little further down-stream to Ballater Caravan Park. I don't know about you. I have never been in a proper earthquake, but I like thunderstorms. They are memorable. Wonderful, scary thunder and lightning in Bangkok. I recall watching a lightning storm with the kids from the eves of a motel over in Cape May. I always took the bairns up to the Velox in our roof to see our Aberdeen storms.

But when I re-read that paragraph some days after writing it, I felt how inadequate it is. What do we in Aberdeen know of the terrors of real weather? Of the ground trembling beneath us? Of lightning darting down, splitting trees close by? Have you ever been terrified by the forces of nature? Can you think what it might be like? That is what David is invoking. Let your imagination go free. Jehovah can, and if necessary will, shout you out of your placid controlled existence.

Is Jehovah's shouting effective? Well, we will know in due course. In the meantime we can pray that God's power strikes home to those who need that message. There's much in the media just now about our rulers, but even closer to home we can all think of some who seem self-reliant and arrogant.

There is evidence that at least the message is heard, whether or not it works. As I was writing these pages Wild TV had a week on 'Wild Weather'. Throughout the natural disasters, earthquakes, hurricanes and tornadoes, storm-surges, lightning and other storms, the audio regularly picked up 'My God! Oh my God!' – the reaction of those caught up in them.

Calvin notes that in this psalm David has selected works of God that not only show God governing – and I quote – 'but which also awaken the torpid, and drag them, as it were, in spite of themselves, humbly to adore him.' Then to my surprise – would you believe it? – Calvin goes on to quote the bulk of an ode by Quintus Horatius Flaccus. Calvin says the works of God awake 'the torpid, and drag them, as it were, in spite of themselves, humbly to adore him as even Horace was compelled, though he was not only a heathen poet, but an Epicurean and a vile contemner of Deity, to say of himself in one of his Odes, — Lib. I. Ode 34. Calvin is quoting *Fortune's Changes*. Listen:

'Once I wandered, an expert in crazy wisdom, a scant and infrequent adorer of gods, now I'm forced to set sail and return, to go back to the paths I abandoned. For Jupiter, Father of all of the gods, who generally splits the clouds with his lightning, flashing away, drove thundering horses, and his swift chariot, through the clear sky, till the dull earth, and the wandering rivers, and Styx, and dread Taenarus' hateful headland, and Atlas's mountain-summits shook. The god has the power to replace the highest with the lowest, bring down the famous, and raise the obscure to the heights. And greedy Fortune with her shrill whirring, carries away the crown and delights in setting it, there.'[4]

Horace died in 8 BC. I don't know if he knew of Psalm 29. It's not impossible. He was well-read. He spent some years studying at the Academy in Athens. But whenever or why-ever he wrote, Horace too had heard the warning from a powerful God to the high and mighty among men.

But tonight here in Aberdeen we end with vv. 9b–11. What happens when the message of the psalm is heard and acted on? Verse 9b: 'In his temple all cry "Glory!" The LORD sits enthroned over the flood; the LORD is enthroned as King forever. The LORD gives strength to his people. The LORD blesses his people with peace.'

Let us also cry 'Glory'.

Gilcomston Prayer Meeting, 11 February 2017.

---

4 Translated by A.S. Kline © Copyright 2003: *Poetry in Translation*.

Psalm 36

The heading tells us that this is a Psalm of David, the servant of God. Note – the word 'servant'. There are only two Psalms thus titled: this one and Psalm 18. The rubric to Ps. 18 says it was the song of David after the Lord had rescued him from his enemies and the hand of Saul. This one also has to do with enemies. Look at the very last verse: 'see how the evildoers lie fallen – thrown down, not able to rise' (v. 12). We'll come back to that. David seems to be thinking of something real, history. And the whole does give the impression that it happened recently, that it is fresh in his mind.

Now as to the Psalm itself. Clearly it divides in two at v. 5. Before that David is writing of the evil-doer. After that he is concentrating upon God.

The start is startling. Like Dvorak's or Mahler's Eighth Symphony it sails straight onto its course – no clearing of the throat. In one translation the first sentence of v. 1 declares: 'I have a message from God concerning the sinfulness of the wicked'. In another: 'A message from God: The transgression of the wicked resides in their hearts'. We don't know whether this was an abrupt irruption into David's mind as God suddenly spoke to him, or whether it was brought home as a conclusion after David thought over particular events.

The Psalm elaborates: 'There is no fear of God before their eyes' (v. 1b). That is the basic – the foundation of the next three verses. 'In their own eyes they flatter themselves too much to detect or hate their sin. The words of their mouths are wicked and deceitful; they have ceased to be wise and do good. Even on their beds they plot evil; they commit themselves to a sinful course and do not reject what is wrong.'

What strikes me is that this is not a denunciation, and it would be wrong to take it as if it were. It is a statement of simple fact about the wicked. And, recall that this is not David speaking: it is a message from God (v. 1a). It is not saying that Man has fallen by deliberate choice with all these consequences. Woe! Woe! It is not saying that sinners are in rebellion against God. It is simply saying: 'there is no fear of God before their eyes'. The wicked are not ignoring him – ignoring is a positive action. They are just so far gone that they have forgotten he really does exist. They go about their lives, their business, their scheming and their plots, without ever taking God into account.

That rings true. As reported by C.S. Lewis, Screwtape, in his 'Address at the Annual Dinner of the Tempters' Training College for Young Devils', said the days of the great sinner seem to be past, but there is still a vast haul of lesser souls. I quote: 'In each individual choice of what the Enemy [sc. God] would call the "wrong" turning such creatures are hardly, if at all, in a state of full spiritual responsibility. They do not understand either the source or the real character of the prohibitions they are breaking. Their consciousness hardly exists apart from the social atmosphere that surrounds them.' So much for Screwtape. His analysis is just a rewrite of Ps. 36: 2–4, with apparent empirical research masking plagiarism. It is not the great sinners that are the standard meat and drink for the demons. Oh, the great sinners are to be enjoyed – see Screwtape's later praise of the blended vintage Pharisee in the wine of the toast at the Tempters' dinner. But the standard fare is the average, the uncaring who has forgotten God, a mind is filled with trivia – the TV soaps and celebrity programmes – with envy, plots to get on at work, schemes to make money or more money, whose interest is gossip and slander in the social media, in the magazines and in their personal life. They commit themselves to a sinful course and do not reject what is wrong. Why? They have got to the stage that they cannot recognise the wrong so as to avoid it.

There is tragic side to this as well. Verses 2–4 do not say that the evildoers have stopped going to church – to use a modern term. People forgetful of God can go through the motions of Christian practice while it makes no impact within them. I can think of manipulative and duplicitous men whose evangelical doctrine is unimpeachable. The tragedy is that they appear quite psychotic as to its application. But, no, I am not going to tell you who I was thinking of as I wrote those words. Still, we do need examples. How about Tariq Aziz, Saddam Hussein's very able Foreign Minister – latterly his Deputy Prime Minister? Aziz is a Chaldean Catholic and who to some extent protected Christians in Iraq while he was in authority. The Chaldean Church is an old, old one – a Uniate church in full communion with Rome, with congregations in the US, Australia and New Zealand as well as in the Middle East. Other examples? Consider various TV evangelists preaching the Prosperity Gospel, the Gospel of Success, who live so well – private jets, expensive houses, and the like. I commend perusal of the ReligionNewsBlog website. In business, remember the company executives of WorldCom, Enron or Tyco who taught Sunday school at their local churches while plotting, rigging, conspiring, defrauding. Men now behind bars and paying huge fines – their families devastated. These were men who were busy, busy, busy. So busy they ceased to be wise and do good as v. 3 puts it. Taking a point from our studies in Joshua – they did not take time to consult God. They just did business as they saw it and took advantage, fast. They flattered themselves as to their business acumen too much to detect or hate their sin (cf. v. 3).

That, then, is the first part of this Psalm. That was the message God sent. Now David turns to God himself. It's a necessary corrective. It is too easy to condemn others – to be the self-satisfied Pharisee. These next verses are a paean of praise. We would need intricate choral polyphony or a massive orchestra and a score by Bruckner, Mahler or Wagner to do it justice. I cannot. So let's just read vv. 5–9: 'Your love, LORD, reaches to the heavens, your faithfulness to the skies. Your righteousness is like the mighty mountains, your justice like the great deep. You, LORD, preserve both people and animals. How priceless is your unfailing love, O God! People take refuge in the shadow of your wings. They feast on the abundance of your house; you give them drink from your river of delights. For with you is the fountain of life; in your light we see light. Continue your love to those who know you, your righteousness to the upright in heart.' This is the God the evildoers ignore. This is the God that David trusts for his protection – v.11: 'May the foot of the proud not come against me, nor the hand of the wicked drive me away.'

Then there is that last comment – v. 12: 'See how the evildoers lie fallen – thrown down, not able to rise.' It's the way David puts it that makes me think the Psalm was written after some actual event, some conspiracy against him, or whatever. But that also makes me think that we should not universalise that comment. The evildoers David was thinking of are fallen, not able to rise. But then we also know of examples of evildoers who have fallen, and then been raised, not by themselves, but by a merciful God – the God that David has just been speaking about. Think of such as Charles Colson (1931–2012) in his years as a Nixon hatchet-man, but later of the Prison Fellowship and the books. What about Jonathan Aitken, government minister, perjurer, and now, it seems, a keen, effective Christian? (Aitken was ordained in the Church of England in 2018 to minister in prisons). We can even pray for Tariq Aziz (who died in 2015, seven years after this was written). With God nothing is impossible.

Gilcomston Prayer Meeting, 15 March 2008.

Psalm 37

God has a droll sense of humour. Mike was arranging the February roster and when he approached me I had a contract to compete by the 10th. So I looked at the later of the scheduled psalms. That was in January, and my eightieth birthday was coming up. And so I came across Ps. 37: 25, 'I have been young; now I am old . . .'. Of course, after that I had no choice. But I have found it difficult to deal with it for tonight. It does not readily lead to prayer, and I am afraid that what follows may be a bit of a lecture. The work-habits of fifty-plus years are hard to shake off.

First, a lateral point. The text in front of us has forty verses. The Bible was not written in chapters and verses. Chapters were first inserted into the Bible in the early Thirteenth century through Archbishop Stephen Langton, who, incidentally, opposed King John and in 1215 helped write the Magna Carta. Verses were introduced in the early 1500s, and for us became standardised in the Geneva Bible of 1560.

To disinter a catch-phrase from the Goon Show, you may be thinking 'I don't wish to know that.' If so, fair enough. But the English versification of this psalm is important. It conceals that this is one of the acrostic psalms, though some versions tell you that in a footnote. They are *tours de force*. It is a difficult thing to do – try it. But this one is more than that. This one's acrosticity (if there is such a word) underlines the importance of what it says.

This psalm is not a prayer of petition. This is not a psalm of praise. It is a psalm of instruction, written to be memorised. For a Jew, this acrostic is a memory aid. Its twenty-two sections each begin with the next letter of the twenty-two letter Hebrew alphabet. That helps you remember it – if you know Hebrew. Our forty verses are not easily memorable. In the NIV and some other versions, however, the forty verses are grouped into twenty-two paragraphs. The form may be less memory-adhesive, but that cannot be helped. We are being taught things to remember. So this not a psalm with a story; rather it has a theme. More accurately it is like a symphony with themes stated, juggled, and intermixed. It is a string of nuggets, which memory can bring to mind as and when needed. And there is no reason to suppose these are not based on the fruits of age and experience (v. 25). So, youngsters, pay attention!

The psalm confronts a problem we have all wondered about: if God is just why do the wicked prosper? Job 21 brings it up. Ps. 73, which you may note is 37 the other way round, poses the question, as does Habbakuk 1. Jeremiah says to God: 'You are always righteous, Lord, when I bring a case to you. But I would speak with you about your justice: why does the way of the wicked prosper, why do all the faithless live at peace? You have planted them, and they have taken root; they grow and bear fruit' (Jer. 12: 1–2).

Before we get stuck into the text I need to say this. The psalm speaks in generalities. It does not lay down specific detail of instant accuracy. It is throwing flashes of light on what is in fact a changing and evolving scene. Thus take that v. 25, 'I have been young, now I am old yet I have never seen the righteous forsaken or their children begging bread.' Look at our world. Look at the world of David's time. There are exceptions to such a statement. Some righteous do suffer and appear forsaken. Some of their children do beg for bread. For such we must pray. But see v. 9, that those that hope in the Lord 'will inherit the land' – an idea implied in v. 3 that recurs in similar form in vv. 11, 18, 22, 27, 29, and 34. As an actual territorial inheritance that was not in David's pupils immediate future, nor in ours. But you will see that v. 11's reference to inheritance, peace and prosperity does in fact point beyond into the eternal. That is why it is the third of the Beatitudes (Matt. 5: 5). So the pictures of Ps. 37 are photos taken of a continuing process, and we have not yet reached its conclusion. That lies beyond.

For me this psalm has four major sections: vv. 1–11, 12–20, and 21–29 and 30–40. The first two are about the relations of the faithful and the godless. Elements of that remain in the two final sections – about half the psalm – but they are far more concerned with the interaction between God and his folk.

Vv. 1–11:

There's that feeling that there's something wrong when you see people 'getting away with it.' Feeling that 'that's not right' is universal, and echoes down the centuries. Political programmes aim at 'justice for all'. Christians and atheists alike try to alleviate, if not solve society's inequalities. The fact remains; down through the centuries, what's right is not being achieved. However, this psalm is not saying to be inactive and just watch. It does say 'watch and see'. It does not say watch and see, but stay out of it. Some righteous are called to help change things. It does not say 'do not try'. It does say 'do not fret' (vv. 1, 7, 8). And note this psalm does not equate prosperity with being wicked. Many Christians do prosper. Similarly it does not equate poverty with righteousness. Some god-haters are poor.

As I read on in the psalm of the godless that prosper, but then vanish (v. 10), I was reminded of the fates of most of those that had been tenants in 'The House of Government'. The House was a large apartment block in Moscow, across the river from the Kremlin, where senior officials, who had come to power as the Communist Party consolidated its hold on the country, were housed. Many had had powers of life or death, either immediate or through sending people to the gulag. Yuri Slezkine traces the career of most of them through the years: most came to a sudden end. [Y. Slezkine, *The House of Government: A Saga of the Russian Revolution*, Princeton, NJ: Princeton U.P., 2017].

Note the warning of v. 8 as to how you react to the godless that prosper. 'Refrain from anger and turn from wrath; do not fret – it leads only to evil.' A curiosity of the English language is how it has imported foreign words to put into one word an idea for which ordinary English would take several. One is 'schadenfreude' – rejoicing when someone gets his come-uppance. It is taking pleasure in the misfortune of others, and particularly can arise if you think they deserve it. Does it apply to this psalm? You will see the wicked vanish and be forgotten, if you wait and see what happens. Some might be tempted to interpret this psalm as a song of anger, bitterness and envy being assuaged, satiated, by the wicked being dealt with. Seeing others 'getting away with it' can stoke anger, bitterness and envy. V. 8 warns. Do not fall into that trap. It will corrupt you. So, in summary, keep a calm sough!

Vv. 12–20:

Basically at best the godless have no time for the faithful. At the worst they actively oppose them, and try to do them down. That was true for David's time, and it is true for ours. There are regimes that prohibit Christianity and people that kill Christians as a matter of principle, even of obligation. Yet, these verses say that through it all God will succour his people. The godless will be dealt with. That takes us on to vv. 21–40, which I will read as a whole:

This starts with a contrast, repeated in later verses as David reflects on the behaviour of each. The godless borrow, and do not give back. God-fearers not only return what is given, they give generously (v. 21). Wrongdoers will lie in wait intent on evil (v. 32), but they will be overturned (v. 28b). Though the wicked and ruthless flourish, they will vanish away (v. 35). They have no future to look forward to (v. 38).

But the major thrust is that God sustains his people. He delivers a more satisfying life to those who are faithful. When the psalm was composed the thought was probably of God's protection in our life on earth. But it goes beyond that. Verse 28 promises that He will care for his people forever – which takes us beyond this life. For the writer, whether he was David or someone else, that must have been a wonderful thing to know – he has just noted in v. 25 that he is now an old man. But it is something for all ages, even youngsters, to cherish.

So finally we come to the summation in vv. 39–40. 'The salvation of the righteous comes from the Lord; he is their stronghold in times of trouble. The Lord helps them and delivers them; he delivers them from the wicked and saves them, because they take refuge in him.' There is comfort in the simplicity of that. It does not say that he saves them because they have been good. It does not say that he saves them because they have learned not to fret. It does not say that he saves them because they have not got angry because of the apparent injustices of the world. He saves them because they take refuge in him, trusting in his promises. That is what we do as we pray.

Gilcomston Prayer Meeting, 28 February 2020.

Psalm 38

I want to take this Psalm two ways. Whether the second is lawful you may decide.

The first is to take this Psalm at its face value. It is a psalm of David written out of anguish. David is praying for deliverance because God is punishing him for his sins.

There can be physical consequences of sin. In this instance the probability is that David has a venereal disease. It is plainer in translations other than the NIV – e.g. the KJV or the RSV. But see v. 3: 'There is no health in my body: my bones have no soundness.' V. 5: 'my wounds fester and are loathsome'. V. 6: 'I am bowed down.' V. 7: 'my back (or my loins) is filled with searing pain; there is no health in my body.' V. 8: 'I am feeble and utterly crushed.' V. 10: 'my heart pounds, my strength fails me, even the light has gone from my eyes.' Why? V. 3; 'because of my sin.' V. 5: 'because of my sinful folly.'

Disease is something that we have to face up to. It is indeed possible to contract syphilis or other venereal afflictions blamelessly. It is possible to get HIV/AIDS innocently. That marvellous tennis player some of us may remember, Arthur Ashe, got it through a blood transfusion during open-heart surgery. He died in 1993. There was that poignant appearance of Kimberly Bergalis before the US Congress in 1991 to publicise the then relatively new problem of AIDS. She was in a wheelchair as her frame was being ravaged by the disease, and she wanted all health care workers to be tested for HIV. She had been infected by her dentist. She died later that year. There are many infected with HIV through blood transfusions or through licit sex – think of AIDS in Africa. These and similar cases must concern us. Why do the innocent suffer?

But that is not David's situation. He acknowledges his sin and his sinful folly. So I am not going to try to cover the question of innocence and disease. But I would comment that not all in illness is punishment for sin, the result of folly and going astray. It may be: but it need not be. Remember Job and the potsherd (Job 2: 8). Remember Paul's thorn in the flesh where the purpose of the affliction was very different (2 Cor. 12: 7). The person who sees every physical malady as punishment for offending against the

Almighty does not know the Almighty you very well – I almost said, not at all. God is not like that. In a way those who reckon – and may delight in telling others – that they have been selected out for special treatment by God through illness or other difficulties are more interested in themselves than in the God of whom they speak. There are those that 'enjoy bad health'.

In this instance God is punishing David as a result or as a consequence of acknowledged sin. We do not know the circumstances, but we have his clear testimony as to what is going on. And note what I just said. The punishment is 'as a result of' or 'as a consequence of' sin. What has happened is in this case physically related to sin. Sometimes we are chastised through something happening to us, but the connection between that something and the need for us to be chastised is evident only to us. If I am right that this psalm has to do with venereal disease, the connection is more immediate. It is a result anyone can deduce.

And of course, as is so often the case, when there is blood in the water the sharks are circulating. The jackals try to cut out the weakened. V. 12: 'Those who seek my life set their traps, those who would harm me talk of my ruin: all day long they plot the deception.' In a sort of a way sin has stirred them up. Vv. 19–20: 'many are those who are my vigorous enemies; those who hate me without reason are numerous. Those who repay my good with evil, slander me when pursue what is good.'

But it is not just the enemies. David's friends and companions avoid him (v. 11). In this case it is because of his wounds, he says. That is often the case. Some of us – by which I mean me – are slow to get alongside someone who is going through an illness even though there is no reason to suspect that it is God punishing. Visit the sick: Matt. 25: 36?? That's not what it says. There are those who seemed to enjoy the bad health or medical problems of others, but the Matthew text says 'I was sick and you looked after me' – the focus must be the ill person, not the preening self-congratulation of the visitor. What about bereavement? That is difficult. There are times not to speak. There are times to speak but not to speak of the dead. But there are times not to stand afar off.

If God is chastising someone, is that not even more time to get alongside? I speak to my condemnation, but see how David analyses his position and responds. First, as already said, he recognizes his punishment is for sin. He does not rail against an arbitrary God. He does not denounce an unfair God. This is not 'why has this happened me? I don't deserve this.'

No. David accepts that what has happened to him is from God because of sin. That recognition doesn't of itself change things. He still has all those symptoms. His enemies still circle. His friends still avoid. But David does not engage with either the enemies or the friends. They are there doing what they do; the friends ignoring, the enemies plotting. Why doesn't David speak to his friends? One answer could be that it was up to them to make the approach – as I indicated above. As for the enemies, David remained as vigilant as usual, as his health permitted. That would be politic. But he does not tackle them face-to-face.

The solution is repairing his relationship with God. David has sinned. He has broken fellowship with God. He wants to get back where he was. That is what is important for David. See it in vv. 13–14 when he repeats twice: he is as someone deaf, that cannot hear, mute, that cannot speak. He will not react to his friends' silence, or respond directly to his enemies. His attention is elsewhere: V. 15: 'I will wait for you, O Lord; you will answer. O Lord my God.' In an odd sort of way being punished for your sin is reassuring. It proves God cares for us as his children – see Hebrews 12: 4–11.

And there is a glow at the end of the psalm. V. 21: 'O Lord, do not forsake me; be not far from me, O my God. Come quickly to help me, O Lord my saviour.' God has not cast David off, just punished him. David still trusts God, even in a sin induced sickness. And for our reassurance note: we have many others of David's psalms some of which must have been written after this one, showing that his trust was honoured. The Lord was indeed his saviour.

The second way I want to take this psalm is briefly to distort it though I have the precedent of Augustine for this comment.

Jesus Christ, our Saviour, was without sin. This is Easter Saturday, the day after the crucifixion. That was not punishment for **his** sin. It was punishment for **our** sin.

Can you see echoes in this psalm of what he went through for us? Vv. 11– 12. Many enemies plotted against him. They sought his destruction. His loved ones and friends did not intervene – Peter's denial. And at the end some stood afar off, though within sight. He was broken. His strength failed as the cross took its toll on his frame. Like David, Jesus does not respond to his enemies (vv. 13–14). He trusted in his God even as he cried 'my God, my God why hast thou forsaken me?' (Matt. 27: 46).

So tonight let David's anguish – which ends in trust – reflect for us the events of Easter.

Gilcomston Prayer Meeting, 26 March 2005.

Psalm 41

I found grappling with this Psalm difficult for a variety of reasons, not all of which are relevant for tonight. As usual I have had a look at Augustine, at Calvin and at Matthew Henry. Should I have gone to more modern books? Perhaps, but while I have lots of books on my shelves, modern commentaries do not figure among them.

To my surprise Augustine is not useful. His commentary on Ps. 41 is a transcription of a sermon delivered on the Day of Martyrs. So he discusses the psalm in terms of the Passion of Christ. While interesting, and not 'wrong', this is a Davidic psalm. We should pay attention to David's struggles. Augustine does not.

Calvin is different. Calvin does write of David and his difficulties. But, Calvin takes 6000 words, so there's a level of detail that's unhelpful if you are looking for 15 to 20 minutes. That said, he's interesting, often following the possibilities of different readings. But he uses a text that does not always match what we have in front of us: it's probably the original Geneva Bible. Different translations can ring alarm bells. You read the NIV – but the NIV may have imposed one view, while concealing the possibility of ambiguity in the basic text. If it could be this, or it could be that, we should know about it. But this is not the place to chase these hares.

Last, Matthew Henry. Helpful as always, he also raises some textual questions, though in general he sweeps through, much as I intend to.

My cardinal problem with this Psalm was this. It thrashes around. It took me a long time to come to terms with that. With diffidence – for I don't know if the modern commentators come up with this solution – I offer this. We should not read it as though David one day sat down and wrote it out. *Per contra*, I see different thoughts written at different times, later rearranged into the final version. How many here have written poems? How many have written prose? You rarely conceive a bit of writing and set it down seriatim in the way it finally appears. Rather a piece of writing is hacked out and reworked. Bits are added. Bits are chopped. Bits are relocated. Cut and paste! The script in front of me is an example of the process. So, I suggest, is this Psalm.

Remember what it was originally. It was not written for those who can read to pore over. It was not for the private musings of the faithful. It was not set down for the lucubrations of the herd of modern scholars. It was finalised and given to the Director of Music for performance, as its title indicates. And, by the way before you confuse the Director of Music with John Rutter or Graham Kendrick, or even the Gettys and Stuart Townend, remember that there was no Temple at this time. The Director would set appropriate music, and his choir would perform it. It was like a sung sermon, intoned for the edification of the people, most of whom could not read, and we don't know if texts were provided for the use of those who could. Maybe I should simply have read it – or sung it – as a sermon or teaching for you to think about.

Look at it. The apparent pattern is blessing on those who help the troubled, sickness, rampant enemies, restoration and lessons from that. But I suggest the origin was the facts of the middle. David was sick, vv. 3b–4. In his illness, his enemies pounced and he hated that, vv. 5–9. He prays, vv. 4 and 10. Then he thinks: God blesses those that care for those who are in weakness, vv. 1–3, and implicitly by contrast, how unblessed the others are. Finally, vv. 11–13, he has come through it all and praises the Lord. Then he puts the bits together in the form we have.

Sticking with that idea, let's look at it.

The middle of the Psalm has to do with David's illness. He acknowledges that it has to do with sin – we have not precise idea of what sin that was. He asks the Lord for mercy (v. 4). But he swiftly passes to his attackers. In v. 5 David tells us his enemies are saying malicious things about him. They hope he is dying. The NIV is too smooth in saying they are speaking in malice. Calvin points out that they were pronouncing maledictions. That is much more extreme than mere malice. It is easy to be malicious. You can do that in an ever so civilised manner. A malediction is an unvarnished expression of hate. It is 'evil-saying' – male-diction. But even that set of syllables may blunt the point. To bring a malediction on someone is to call down a curse on them. The enemies were cursing him in his weakness. No wonder David was hurt. Even his close friend had betrayed him (v. 9). It hurts to be attacked – cursed – by those you thought were your friends. That isn't just being let down. This isn't even some sort of call for a change away from a President that has been too-long-in-office. This was an attack on the King, who knew that he had been placed there by God. So it was also an attack on God. And it hurt. In art terms David's reaction reminds me of Francis Bacon's series of Screaming Heads.

Now, go back to the beginning. Given what David has gone through you see why he realises that: 'Blessed is he who has regard for the weak; the Lord delivers him in times of trouble. The Lord will protect him and preserve his life; he will bless him in the land and not surrender him to the desire of his foes. The Lord will sustain him on his sickbed and restore him from his bed of illness' (Ps. 41: 1–3).

You can take that passage two ways. It could be a general thought, pointing to the compassion of the Lord who protects those that have regard for the weak. Or it could be that David has a feeling that he was succoured because he himself had succoured – perhaps even including succouring that traitorous friend of v. 9. Calvin and Henry would accept either. But really this is one of those useful ambiguous bits. Both can be true.

David saw this particular illness as tied up with sin, v. 4b. It was not primarily a testing – we know from elsewhere in the Bible that that can happen, and there may have been a testing element in it – but David recognised that he needed to be healed because he had sinned against the Lord, v. 4. However, let me step sideways and make a further comment. Testing happens. But the Lord does not test so that he may know whether we stand up to it or not. He knows us through and through. He tests so that we know ourselves.

One thing more from that passage. The NIV has 'the Lord will … restore him from his bed of illness'. Calvin, so generally assumed to be stern, cold and lacking in empathy, says that in the original the sense has to do with the bed, not directly with David. Two possibilities. God may be changing David's bedding, making him more comfortable – a lovely thought. Others, whom Calvin prefers, see the bed that once was David's sickbed being turned by God into a couch as David came back to health. Please yourself. Either thought is worth thinking. They show the care of God for those being trained or disciplined through affliction.

So, David has gone through illness, and his enemies have taken the chance, they hoped, to do him down. They have not sympathised. They have not helped. They have not fluffed up his pillows. Instead they have cursed him and hoped for his demise.

David calls on God to raise him up so he may repay those that have proved to be against him, v.10. And God does sustain and then restores him,

v. 3. Obviously David recovers – after all he wrote the Psalm commenting on the events. So we have vv. 11–12. David knows that God is pleased with him because his enemies do not triumph. God upholds him in his integrity and sets him in his presence forever. No wonder that in the last verse David is full of praise. 'Praise be to the Lord, the God of Israel, from everlasting to everlasting'.

We should echo that.

Gilcomston Prayer Meeting, 25 June 2011.

Psalm 46

My archives show that I agreed to tackle this psalm on 14 April 2017. Since then we have had the terrorist bombing of a pop concert in Manchester, the London Bridge attack and a General Election. Daily, TV, radio and the papers tell us of dreadful doings. Yet this psalm contains v. 10. 'Be still and know that I am God; I will be exalted among the nations; I will be exalted in the earth.' In the ultimate, that is what we stand on. This is a psalm to encourage, to reassure. Apparently 'be still' implies even a limpness. We are as clay in the hands of the potter. Fret not. Trust your Maker. We are told it was Luther's favourite psalm. Very understandable, given what he went through.

The Psalm has three sections, separated with that word 'selah', which may mean pause and think, or pause for a musical interlude. But I am not going to stick to that programme.

Calvin thinks this Psalm was probably triggered by deliverance from a crisis. Jerusalem, in great danger, had been saved. That is why the faithful are being exhorted to rely on God as their protector. But we do not know for sure which event could be its root.

The Psalm was written by one or more of the Sons of Korah, one of the divisions of the Kohathites who were entrusted with the praise in the Temple and are not to be confused with the Australian gospel group that has pinched the name. We don't know what 'according to alamoth' means. Alamoth might be an instrument, or a common and well-known tune. I wonder Psalm 46 sounded like when performed by the Sons of Korah. Western ears might be appalled.

The Korah connection provides a possible source for the Psalm. Look at 2 Chron. 20. Faced by an invasion, Jehoshaphat prayed to God (vv. 6–12). God responded through a prophet, Jahaziel. God would act. Then 'some of the Levites from the Kohathites and the Korahites stood up and praised the Lord, the God of Israel, with a very loud voice' (2 Chron. 20: 19). Next day Jehoshaphat exhorted the people to rely on the Lord, and appointed singers to praise the Lord as they led the people out (2 Chron. 20: 20–21). God induced the invaders to fight among themselves, and the kingdom was saved without it having to fight.

So 2 Chronicles 20 could lie behind the psalm. The Kohathites, the Sons of Korah, knew all about it. They had been there on the scene, singing. Calvin has a different suggestion, but we will get to that.

Verse 1 starts with a succinct, confident assertion: 'God is our refuge and strength, a very present help in trouble' as the KJV has it. It is a trumpet call. Imagine the 'very loud' voices of the Brothers Korah belting out v. 1! Were I orchestrating it I would adapt a few bars from Stravinsky's magnificent *Oedipus Rex*, and recapitulate that solemn but explosive fanfare for vv. 7 and 11. 'The Lord Almighty is with us; the God of Jacob is our fortress' : 'God is our refuge; God is our fortress' – both reflecting the confidence of v. 1.

Verses 2 and 3 go to specifics: 'Therefore we will not be afraid', even though earthquakes and fierce floods may happen. Concentrate on that 'therefore'. Be confident and trust. The last time I was taking this meeting I quoted Calvin's use of an Ode from the Roman poet Horace – probably the first time Horace was cited within these walls. I am pleased do so again tonight. Writing on vv. 3–5, Calvin, who, did not just read theology, quotes again from Horace, this time Book 3, Ode 3, an Ode entitled 'Stand Firm'.[5] Though acknowledging that Horace was a pagan, Calvin associates Horace's words with the Psalm. It's better in the Latin than the English.

Dux inquieti turbidus Adriae, Nec fulminantis magna Jovis manus, Si fractus illabitur orbis, Impavidum ferient ruinae.

The passion of the public, demanding what is wrong, never shakes the man of just and firm intention from his settled purpose, nor the tyrant's threatening face, nor the winds the stormy masters of the troubled Adriatic, nor Jupiter's mighty hand with its lightning: if the heavens fractured in their fall, still their ruin would strike him, unafraid.

Paraphrasing, Horace is saying, 'Stand firm on your beliefs. Be confident and unafraid though you are threatened by tyrants or by storms.' Tyrants and storms. Nature and human conflict. The Psalm speaks of threats from both.

Verses 2 and 3 speak of raging waters and earthquakes, mountains collapsing into the seas. Verse 6b says that God lifts his voice and the earth melts. We know more than the Sons of Korah. The TV can show us raging waters, even in the UK. We have seen earthquakes – Italy 2016. We have

5   Horace, Book 3, Ode 3, Translated by A.S. Kline © Copyright 2003.

seen eruptions, Mount St Helens, Pinatubo, Monserrat. Recall the Japanese and Indian Ocean tsunamis. This psalm contrasts the threat of all such with the tranquillity of Jerusalem, the city of God, irrigated by a peaceful river (vv. 4–5). God will defend his city from natural disaster.

The other threat comes from humanity. 'Nations are in uproar, kingdoms fall' (v. 6a).

When we began I pointed to the events of 2 Chronicles 20 as a possible source for the Psalm. Calvin took a different view. He suggested the destruction of Sennacherib's army (2 Kgs 19: 35–36 and Isa. 37). Maybe. You will recall that Sennacherib, besieging Jerusalem, sent a letter to Hezekiah detailing how so many other kings and their gods had failed to stop him. Hezekiah took the letter, spread it before the Lord, and prayed for help. Isaiah sent a message to him. God had heard and would act. That night the Lord smote the Assyrian army. Sennacherib retreated to Nineveh, soon after to be assassinated.

We have been hearing a lot about Iraq and the re-taking of Mosul. Mosul once was Nineveh. The Islamic State (ISIL) took it over in June 2014. On 24 July 2014 ISIL blew up the reputed Tomb of Jonah at the city's edge. They said it was an idolatrous abomination. The area was retaken in December 2016, and, lo and behold, thanks to that cultural crime and the tunnels ISIL made to defend Mosul, archaeologists have found the ruins of Sennacherib's Palace underneath the old tomb. A magnificent building, extended by his successors Esarhaddon and Ashurbanipal, Sennacherib's Palace was buried and forgotten when Nineveh was destroyed in 612 BC. 'Come and see what the Lord hath done, the desolations he has brought on the earth. He makes wars cease to the ends of the earth. He breaks the bow and shatters the spear; he burns the shields with fire.' (vv. 8–9). (Cf. http://www.telegraph.co.uk/news/2017/02/27/previously-untouched-600bc-palace-discovered-shrine-demolished).

So finally we come back to v. 10. 'Be still and know that I am God; I will be exalted among the nations; I will be exalted in the earth'.

There is a question whether Ps. 46: 10 is addressed to the heathen or to the God-fearers. No. We do not always see it. But we can stand firm. Thanks to the death of Christ we can grasp this Psalm for ourselves, 'God is our refuge and our strength.' With the Sons of Korah we can affirm the final verse of the Psalm. 'The Lord Almighty is with us; the God of Jacob is our fortress'.

Gilcomston Prayer Meeting, 10 June 2017.

Psalm 47

There is an irony in my tackling this Psalm. It is a psalm by the sons of Korah. Remembering Korah's rebellion against Moses in Num. 16, and thinking 'that can't be right', I looked up that 'Korah' to see if there was a connection. It appears not. A different family produced the composers of this psalm. The sons of Korah were a division, a sept of the Kohathites, the door-keepers and singers in the Temple. Apparently there is also an Australian Christian Pop group that use the name. So far so good. The sons of Korah are responsible for eleven psalms, psalms 42, 44–49, 84–85, and 87–89. Then I noticed that some Talmudic scholars explain the name 'Korah' as 'ice' 'hail' 'frost' – curious as a name, eh? But it can also mean 'baldness'. So here in front of you is a bald man talking about the songs of baldies.

Obviously this is a composition for a ceremonial occasion – the equivalent of Handel's 'Zadok the Priest', which we use in the Coronation. We do not know what first evoked Psalm 47, but clearly it was something special. Maybe it had to do with bringing the Ark into Jerusalem. Remember David dancing before the Lord in that procession, to the disgust of his wife, Michal (2 Sam. 6: 14–22). Some have suggested it was composed for the coronation of Solomon (2 Chron. 29: 21–5) or for the inauguration of Solomon's Temple (2 Chron. 3 to 7). At any rate vv. 3–4 would indicate that at its time Israel was in the ascendant. God had 'subdued nations under us, peoples under our feet. He chose our inheritance for us, the pride of Jacob, whom he loved.' Others have thought that it may have had to do with the restoration after the Exile. Ezra 3: 10–13 speaks of the joy and praise as the foundation of the Second Temple was laid when the Levites, the Sons of Korah, were involved in the joyful celebrations (Ezra 3: 10). But, given the extravagance of expression of Ps. 47, and the fact that the restoration left the people as part of the Babylonian Empire, that connection seems unlikely. Ezra 3: 10 also says that the praise offered was prescribed by David. So, while this Psalm may have been used then, it certainly was not written for the restoration.

Of course, there is a possible transcendental application to the Second

Coming. However, to jump straight to that could invite us merely to wallow in mushy feelings. There is more to this psalm than a warm emotional bath.

I divide this Psalm into three chunks, although there is a case for a single split at the Selah after v. 4. My reason is that vv. 1–2 are general while vv. 3–4 focus on the nation. Thereafter vv. 5–9 are again general, calling the whole world together in praise.

So, vv. 1–2: 'Clap your hands, all you nations; shout to God with cries of joy. For the LORD Most High is awesome, the great King over all the earth.' That is a mighty summons. 'All you nations': you cannot go wider than that. Yes, there are other psalms that speak of the whole of creation praising the Lord – 'The heavens are telling the glory of God' as you find in Papa Haydn's marvellous 'The Creation'. But this is a call to the sentient peoples of the world. See v. 9 – all nations assemble as the peoples of the God of Abraham. It applies also to you and to me. Two things about vv. 1–2.

First, it is a call to take part. It is an invitation. It is not an instruction. What do I mean by that? Simply this. It is a call to be joyful. True joy is not synthetic. It bubbles from deep within. Joy is genuine, a fundamental feeling. Not something to be turned on. By way of contrast think of those parades in North Korea, though I would not underestimate what brain-washing can do. What about the Hitler rallies at Nuremberg, orchestrated by Albert Speer, and brilliantly presented in Leni Riefenstahl's film 'The Triumph of the Will'? What of the ovations that greeted Stalin's speeches, with Uncle Joe, a former trainee priest, watching to see who would stop clapping first. No. Take part. But be real!

Secondly, it is a call to Joy. Not to Fun. Despite v. 1, this is not happy-clappy or jumping around. It is praise, not entertainment. The focus is God the Lord, not the self-centred emotional release of the participant. Joy, true joy, has a different feel. Terry Pratchett puts it well. 'Joy is to fun what the deep sea is to a puddle. It is a feeling inside that can hardly be contained.' (T. Pratchett, *A Hat Full of Sky*, (London: Doubleday, 2004) 349).

My second chunk is vv. 3-4: 'He subdued nations under us, peoples under our feet. He chose our inheritance for us, the pride of Jacob, whom he loved. SELAH.'

Here are problems. Augustine simply slides straight past what could be seen as assertions of power, hegemony, and a tribal triumphalism. He relates this passage to the authority of the Apostles, and also comments on Jacob being preferred over Esau, the younger over the elder. His point, I think, is that God chooses as he will. Calvin is more sensible. For him in these verses the people are acknowledging God's favour. Matthew Henry also takes us along that line of thought, though first rehearsing God's choice of the Land for the Jews. For Matthew Henry we can trust God's choosing of our way for us. So, in sum, let me put my thought like this: to think you are the 'Chosen People' can lead to arrogance and self-regard. Do you, self-styled Christian, think like that? You need not. You can celebrate along with this psalm, just recognising a simple statement of fact. Through Christ we too can join in praise. God loves us. He has chosen our inheritance for us. His Son died to make it so.

Then we come to that little word, Selah. The scholars don't know what it means. It certainly indicates that there should be a break at this point. It may indicate a pause for a musical interlude. In a psalm like this it might even indicate 'pause for fanfare' – see v. 5. It could also mean 'pause and think about that', which would also fit. So, think about it.

My last chunk, vv. 5–9, fits together.

God has ascended amid shouts of joy, the LORD amid the sounding of trumpets. Sing praises to God, sing praises; sing praises to our King, sing praises. For God is the King of all the earth; sing to him a psalm of praise. God reigns over the nations; God is seated on his holy throne. The nobles of the nations assemble as the people of the God of Abraham, for the kings of the earth belong to God; he is greatly exalted.

How can we gloss that? I would start by citing 2 Chron. 20: 19. Jahaziel, son of Zechariah, the son of Benaiah, the son of Jeiel, the son of Mattaniah, a Levite, and interestingly, given our Psalm, a descendant of Asaph, the author of so many other psalms, but not a son of Korah, was encouraging Jehosaphat to march against the invaders. Jehosaphat accepted the instruction as from God via Jahaziel: 'Then some Levites from the Kohathites and Korahites stood up and praised the LORD, the God of Israel, with a very loud voice' (2 Chron. 20: 19). I think that is the only place in the Bible that comments on the sheer volume the Sons of Korah could produce. That said, I think that that praising could be eclipsed by a proper performance of our psalm, or something inspired by it.

The Internet has made all sorts of material available. Praising the gods is, of course, a part of all religions. Nowadays you can call up on the web hymns of praise to a slew of Sumerian, Assyrian or Babylonian gods, to Anu, Enlil and Enki, to Inanna or Anna the patron god of Abram's Ur, or to Marduk, patron of Babylon (http://etcsl.orinst.ox.ac.uk/index1.htm). I looked some of them up. Among other Near Eastern religious songs of praise I have not come across a fit competitor for Ps. 47. They are formal, courtly, detached. There are echoes, but in my reading this explosion of praise is unrivalled.

So, in its original use, what we have in Ps. 47 is a psalm of celebration for a formal occasion. Link it to a procession, a coronation, whatever. David dancing.

Tonight we can transport these words forward to our time. We can praise our Lord in these terms. We do so not as individuals, but as part of the Church. This is a group, together praising our God. We are in the great parade, together with many others, – no doubt with others whom we might view askance on seeing them in the parade – and they us – we together are the Church, the Bride of Christ. Look at Pope Francis's 2013 Apostolic Exhortation on 'The Joy of the Gospel', *Evangelii Gaudium*, – an intriguing reference to Joy. Papa Frankie/Pope Frank says a lot. Shed your blinkers!

Back to our Psalm. Translate it into music, that greatest expression of profundities. What might composers have made from these last verses? Monteverdi's Vespers of 1610, Verdi's Requiem, Mahler 2 or 8, Elgar's 'The Dream of Gerontius', Tchaikovsky or Rachmaninoff's settings of the Orthodox texts. Maybe not Rutter or Taverner. Certainly not Getty or Kendrick.

Our Lord: 'has ascended amid shouts of joy, the LORD amid the sounding of trumpets. Sing praises to God, sing praises; sing praises to our King, sing praises. For God is the King of all the earth; sing to him a psalm of praise. God reigns over the nations; God is seated on his holy throne. The nobles of the nations assemble as the people of the God of Abraham, for the kings of the earth belong to God; he is greatly exalted' (Ps. 47: 5–9).

Remember the Catechism, Question 1? Man's chief end (sc. main purpose) is 'to glorify God and enjoy him forever.' It's what we are for. So: Let us praise.

Gilcomston Prayer Meeting, 28 June 2014.

Psalm 48

This is a celebratory psalm, and a special one. Practice in Jewish synagogues is to recite one particular Psalm each day of the week, each connected with the seven days of creation. Psalm 48 is linked to the second day of Creation, the day God separated the firmament from the waters (Gen. 1: 6–8), and is recited at the end of Monday morning prayers. How does that fit tonight?

We often get more out of a psalm when we can link it to a background. This song is a celebration of being protected by God. So, who wrote Ps. 48, why and when? We are told the 'who' – but only in general terms. It is a song of the Sons of Korah. They were a division of the Kohathites, the door-keepers and singers in the Temple. All well and good, but that does not take us very far. There were a lot of them. However, and without having delved into modern scholarship, I will stick my neck out and later suggest a name.

'Why' and 'when' may go together. Ps. 48: 4–6 tells us that kings had come against the city of God, but had been blown away as if by a gale. God had intervened. But when? Of course this psalm may have been written as a general tribute to the power of God to defend Zion. I find that unacceptably vague. So here are four options.

First, 2 Chron. 14: 9–12. Zerah the Cushite invaded when Asa was king. Asa's army defeated the intruders. Jerusalem was protected, but the defenders had had to fight. That does not fit. Second, 2 Kgs. 16: 5–9; 2 Chron. 28: 1–27. Rezin of Syria and Pekah of Israel tried to conquer Jerusalem when Ahaz was king. Isaiah's advice was to trust in God, not in man (Isa. 7: 1–12). Instead, Ahaz bribed Tiglath–Pileser of Assyria to help, but from then on he was under Tiglath's control. The kingdom was free from further incursions, but only under foreign protection. However, when Ahaz visited Damascus to pay his respects the architecture impressed him, so he ordered a new altar and sacrifices in the Temple. Ahaz said he would there seek God's guidance (2 Kgs. 16: 15). Had Ahaz got a scare and in some measure returned to the Lord? Maybe yes, maybe not. He was notorious, and when he died he was not buried with the kings of Israel (2 Chron. 28: 27). Even so, we can pray that Covid-19 would turn some to God. But that story does not fit Ps. 48.

Third, 2 Kgs. 18 and 19, 2 Chron. 32, Isa. 37 – the destruction of Sennacherib's army. Besieging Jerusalem, Sennacherib sent Hezekiah a letter boasting how the gods of so many other kings had failed to stop him. Hezekiah went to the Temple, spread the letter before the LORD, and prayed for help. Now, intriguingly, Hezekiah was Ahaz's son (2 Kgs. 18: 1). Had father taught son? We don't know, but clearly Hezekiah knew to rely on God for help. Isaiah sent a message. God had heard and would act. That night the LORD smote the Assyrian army (2 Kgs. 19: 35–36). In the older wording, 'when they arose early in the morning they were all dead' (v. 35). Sennacherib retreated to Nineveh, and soon after was assassinated (2 Chron. 32: 21). In that case salvation came by the arm of the LORD, not by force of arms. Calvin thinks that story may lie behind Ps. 46, but no clear evidence ties it to Ps. 48.

Last, somewhat earlier we have 2 Chron. 20: 1–30. When Jehoshaphat was king – incidentally the son of Asa (1 Kgs. 22: 41: 2 Chron. 17: 1) – a heterogeneous group, an alliance of Moabites, Ammonites, and Edomites from Mount Seir, invaded. That was an attack by kings, plural, precisely what is spoken of in Ps. 48: 4–6.

Knowing the attack was coming, Jehoshaphat and the people got together in a new courtyard in the Temple and prayed to God (2 Chron. 20: 5–13). Among them was someone whose name means 'God sees' or 'God looks'. According to v. 14 this was 'Jahaziel, son of Zechariah, the son of Benaiah, the son of Jeiel, the son of Mattaniah, a Levite, and a descendant of Asaph' (2 Chron. 20: 14). He got to his feet and prophesied. God would take care of things. Indeed, Jahaziel transmitted precise instructions. The army was to march to where the invaders would be, at the end of a gorge in the Desert of Jeruel. But the troops would not have to fight. They were there only to observe. The LORD was going to act (2 Chron. 20: 15–17).

Jehoshaphat and the people accepted his message and worshipped God. But then the narrative goes further. 'Some of the Levites from the Kohathites and the Korahites stood up and praised the LORD, the God of Israel, with a very loud voice' (2 Chron. 20: 19). I think that is the only place that comments on the sheer volume the Sons of Korah could produce.

Next day, Jehoshaphat exhorted everyone to rely on the LORD, and detailed off singers to praise the LORD as the troops left Jerusalem – Sons of Korah, no doubt (2 Chron. 20: 20–21). When the army reached the invaders they found them already dispersed and defeated. God had induced them to fight among themselves, first the Moabites and Ammonites against the Edomites, and then Moab against Ammon. So, the kingdom was saved without a fight (2 Chron. 20: 22–23).

In short, 2 Chron. 20 looks to me the event that lies behind the Ps. 48. As with Sennacherib the people did not have to fight. But here we see that the Kohathites, the Sons of Korah, knew all about it. They had been there, singing, loudly. Certainly they would have been involved in the joyful return, with 'harps and lyres and trumpets' (2 Chron. 20: 27–28). Agreed, singing is not mentioned in the brief note of the return to Zion, but were the Sons of Korah silent? I doubt it.

Ps. 48 is a Psalm of the Sons of Korah. But I don't think a committee wrote it. So, who is the author? I suspect Jahaziel. Not to the level of 'beyond reasonable doubt'. Nor even 'on the balance of probabilities'. But it is a 'reasonable possibility'. Consider. According to 2 Chron. 20: 14 Jahaziel was a Levite, not a Kohathite or a son of Korah. But he was of Asaph's line, and we have seen so many other Psalms by an Asaph. His family had the psalmist gene, if I may put it like that. Imagine how he would feel after what had happened? He was the conduit for that crucial prophecy. Having seen its fulfilment, wouldn't he be joyful? Wasn't he the person best fitted to compose a celebratory anthem for the Sons of Korah to sing. And so it got into their hymn-book – we are told it is a psalm 'of' the Sons of Korah, not a song 'by' the Sons of Korah. In other words it's one that they sang. And so it came to us. What do you think?

Now, what does all this teach us? Overarchingly this psalm speaks of protection and salvation, and that immediately takes us to our Saviour. He stands behind and above all this. As examples we can celebrate three categories of God's protections. First, equate protection of Mount Zion with the protection of Christ's Church. Second, the protection of particular congregations. Third is the protection of each of us as individuals.

Protecting Mount Zion. Link that down through history. Yes, there are occasions when, because of sin, God's protection was withdrawn, and enemies had a very free rein. There was the Exile to Babylon, and the rule of various empires, culminating with the Romans. But on the plus side run through these. Noah and the Flood. The career of Abraham. Joseph. The Exodus. The Hezekiah and Jehoshaphat incidents. Consider the Book of Esther. The Return from Babylon, and Ezra and Nehemiah. Jump to the survival of the nascent New Testament church. Saul, a major persecutor, was stopped in his tracks. The Church was protected as it spread in the Roman Empire. The Reformation. Last week we remembered VE Day. I could go on, but you can make your own list. God protects his church.

Second, the protection of particular congregations. A congregation is a gathered flock. Take the word apart: in Latin 'con' means together, 'grex, grecis' is a flock, and the 'ation' bit is the Roman for action. Con-greg-ation. The Good Shepherd looks after his flock. So, quite solipsistically, consider the Gilcomston congregation. Two hundred and fifty years ago we were coming together and building a place to worship. Subsequently we might have ceased to exist several times. There was the 1843 Disruption. The congregation might have been dissolved in 1938 when the minister, James George Lunn, left for Scone. In 1943 Lindsay Stewart resigned during his secondment as an RAF chaplain. Again that might have been the end. From the 1970s on the Presbytery of Aberdeen united or dissolved several city centre churches, but Gilcomston survived various scrutinies. We have been protected through our leaving the Church of Scotland.

Finally on this track, I leave to each of you to remember occasions on which the Lord has preserved you, from attacks whether minor or major.

So there is much in Ps. 48 to echo and embrace. Like a well-cut diamond it reflects and transmits many truths. The LORD **is** worthy of praise as we contemplate his city, whatever the content you see in Mount Zion (Ps. 48: 1). It is beautiful, and, with God in its citadels, he is its fortress (Ps. 48: 3). We have heard, we have seen, that he is its security (Ps. 48: 9). Think of his unfailing love (Ps. 48: 10). In prayer we can go about – I would even say wander about – his City. See its towers, ramparts and citadels, however you want to interpret that imagery. Why? So that we may tell future generations all about it (Ps. 48: 12–14). This God is our God for ever and ever. Our guide and protector even to the end (Ps. 48: 14). And, finally, recall that Jewish link of Ps. 48 to the second day of creation. To adapt Churchill's words after El Alamein, for us that end is just an end of a beginning. Like the Sons of Korah, we have good reasons to praise God.

Gilcomston Prayer Meeting, 16 May 2020.

Psalm 49

I was given a choice of dates and therefore of Psalms. I chose this one. Some may remember two screaming psalms that I have dealt with in the past. Ps. 35 in particular was ground into me as I recalled my experience and David shouted his anguish and I called it the 'Song of the screaming Dean'. And I found that it must have gone deep within me, that experience of Ps. 35, for it is the main reason I asked for Ps. 49 when I had to read it and the alternative choice. My archive shows that Ps. 35 was on 4 December 1997, just after my second deanship.

This Psalm also has to do with 'when evil days come' and wicked deceivers surround (v. 5). But how different it is from Ps. 35. Yes Ps. 35 won through at the end – but only at the end. The rest of it was 'where are you Lord?' not unakin to 'my God, my God why hast thou forsaken me?'

Here there is a poise, composure and a deep tranquillity. The writer, one of the sons of Korah, or at collaboration between some of them – is preaching. 'Hear this all of you peoples; listen, all who live in this world both low and high, rich and poor alike. My mouth will speak words of wisdom' (vv. 1–3a). He is going to expound a dark saying, a riddle' (v. 4) to which the answer is wisdom

What is this wisdom? It is the wisdom of God. It is the wisdom that is foolishness to some. It is that God alone is safety and security when it really comes down to essentials – when things get really bad. Jeremiah says the same thing. In Jer. 9: 23–24 I read 'This is what the Lord says: Let not the wise man boast of his wisdom, or the strong man boast of his strength, or the rich man boast of his riches but let him who boasts boast about this: that he understands and knows me, that I am the Lord who exercises kindness, justice and righteousness on earth, for in these I delight" declares the Lord.' At the end of Daniel (Dan.12: 9–10) reading selectively 'Go your way Daniel ... Many will be purified, made spotless and refined but the wicked will continue to be wicked. None of the wicked will understand, but those who are wise will understand.' Take Ps. 111: 10 or Prov. 9: 10, the first part being the motto of my University: 'The fear of the Lord is the beginning of wisdom'. The phrase is echoed in Prov. 1: 7: 'The fear of the Lord is the beginning of knowledge but fools despise wisdom and discipline.'

But see what our Psalmist is saying. He raises the question – why should I fear when evil days come (v. 5). He is not saying that in evil days he is frightened. Unlike David in Ps. 35 he is not screaming for help when wicked deceivers surround him – men who trust in their wealth well and great riches (v. 6). Is that because he has not gone through what David went through? Perhaps. Maybe he has been through the experience of the writer of Ps. 73 who was puzzled about the way the wicked prosper until he went in to the sanctuary of the Lord. 'Then I understood their end' (Ps. 73: 17). Maybe he has the wonderful serenity of David writing Ps. 37 as an old man, that other great exposition of the same point. It does not matter tonight, our Psalmist is just simply and clearly say that he himself does not in fact fear. All men will die. And in that framework there is a certain detachment to be found. But more than that. This man has seen, perhaps vaguely, but nonetheless reliably, something else.

Vv. 7–9: 'No man can redeem the life of another or give to God a ransom for him – the ransom for a life is costly, no payment is ever enough – that he should live on forever and not see decay. All can see that wise men die, as do the foolish and senseless. They leave their wealth to others (v. 10). Even if they had named lands after themselves (v. 11). And then you get verse 15: 'But Lord will redeem me from the grave; he will surely take me to himself'.

What has happened here? He has just said that all die and no one can redeem another: the ransom for a life is costly (v.8). But: 'God will redeem my soul from the grave' (v. 15). This man has seen his Redeemer, even as Job did. Job also had gone through the mill. He had been praised by men (Job 7: 17). Men praise you when you prosper, as our Psalmist notes in v. 18. But then there came the trials and temptations – Job's comforters not being the least of the trials. And through all that Job sees through to his Kinsman Redeemer (Job 19: 25): 'I know that my Redeemer lives … After my skin has been destroyed, even yet in my flesh I will see God; I myself will see him with my own eyes – I and not another. How my heart yearns within me!'

That is what our Psalmist also sees. His redeemer is his God (v. 15), and that puts everything into a true light, and balance, a reality. God will redeem him. God can and will pay the ransom.

So this psalm is going through the facts. Men die. Those who trust in themselves and not in God pass into the grave, leaving all their prized possessions, their splendours, their dignities, behind. There is no hope for them. They will not be taken by God to himself. Think the Rich Man and Lazarus (Luke 16: 19–31).

So do not be overawed when a man grows rich, when the splendour of his house increases, for he will take nothing with him when he dies, his splendour will not descend with him. On the contrary, the Psalmist sees past all the trumpery, be it ever so thick and clotted. What is essential is to know God so well that you are quietly confident that he will redeem your soul from the grave and take you to himself (v. 15).

Of course we know a bit more than the Psalmist did. And maybe Job saw a bit farther than our Psalmist (not all insights recorded in the Bible are cumulative). We know of Jesus and how our redemption was procured. We also know that not all trust in him. Rather they trust in themselves, as did the contemporaries of the psalm (v. 13). Paul speaks of it as the foolishness of the Cross and the reaction of some to it (I Cor. 1: 18 – 2: 5).

But note this in our Psalmist. His reaction to all these deep truths is cool, clear-sighted, clinical. These are facts: live by them. Men who trust in themselves are without salvation. But there is no superiority here. There is no 'We're right. They are wrong. Ha! ha!. They think we are foolish but it's really them that's the mugs. Nya! Nya! Nya!.' I regret that you can find that attitude among some evangelicals as they talk among themselves. But that is the Pharisee in the Temple despising the Tax Collector (Luke 18: 9–14). It almost makes you wonder whether such do really know the God they say they are following.

No. Here there is a quiet simple confidence, which is what we need to get through to, even today. I remember that magical point when John Freeman was interviewing the agent Carl Gustav Jung. The austere Freeman edged round to asking 'Do you believe in God?' The old man twinkled at him – round the bowl of his pipe if memory serves – and said: 'Believe? I know!'.

That I submit is that kernel of this psalm. This is a man who is as taken up with God as was the writer of Psalm 119: 57–64: 'You are my portion O Lord … I have sought your face with all my heart' (Ps. 119: 57–58). The Korah message is this: 'Hear all you people, list all who live in this world, both low and high, rich and poor alike' (vv. 1–2). 'I will expand my riddle' (v.

4). To have your life redeemed is not a matter of the riches. The ransom for our life is costly. No payment ever enough (v. 8). But know God and he will redeem. He will take us to himself through the Redeemer himself, he for whose work in this world we have gathered tonight to pray.

Gilcomston Prayer Meeting, 8 December 2001.

Psalm 50

This Psalm should come with a health warning. If you are prone to beat yourself up there is much in vv. 16–22 to wallow in. This psalm is instruction, reproof and warning, and it can give you a real dunt. You need to be careful with it. If you love God do not let it attack good practice. I can say this in a body like tonight. I am not saying don't take it seriously. But do not let it become a disturbing incubus. Remember Jesus. He, not our 'performance', is our security.

The Psalm divides into three. Verses 1–6 show God coming and summoning the people. Verses 7–17 are a celebration or statement of his Power. Verses 16–22 rebuke the wicked.

That third section is the one that can really get to you. It is an attack on insincerity. In his commentary on this psalm Calvin writes:

> There have always been hypocrites in the Church, men who have placed religion in a mere observance of outward ceremonies, and among the Jews there were many who turned their attention entirely to the figures of the Law, without regarding the truth which was represented under them. They conceived that nothing more was demanded of them but their sacrifices and other rites.

That section has to do with those who go through the motions of Christianity without allowing it to penetrate and change their hearts.

We have often found it helpful to look and see whether the circumstances under which a psalm is birthed can help us understand its message. This is one of those. The superscription tells us that it is a Psalm of Asaph. The Bible names three Asaphs, and needless to say scholars debate. One stands out. In 1 Chron. 15: 16–17 we read that when the Ark was brought to Jerusalem David told the Levites to appoint from their number musicians who were 'to make a joyful sound with musical instruments, lyres, harps and cymbals'. The Levites accordingly chose Heman, the grandson of Samuel, Asaph and Ethan, and their descendants, those three being particularly detailed off to 'sound the bronze cymbals' (1 Chron. 16: 19). Under those circumstances, as a leader of the praise it seems probable that that Asaph would contribute to the praise by writing psalms. At any event, by the time of Hezekiah, Asaph the psalmist was on a level similar to that held by David. In 2 Chron. 29: 39 we read: 'King Hezekiah and his officials ordered the Levites to praise the Lord with the words of David and of Asaph the seer. So they sang praises with gladness and bowed down and worshipped.'

Was Asaph the seer the virtuoso of the bronze cymbals of 1 Chron 15: 17 and 19? I think so, for that would shed light on tonight's psalm. Given his role in worship that Asaph was well placed to see people at church, as it were, and also in what we might term civil life.

Think how a psalm comes to be written. Yes. There may be a sudden revelation. God can abruptly inspire. Some psalms give you the feeling that that was how they were birthed. But we have also seen many that have their origin in actual events. I suggest that Asaph as Head of Music grew tired of seeing rampant formalism, Temple officials and other worshipers going through the motions, but living not very righteous lives. Verses 16–22 could have sprung from stewing over what he saw, and God worked on that, resulting in the glories of the first verses. I am bolstered in that thought by John Calvin. In his time he was in a good position to see discrepancies in the Geneva church between profession and actuality. And, of course, modern examples come to mind. There are those who go to church and then join with thieves (v. 15). Think of the Enron and Tyco scandals of 2001/2. Think of executives who taught Sunday School each week, and at work juggled accounts to conceal their depredations. There are embezzlers holding office in kirks. There are adulterers, ministerial and others (v. 15). There are those that use their mouths for evil, who deceive, and testify against and slander their brothers, vv.19–20. There are those who hate God's instruction and cast his words behind them (v. 17). The façade of religious observance is there, but it is only a façade. How does that fit with recent decisions in various denominations?

Verses 16–22 are a severe rebuke. Yet this psalm made it into the regular praise of the Temple, and has come down to us as part of the Bible. How many sang it, and remained heedless of its message? Makes you think, doesn't it?

But for us, let us recall the rest of the Psalm. First, God is coming, vv. 1–3. He is coming to judge, for he is a God of justice, vv. 4–6. He summons the consecrated – those who made a sacrificial covenant with him. That is an important qualification. This psalm is not about general judgement. It is specifically about the 'consecrated', though, as is obvious from the section we have just looked at, not all the consecrated are what we would term converted.

We are to realise that God does not need our worship. He does not need elaborate ceremonies or flowery language, rigmarole and falderal. The Lord's Prayer is very simple – almost terse. See Matt. 6: 9–13, or the even shorter version in Luke 11:2–4. Paul's wording of the Lord's Supper in I Cor. 11: 17–34 is also short. The God who is coming is Lord of all. 'I have no need of a bull from your stall or of goats from your pens, for every animal of the forest is mine, and the cattle on a thousand hills. I know every bird in the mountains, and the insects in the fields are mine. If I were hungry I would not tell you, for the world is mine, and all that is in it', Ps.50: 9–12.

God does not bring charges about sacrifices and burnt offerings, though there might be a hint that they can be boring – they are ever before him, v. 8 *ad fin*. Indeed, other Bible passages indicate that he tires of sacrifices. There are many examples. Hosea 6: 6 ff, God desires mercy, not sacrifice. Samuel tells Saul that the Lord prefers obedience to sacrifice (1 Sam. 15: 22–23). Sacrifices and burnt-offerings, feasts and festivals are meaningless when the heart has gone astray.

That is the message we should take from tonight. We add nothing to God, but we can be faithful. Vv. 14–15: 'Sacrifice thank-offerings to God, fulfil your vows to the Most High, and call on me in the day of trouble; I will deliver you, and you will honour me.'

Gilcomston Prayer Meeting, 8 July 2017.

Psalm 50

This Psalm should come with a health warning. If you are prone to beat yourself up there is much in vv. 16–22 to wallow in. This psalm is instruction, reproof and warning, and it can give you a real dunt. You need to be careful with it. If you love God do not let it attack good practice. I can say this in a body like tonight. I am not saying don't take it seriously. But do not let it become a disturbing incubus. Remember Jesus. He, not our 'performance', is our security.

The Psalm divides into three. Verses 1–6 show God coming and summoning the people. Verses 7–17 are a celebration or statement of his Power. Verses 16–22 rebuke the wicked.

That third section is the one that can really get to you. It is an attack on hypocrisy and insincerity. In his commentary on this psalm Calvin writes:

> There have always been hypocrites in the Church, men who have placed religion in a mere observance of outward ceremonies, and among the Jews there were many who turned their attention entirely to the figures of the Law, without regarding the truth which was represented under them. They conceived that nothing more was demanded of them but their sacrifices and other rites.

This section has to do with those who go through the motions of Christianity without allowing it to penetrate and change their hearts. How was that so clear in the mind of the writer?

We have often found it helpful to look and see whether the circumstances under which a psalm is birthed can help us understand its message. This is one of those. The superscription tells us that it is a Psalm of Asaph. The Bible names three Asaphs, and needless to say scholars debate. One stands out. In 1 Chron. 15: 16–17 we read that when the Ark was brought to Jerusalem David told the Levites to appoint from their number musicians who were 'to make a joyful sound with musical instruments, lyres, harps and cymbals'. The Levites accordingly chose Heman, the grandson of Samuel, Asaph and Ethan, and their descendants, these three being particularly detailed off to 'sound the bronze cymbals' (1 Chron. 16: 19). Under those circumstances, as a leader of the praise it seems probable that that Asaph would contribute to the praise by writing psalms. At any event, by the time of Hezekiah, Asaph the psalmist was on a level similar to that held by David. In 2 Chron. 29: 39 we read: 'King Hezekiah and his officials ordered the Levites to praise the Lord with the words of David and of Asaph the seer. So they sang praises with gladness and bowed down and worshipped.'

Was Asaph the seer the virtuoso of the bronze cymbals of 1 Chron 15: 17 and 19? I think so, for that would shed light on tonight's psalm. Given his role in worship that Asaph was well placed to see people at church, as it were, and also in what we might term their civil life.

Think how a psalm comes to be written. Yes. There may be a sudden revelation. God can abruptly inspire. Some psalms give you that feeling. But we have seen many that have their origin in actual events. I suggest that Asaph as Head of Music grew tired of seeing rampant formalism, Temple officials and other worshipers going through the motions, but living not very righteous lives. Verses 16–22 could have sprung from stewing over what he saw, and God worked on that, resulting in the glories of the first verses. John Calvin bolsters that thought. In his time he was in a good position to see discrepancies in the Geneva church between profession and actuality. And, of course, modern examples come to mind. There are those who go to church and then join with thieves (v. 15). To stay with remoter history, how many now remember the Enron and Tyco scandals of 2001/2? If they mean nothing to you look them up in Wikipedia. Think of company executives who taught Sunday School each week, and at work juggled accounts to conceal their depredations. There are embezzlers holding office in kirks. There are these awful cases of child abuse and sexual harassment. There are adulterers, ministerial and others (v. 15). There are those that use their mouths for evil, who deceive, and testify against and slander their brothers, vv.19–20. There are those who hate God's instruction and cast his words behind them (v. 17). The façade of religious observance is there, but it is only a façade. How does that fit with recent moves in various denominations?

Verses 16–22 are a severe rebuke. Yet this psalm made it into the regular praise of the Temple, and has come down to us as part of the Bible. How many sang it, and remained heedless of its message? Makes you think, doesn't it?

But for us, let us turn from that turmoil and recall the rest of the Psalm. First, God is coming, vv. 1–3. He is coming to judge, for he is a God of justice, vv. 4–6. He summons the consecrated – those who made a sacrificial covenant with him. That is an important qualification. This psalm is not about general judgement. It is specifically about the 'consecrated', though, as is obvious from the section we have just looked at, not all the consecrated are what we would term converted.

We are to realise that God does not need our worship. He does not need elaborate ceremonies or flowery language, rigmarole and falderal. The Lord's Prayer is very simple – almost terse. See Matt. 6: 9–13, and the even shorter version in Luke 11: 2–4. Paul's wording of the Lord's Supper in I Cor. 11: 17–34 is also short. The God who is coming is Lord of all. 'I have no need of a bull from your stall or of goats from your pens, for every animal of the forest is mine, and the cattle on a thousand hills. I know every bird in the mountains, and the insects in the fields are mine. If I were hungry I would not tell you, for the world is mine, and all that is in it', Ps.50: 9–12.

God does not bring charges about sacrifices and burnt offerings, though there might be a hint that they can be boring – they are ever before him, v. 8 *ad fin*. Indeed, other Bible passages indicate that he tires of sacrifices and other ceremonies. There are many examples. Hos. 6: 6 ff, God desires mercy, not sacrifice. Samuel tells Saul that the Lord prefers obedience to sacrifice (1 Sam. 15: 22–23). Sacrifices and burnt-offerings, feasts and festivals are meaningless when the heart has gone astray. Be faithful, and approach him as your Saviour and friend rather than someone you can placate by formalities and otherwise someone you can ignore. But also, don't beat yourself up.

That is the message we should take from tonight. We add nothing to God, but we can be faithful. Vv. 14–15: 'Sacrifice thank-offerings to God, fulfil your vows to the Most High, and call on me in the day of trouble; I will deliver you, and you will honour me.'

Gilcomston Prayer Meeting, 30 May 2020.

Psalm 55

David is in turmoil. Things have been going ill. Enemies are active. A friend he thought a true friend has proved untrustworthy. David is struck all of a heap. Vv. 2b–4: 'My thoughts trouble me and I am distraught at the voice of the enemy, at the stares of the wicked; for they bring down suffering upon me and revile me in their anger. My heart is in anguish within me; the terrors of death assail me.' David is stressed out.

How true to life that is. Given health we are strong and glowing. Opposition can make you conscious of your body. A gut infection, intimations of mortality, and we succumb to gloom. All going well – fine. Not going well – opposition – rummy tummy – betrayal or inadequate support by those we thought were friends and supporters. Depression comes in like a tidal wave.

I first want to draw something else from this Psalm. It is how we affect others. David has been badly affected by the faithless friend – the duplicitous words which we will come to. What we do or say can affect our friends.

When I first read this Psalm while preparing for tonight the last words of v. 4 – 'the terrors of death assail me' – brought up from memory a teacher of mine at the Grammar School, 'Pazzy' Walker. A real pre-War-style school-master – a species now perhaps extinct. (I later met his brother, who was Professor of English at McGill University, and had a cottage at the north-west corner of Dinnet Loch). His room was at the end of the west-most southern corridor on the ground floor of the old building in the Grammar before the blaze. Long face, ill-fitting suit – he must have been younger than I now am – he instilled in me an interest in accurate history, accuracy which not everyone likes – see later.

One day in 1956 in the Higher History class Pazzy declaimed – I use that word deliberately – Pazzy declaimed to the three of us in the class (one became a Professor of History in St Andrew's, and I cannot recall who else was in the class) – Pazzy declaimed William Dunbar's 'Lament for the Makars'. It has stuck. (See William Dunbar (c. 1460-c. 1520) 'Lament for the Makars', in *The Oxford Book of English Verse: 1250–1900*, Arthur Quiller-Couch, ed. 1919).

I that in heill (health) was and gladness Am trublit now with great sickness
And feblit with infirmitie:— *Timor Mortis conturbat me.*

Our plesance here is all vain glory, This fals world is but transitory, The
flesh is bruckle, the Feynd is slee:— *Timor Mortis conturbat me.*

The state of man does change and vary, Now sound, now sick, now blyth,
now sary, Now dansand mirry, now like to die:— *Timor Mortis conturbat me.*

No state in Erd here standis sicker; As with the wynd wavis the wicker So
wannis this world's vanitie:— *Timor Mortis conturbat me.*

Unto the Death gois all Estatis, Princis, Prelatis, and Potestatis, Baith rich
and poor of all degree:— *Timor Mortis conturbat me.*

There are sixteen further verses, all ending with that tolling bell, '*Timor Mortis
conturbat me*' – the fear of death grips me / disturbs me. Or better – the fear
of death messes me up / screws me up. The Latin is from the Catholic
Office for the Dead. A tocsin indeed.

Remembering Pazzy thus, underlined to me how, often inadvertently, we
can affect and influence others. Several times in recent weeks it has been
salutary to have quoted to me things I said years ago. Has it happened to
you? Others remembered: I had forgotten. Teachers, and not just teachers,
– you and me – can stow time-bombs in the memories of and beliefs of
everyone we encounter. For good: and for otherwise.

It's the same with David. David had no notion of us reading his words
so many centuries later. How much we learn from the Davidic Psalms.
David lets it all hang out. Have you ever wondered if David was a manic-
depressive? It was reassuring to hear David Knight have similar thoughts
about David a couple of Saturdays ago. Certainly the ups and downs of
David's life would aggravate a manic tendency. David is honest. If he is
feeling bad, he lets God (and us) know. He is real – no plaster saint. He does
not conceal his anguish. So far as we know he does not have a 'public face'
– always saying the 'right thing' – that off-putting, venal unreality. You know
the type – you can see the wheels calculating behind the eyes. That's not to
say David always disclosed to people all that was in his mind. But he was not
like this former friend whose talk, v. 21 tells us, was smooth as butter, more
soothing than oil, concealing the war in his heart. A wee bit of reserve can
be an alternative to duplicity – and is preferable. But always, note, whatever
is going on David turns to his God.

We do not know what triggered this particular Psalm. Who were the enemy, the threatening wicked of v. 3 – those prowling the city walls and going about its streets – vv. 10–11? Some have suggested Absalom and his cronies. Perhaps. Perhaps not. Look at vv. 12–14: 'If an enemy were insulting me, I could endure it; if a foe were rising against me, I could hide. But it is you, one like myself, my companion, my close friend, with whom I once enjoyed sweet fellowship at the house of God, as we walked about among the worshippers.' That does not sound like a son – more like a contemporary. But it does not matter. The point is that someone close has betrayed the friendship.

And David is in turmoil. Vv. 5–8, 'Fear and trembling have beset me; horror has overwhelmed me. I said, Oh, that I had the wings of a dove! I would fly away and be at rest. I would flee far away and stay in the desert; I would hurry to my place of shelter, far from the tempest and storm.' How many heard Mendelssohn as I quoted those verses? Mendelssohn's 'Hear my Prayer' is based on Ps. 55.

There is an acute contrast here. Consider vv. 20–21: 'My companion attacks his friends; he violates his covenant. His talk is smooth as butter, yet war is in his heart; his words are more soothing than oil, yet they are drawn swords.' Think of the interplay of politicians, apparently best of buddies, and then their biographies reveal a different picture – recently Prescott, Levy, Cherie Blair. But look at David's response to betrayal in vv. 16–19, and then v. 22. Verse 16: 'As for me, I call to God, and the LORD saves me. Evening, morning and noon I cry out in distress, and he hears my voice. He rescues me unharmed from the battle waged against me, even though many oppose me. God, who is enthroned from of old, who does not change – he will hear them and humble them, because they have no fear of God.' Then go to v. 22: 'Cast your cares on the LORD and he will sustain you; he will never let the righteous be shaken.' Does that not sit oddly with the cries of v. 17: 'Evening, morning and noon I cry out in distress'? No. The Bible does not say Christians will escape distresses. It says that God hears, and, v. 18, rescues. It is entirely possible to be in acute distress and yet not to be shaken. God sustains (v. 22).

See also this. God is not indifferent to those who cause the distress. Verse 23: 'But you, God, will bring down the wicked into the pit of decay; the bloodthirsty and deceitful will not live out half their days.' At this point I hear Pazzy's voice again: '*Timor Mortis conturbat*'. Consider Stalin. Latterly Stalin had a miserable life. See his daughter Svetlana Alliluyeva's account, or Khrushchev's Memoirs. (S. Alliluyeva, *Twenty Letters to a Friend*, trans. P. Johnson, (London: Penguin, 1968); *Khruschev Remembers: (1894-1971)*, S. Talbot trans. (London: Andre Deutsch, 1971)). Think, if you can – maybe I am too old for my audience – think of Stalin's paranoia and his grim death – though, notwithstanding v. 23, Stalin was seventy-four when he died. And, as we are thinking of apparent friends now become enemies, factor in Stalin's theological training in the Georgian Orthodox Seminary at Tiflis (Tblisi) Georgia, where incidentally Anastas Mikoyan (1898–1978) one of Stalin's collaborators who survived, actually graduated in theology though it led him to aetheism. Georgy Malenkov (1902–1988), Stalin's immediate successor, maybe went the other way, for in his last years he was a singer in a cathedral choir in Moscow. Still, all that is by the way – thanks to Pazzy.

V. 23 is bleak. 'God will bring down the wicked into the pit of decay'. It is balanced by the last line of the Psalm. 'But as for me, I trust in you, my God'.

So where does that take us? It takes us in two directions. This Psalm has a personal application to all Christians, to every one of us. I detail no more. It is for each to take the elements of this Psalm that apply to our own situation, to our own life. The Psalm also applies to the Church eternal. She has been betrayed by her former friend – the close friend with whom she 'once enjoyed sweet fellowship at the house of God, as we walked about among the worshippers' to quote from v. 13. We are here in part at least to pray for Jesus' bride, who certainly is under attack throughout our society, our world, and even by those who posed as her friend in the past. We are heading deep into the secular society. The relationship between the church and the state, between church and society, has always had duplicitous elements. There never was a golden age of a Christian society. If you think that there was you don't know real history, but only the dewy-eyed inventions of the hagiographers. But, that said, recognise that it may be good for the Church to have a clear knowledge of the way society thinks of her. It is the past privileges of, and the abuses by, the visible Church or churches, that have brought us to the present situation. Betrayal by a supposed friend is bruising – but then at least you know who your friends are.

Verse 22 again: 'Cast your cares on the LORD and he will sustain you; he will never let the righteous be shaken.'

Gilcomston Prayer Meeting, 26 July 2008.

Psalm 61

Before we read this Psalm, I want to insert something in your mind. I do that by giving you two examples to work from. The one is from television or film. Occasionally you get a shot of something fairly close, such as a hedge or a lattice. The foreground image fills the screen. And then the focus shifts, and you see beyond. Through the hedge you see the pasture, and the hedge itself disappears from your senses as anything other than a faint blur. The other example comes from memory. In the days when I used my garage for the car, and before it filled with assorted treasures, including my son-in-law's Kawasaki, there were occasions of a morning when I would dash out of the back door, hashed as usual, and trot, well, walk, through the garden, open the garage door, get in the car, back it out, and get out to close the garage door. Then, suddenly, a blackbird would start to sing. And the morning would change. Do you know what I am talking about? When last did you stop to hear a blackie in full-throated salute to the new day?

Two impressions then. Both instants when things out broaden out, and trivia fall into their true character as trivia. See that at work also in David's psalm at verses 3 to 5, where he sees the bigger picture.

When I was allocated this psalm, of course, I read it. I read it first in the RSV version I have at Kings. As I read it, various thoughts – emotions really – went through my mind. It spoke off the page. When I went home and had another look, this time in the NIV, I chuckled. If you have it, look at the rubric. This Psalm was written to be sung with stringed instrument accompanists. My RSV does not carry that data.

You see, when I was reading it out in the jumble of my room at Kings my impression was that this is a piece that could be sung – that should be sung. I could set it to music – or better I could see/hear it set by the Strauss of the 'Four Last Songs'.

I could dance it. Or, not to embarrass my family, and anyone else of tender sensitivities here tonight, I could choreograph it, and get its message over to you quite readily in a dance sequence. The psalm begins with David in the dumps. He needs help. He talks about that, and the future he hopes for. He is faint. He is yearning. We can all put music to that sort of thing.

But note that you can see that the psalm is unequal in the 'time' it covers. The time comprised in vv. 1–2 must be extensive. It takes time to become faint with anxiety. Choreographically we would need several minutes at least to show apprehension growing, the feeling of being alone.

Of course David gets through it. At the end he is asking to stay in God's presence, preserved by true and constant love (v. 7). 'So I will ever sing praise to your name and fulfil my vows day after day' (v. 8). That conclusion says it all: need more be said? We too have such hopes.

But there are other things to say. That ending is the ending. It comes after earlier verses, where David expresses his desolation. Then, particularly in verses 3 to 5, you see him seeing through the hedge – hearing the blackbird. These verses are the peaks, or perhaps the pass through which he gets to the broad and well-watered plains. They are where the focus shifts. That is when I heard the blackie sing. These verses and their shift in focus bring resonances in my mind from music, from Britten, Bliss, or Liszt, and from works of art – Vermeer, Picasso or Renoir, for example, or sculpture by Rodin or Epstein, the Nefertiti head in the Neues Museum in Berlin. – instances where you suddenly see things differently, in a wider and broader perspective. When things fall into what you just know is their right place.

So, do not underestimate the start of this Psalm. It is compressed. Do not rob it of impact because there are only 26 words in vv. 1–2a. They set the scene. There is real anguish – David is deep in difficulties. He is at the end of himself – or at what feels like the end of the earth, v. 2. He yearns to be lifted up out of the mess and set on a rock (v. 2). But he has the knowledge of God's dealing with him. That helps him see things differently. '[Y]ou have been my refuge, a strong tower against the foe' (v. 3). So David will 'take refuge in the shelter of [God's] wings' (v. 3). He will make God's tent, his home (v. 5). Recall Jesus' simple and overwhelming statement: 'If anyone loves me, he will obey my teaching. My Father will love him, and we will come to him and bide with him' (John 14: 23, altered).

David knows, and sees again the reality that had gotten out of focus in v. 1. 'God has heard my vows, and granted the wish of all who revere his name' (v. 5, altered). These truths – the shelter, the tower, the cover of God's wings, the knowledge that God hears and grants the wishes of those who revere him – these are David taking a step back, and all his pains and frustrations suddenly drop into true perspective. Yes, there is the pain, but then there is the Big Picture that is the real truth of things.

For me that evokes those parallels – the focus shift, the blackbird singing, and the music and the art. Stand back from your problems – your concerns for yourself, or even for others – and rest in God. Lift your nose off the canvas and see the whole picture, the real picture. You will survive through the turbulence, and go through into rest. Back there was the narrows, the current and rapids that threatened stability, but here is the expanse of true reality. Back there were the sodium lights: here is the majesty of the starry night.

That is what has impelled David in this Psalm. We do not know what is oppressing him on this occasion. His is praying with urgency, v. 1. His heart is fainting – he is discouraged, v. 2. He wants to be raised up and set on a rock, v. 2b. But then he remembers. God has done it before. 'You have been 'my shelter', and 'a tower of refuge' (v. 3, NIV). God has heard his vows in the past, and granted the wish of all who revere his Name, v. 5.b. God has promised.

From elsewhere we know of God's promises to David. I could be wrong as to the chronology of this Psalm, but remember David's life. In 2 Sam. 7 he had wanted to build a house for God, and Nathan had immediately, and without thought, encouraged him. But Nathan had got it wrong, so God sent Nathan to David with the correction that contained all those promises. Why didn't God speak directly to David? Why do we want God to speak direct to us? Why do we want our prayers answered direct? Well, an intermediary avoids one possible problem – that what we grasp at as an answer might just be a chemical reaction in our liver. David knew that Nathan was a Man of God. Nathan was not one of those power-hungry people who always know what God wants other people to do. So David had, in a way, an objective answer to his prayer – and, being 'objective', one that he could rely on. In a way, God in correcting Nathan, together with David's conversation with God in 2 Sam. 7: 18–20, laid a sure foundation for the end of our Psalm.

This Psalm must have been written after the promise came through Nathan – how long after I don't know, but here David clings to the promises. David is faint, but then remembers. The music drops a tone, as it does in Britten's 'War Requiem' when the boys' choir enters so marvellously at intervals throughout that wonderful work. David, floundering in the bog, suddenly hits bedrock and a sure footing. God has heard his vows, and will grant the wishes of those who fear him, v. 5. He will indeed grant length of days, and the Psalmist will dwell in God's presence forever, v. 7, as we will.

God's Love will preserve him, v. 7b, as it will us.

So, let us copy David. Let us take our minds off whatever immediate self-centred concerns we have brought with us tonight. Remember the promises of God. Take that step back from the turmoil, shift focus, drop a tone, remember the blackbird. Let us also 'sing praises in honour of God's name as we fulfil our vows, day after day', v. 8.

Gilcomston Prayer Meeting, 2 March 2002.

Psalm 61

So I come downstairs early. It's the second day of waiting for the reentry of the space shuttle 'Discovery' and I'm down to see it. But they've deferred it for one more orbit. So I open up my email, and there's a message timed at 11.12 the previous evening. The Session Clerk was still at work while sensible people were in bed. I had been out the back looking to see if there were any signs of the Perseid meteors.

'Dear Frank, I wonder how you would be placed for taking the Psalm at the Prayer Meeting before too long? Would Saturday 3 September be a possibility? It would be Psalm 61. Mike.'

3 September – more than a month away. Should be possible. So I email back – Yes, ok.

Later memory, which has been flickering, kicks in. Ps.61 sounds familiar. So I check the Bibstud files, and there it is. Ps.61, 2 March 2002 – 1523 words. I read them.

Do I cancel? Well, I am here at this side of the Hall tonight. Am I just going to repeat what I said thirty months ago? The answer is, in substance yes, but a wee bit differently.

Before we read the psalm I want to insert some parallels in your mind. First, from TV or film – the dissolving shot. The camera shows a leafy branch, and then the focus shifts. You see what lies beyond, and the foreground becomes hazy. Second, from music – real music, that is. The composer drops a full tone, and the music broadens out – the entry of the choir at the end of Liszt's 'Faust' Symphony, or the boys' choir entries in Britten's 'War Requiem'. Third, from Art – when you go into that first floor room in the Mauritshuis and see Vermeer's 'View of Delft' or the 'Girl with the Pearl Earring' on the facing wall, or you see the Nefertiti Head in the Neues Museum in Berlin, or Renoir's 'The Luncheon of the Boating Party' in the Phillips Gallery in Washington. Or last, nature – when there's a blackbird pouring out his soul. I am talking about those instants when things quieten and broaden out. You see the bigger picture. Trivia fall into their true character as trivia. See that at work in this psalm as you read it.

Psalm 61 was written to be sung with accompanists on stringed instrument – see the rubric. It could be sung – it should be sung. You could choreograph it, and get its message over quite readily in a dance sequence. The psalm begins with David anxious and faint. He needs help. We could put that to music to that. But note that the psalm is unequal in its balance. You can read it straight through, but in setting it to music you would have to take account of the content of the words. The time comprised in vv. 1–2 may be extensive – more so than the turn-around of the later verses. It usually takes time to become faint with anxiety. Choreographically we would need several minutes at least to show apprehension growing, the feeling of being alone. Musically some of the anguished bits of Shostakovich come to mind.

Of course David gets through it. At the end the king will stay in God's presence, preserved by true and constant love – v. 7. 'Then will I ever sing praise to your name and fulfil my vows day after day' – v. 8. That conclusion says it all. Need more be said? We too have such hopes.

But there are other things to say about Ps. 61. The ending is the ending. It comes well after verses 1 and the first half of 2, verses where David expresses his desolation.

Do not underestimate the start of this Psalm. It is compressed. Do not rob it of impact because there are only 26 words in vv. 1–2a. They set the scene. There is real anguish. David is deep in difficulties. He is at the end of himself – at what feels like the end of the earth (v. 2). David yearns to be lifted up out of the mess and set on a rock (v. 2 again). He knows of God as his fortress – v. 3. That's not a new thought. With due apologies to whoever is 'on' next week, and without arguing that Pss. 61 and 62 are in chronological sequence, drop down to the next Psalm, Ps. 62, and its v. 2. God is a rock and fortress. You get the same thought in Pss. 18: 2, 31: 2 and 94: 22.

David does not wallow in his misery. He is not a masochistic self-flagellant. There are those who enjoy 'being down' and 'needy', or 'attacked by the Devil' – however you want to put it – but who seem never actually properly to turn to God. David is different. God has dealt with him in the past. That helps him see things differently. Verse 3 looks back, not forward: '[Y]ou have been my refuge, a strong tower against the foe'. On that basis David yearns for the future and does not relax into the comfortable sludge of self-pity. His 'get up and go' has not 'got up and went'. He longs to 'take refuge in the shelter of [God's] wings', v. 3. He will make God's tent his home, v. 5. On the basis of his experience of God, he looks forward. And he looks forward to familiarity – almost to domesticity. Heaven is not run by the National Trust, a place to visit and then leave. It's a place to live in and enjoy with its owner. Recall Jesus' simple and overwhelming statement in John 14: 23: 'If anyone loves me, he will obey my teaching. My Father will love him, and we will come to him and we will bide with him' (altered).

As David realises he knows that, he sees the reality that had gotten out of focus in v. 1. God has heard his vows, and has given David the heritage of all who fear God's name, v. 5. And that makes this Psalm ours as well. We too share in the heritage of all who fear God's name, don't we? These truths – the shelter, the tower, the cover of God's wings, the knowledge that God hears and grants the wishes of those who revere him – these lead David into taking that step back from the detail. All his pains and frustrations are dropping into perspective. Yes, there is pain, but there is the Big Picture – the real truth of things.

For me that evokes those parallels – the focus shift, the music, the art, the blackbird. Stand back from your problems – your concerns for yourself, or even for others – and rest in God. Lift your nose off the canvas and see the whole picture, the real picture. You will survive through the turbulence, and go through into fulfilment. Back there were the narrows, the rocks and rapids that threatened stability. Here is the expanse of true reality. Back there were the sodium lights: Here is the majesty of the starry night.

That is what has impelled David in this Psalm. We do not know the circumstances of this Psalm. It has similarities to Ps. 18, where the title speaks of David singing when God had delivered him from all his enemies and the hand of Saul. In this one he is 'down', actually in bad times, not just remembering them. His is praying with urgency, v. 1. His heart is fainting – he is discouraged, v. 2. He wants to be raised up and set on a rock, v. 2b. We do not know what triggered this. It might have been when he was driven out by Absalom – the translation in the Psalter speaks of him crying from 'the utmost corner of the land'. No matter. But then he remembers. God has done it before. 'You have been 'my shelter', and 'a tower of refuge' (v. 3, NIV).

David clings to the promises. David is faint, but then remembers. The music drops a tone, as it does in Britten's 'War Requiem' when at intervals the boys' choir enters so marvellously throughout that wonderful work. David, floundering in the bog, hits bedrock and a sure footing. Past experience. God has heard his vows, and will grant the wishes of those who fear him, v. 5. He will indeed grant length of days – though perhaps we should note that length of days may not be a huge number of days. It is a matter of quality, not quantity. And then the Psalmist will dwell in God's presence for ever, v. 7, as we will. God's Love will preserve him, v. 7b, as it will us.

I am not saying we are all at the same stage among such things. That is impossible. Some are in deep waters. Some may never fall into the depths of the state that David was in when writing it, and will not be called to that. Be glad if that is true for you. But wherever we are in the stages of this Psalm, let us copy David for the rest of this evening. Let us take our minds off whatever immediate or self-centred concerns we have brought with us tonight. Remember the promises of God. Take that step back from the turmoil, shift focus, drop a tone, and remember the blackbird. Let us also 'sing praises in honour of God's name as [we] fulfil our vows, day after day', v. 8.

Gilcomston Prayer Meeting, 3 September 2005.

Psalm 62

'For the Director of Music. For Jeduthun.' Jeduthun was one of three masters of music appointed by David to lead public worship (1 Chron. 16: 41–42; 25: 1–6). Some think he supervised the choir, though in 1 Chron. 16, he and Heman were in charge of banging the gongs and cymbals – the orchestra, to stretch the term. David entrusted three psalms to him by name; the other two are Pss. 39 and 77. There's no time tonight to explore their similarities and differences. Suffice it to say that in all three David reveals himself, and his relations with God.

This psalm is unlike many other Davidic psalms. Here David is serene, secure with his God. I have been thinking about it since I was assigned it, and one watchword has been coming regularly to mind. 'Keep a calm sough'. Non-Aberdonians know that as: 'Keep Calm and Carry On'. This psalm does not praise God. It does not ask God to rescue or protect. It does not ask Him to do anything. It does not even pray. It is just a series of simple statement of facts and principles. David is secure. Keep Calm and Carry On.

I have used the Gateway Bible translation deliberately. It has significant signalling words, words noted by John Calvin. Truly appears three times. Surely appears twice. They are like Wagnerian motifs. Were this psalm music they would be specially presented. 'Truly' would be a distinctively affirmative phrase, reappearing as counterpoint in the verses that come after it, carried first in the strings. 'Surely' would also be recognisable, more solemn, perhaps in the lower brass registers, maybe even in the tympani – at least three of those. A modern Jeduthun, the orchestra man, would know how to do that. If you think about it 'Truly' and 'Surely' recur throughout the whole biblical message. They are its underlying geology. God is reliable, truly and surely. On them David hangs that message: Keep Calm and Carry On.

When and why was this psalm written? In one sense we don't know 'when'. Similarly, in one sense we don't know 'why'. And yet both questions do have an answer. Why did David write it? He wrote it to affirm his basic faith in God. He gave it to Jeduthun to share with the people. When did he write it? He wrote it knowing that some were trying to undermine him, v. 4.

That happened frequently, but we do not know which time this was. In any event, he was not upset. God is his fortress, v. 2. In some translations v. 2 goes on to say, not that he 'will not be shaken', but that he 'will not be _greatly_ shaken'. That is an important difference. If you are under pressure, feel a bit shaky, open your Bible and read 'I will not be shaken', you could get a dunt. The spiral would go: 'David was not shaken. I am shaken. I am falling short in my trust in God!' No. David wrote to counter feeling inadequate. He knew of enemies, but he was secure, if perhaps a little bit shaken.

Look at the psalm. In some versions it divides into three parts, with that enigmatic Selah at the ends of vv. 4 and 8. The psalm starts very abruptly with straight affirmations. Truly my soul finds rest in God; my salvation comes from him. Truly He is my rock and my salvation; he is my fortress, I will never be shaken vv. 1–2. These are the Trulys that David holds on to. He is under covert attack, vv. 3–4. He may sometimes feel like a leaning wall or a tottering fence, v. 3b – which adds weight to the 'not _greatly_ shaken' interpretation – but no matter. Press on. Then we come to the first 'Surely'. Surely the anonymous attackers are duplicitous. They are intent on toppling him, but they lie, outwardly offering him blessings while inwardly cursing, v.4. Selah: think about it.

David's response is his rest in God, who is 'truly' his rock, his salvation, his fortress, his refuge. Ultimately he will not be shaken, v. 6. We are again in the realm of the Trulys. David's honour and salvation depend on God, not on himself, v. 7. And that, of course, is precisely our situation. Our honour, our salvation, do not depend on us, on what we are, or what we do. Our honour and salvation depend on Christ. So David tells the people to trust in God at all times, to pour out their hearts to him – for God is their refuge too, v. 8. Surely that can speak to us. Selah: think about it.

The third part of the psalm gathers together a bouquet of related thoughts, vv. 9–10. The second 'Surely' invites you to look around. The lowborn are but a breath, the highborn are but a lie. Weighed on a balance, they are nothing; together they are only a breath, v. 9. Yet we all tend to strive. So, in v. 10 David warns not to trust in extortion or hope in stolen goods. If our riches increase, we are not to set our heart on them. In modern terms, ultimately, what is illegitimate or legitimate gain going to do for you when you face your Maker? Implicitly, David refers us back to v. 8, to trusting in God at all times, for, doing that you won't do those.

And so to the final verses, vv. 11–12. 'One thing God has spoken, two things I have heard' could puzzle, particularly as the verses go on to speak of three. But we need not go corybantic about it. There is something similar in Job. In Job 33: 14 Elihu notes that 'God does speak – now in one way, now in another – though no-one perceives it.' I think that's right. We need not get a cranial hernia trying to identify the 'one' and the 'two'.

God does speak, sometimes in one way and sometimes in another. As a result we do know, as David does. Power belongs to God. In Him there is unfailing love. He rewards everyone according to what they have done. And if you think about it, these are not intrinsically three. They are but aspects of the God who has revealed himself to us. I go back to the Trulys and the Surelys. God is reliable. In this psalm we see David serene under pressure. His remedy? Trust in God. So should we. But there is something else inherent in the psalm. Trusting is not attained by effort. Rather, by His grace, you relax into it, as David does here. Remember. 'Come unto me, all ye that labour and are heavy laden, and I will give you rest. Take my yoke upon you, and learn of me, for I am meek and lowly in heart; and you will find rest unto your souls. For my yoke is easy, and my burden is light', (Matt. 11: 28–30 KJV).

Know this God. Know Him. Keep a calm sough.

Keep Calm and Carry On.

Gilcomston Prayer Meeting, 22 August 2020.

Psalm 68

This is a long psalm. Two preliminaries: First, normally I would read the psalm and then comment. Tonight is different. I am going to take each bit separately. Second, it seems the scholars do not know what some bits mean. Translations vary. And therefore so do commentators. I am going to use variants as seem best for tonight. But in places I am floundering.

This psalm has three examples of that curious word, 'SELAH'. They are at the end of vv. 7, 19 and 32. These split the text into four and provide a key for us. As we know, scholars debate what 'SELAH' means. The consensus is that it indicates a pause, filled by a variety of reasons.

Working on this psalm I found myself wondering. Might it be wrong to read this psalm straight through. It certainly needs pacing. Indeed, maybe it's wrong to attempt to deal with it between now and about half-past seven. It needs more time, with pauses – the SELAHS – between the sections. The text in front of me is terse – unduly so. And then maybe it's wrong to read it. It is a song. Maybe I should sing it! Try that at home.

The psalm is a series of four tableaus, marked by each SELAH. But you will see that these SELAHS come within a verse. They are like the running head you get in some books – at least I am going to treat them like that.

Verses 1–6 are about God and what he does for people; vv. 7–18 are about God leading the Israelites from Egypt to the Promised Land; vv. 19–31 are about God and a 'procession'. Finally vv. 32–5 instruct us to praise God for what he has done. Fundamentally, then, each part is about God. God, our God, is the focus.

What occasioned the psalm? Scholars debate – their careers require it. Some think that it followed upon some great victory or other, but don't know which. Others, considering in particular the procession described in vv. 24–27, think that it was composed for the bringing of the Ark up to Jerusalem II Sam. 6 and I Chron. 15 tell us about that. Either way David is splurging in relief and thankfulness.

An alternative is that the psalm does not have a single origin. Maybe it is a compilation, assembled over a period and taken out of a number of psalmic sequences that have different bases. For example, v. 29 refers to the 'temple at Jerusalem'. Did a later hand add that passage? Or was David dreaming of the temple which he was later to be forbidden to build because he was a man of blood? (I Chron. 22: 7–8; I Chron. 28: 3–4).

But we need not pursue these controversies. What is important for us is what the psalm says – or what we think it says. It is a glorious paean of praise, both an abstract celebration of God, and as a set of four examples of Him at work, defending, preserving and encouraging his people.

In vv. 1– 6, first note he 'who rides on the clouds'. One commentary says that 'Cloud-Rider' was the name of some local god or other and that this statement is a claim that our God is the real Cloud-Rider. Maybe. Whatever. But think of that title the next time you see the clouds storming in. God is our Cloud-Rider.

Second, 'May God arise' is also translated as 'Let God arise'. The point is not getting God to get up. The point is that when he arises, his enemies flee. As we see in vv. 1–4 our God is active. He is not passive, disinterestedly watching what is going on. He intervenes. He scatters his enemies. They flee. The righteous can be happy and glad. Rejoice before him. He is a caring God, caring for individuals. He is: vv. 5–6:

'A father to the fatherless, a defender of widows, is God in his holy dwelling. God sets the lonely in families, he leads out the prisoners with singing; but the rebellious live in a sun-scorched land.'

As one of the fatherless, raised by a widow, these verses speak to me. As for 'setting the lonely in families', that does not always happen. Why? Are we insufficiently generous in hospitality? But the footnote alternative is that God sets 'the desolate in a homeland'. To me that fits better, for the verses contrast God's care for the desolate with the fate of the rebellious. The desolate are cared for with a homeland. But the rebellious are in a `sun-scorched land'. Not a happy place to be. Do you ever detect an emptiness, a 'whistling in the dark, cheerfulness' in some who reject God? I expect you have met such insouciance. But, there is a desert emptiness in them. In contrast, God leads prisoners out. Prisoners may be prisoners from war, but they could be prisoners of other gaolers – of illness, physical or mental.

The second section is vv. 7–18. It then has its 'SELAH'. Let your imagination work. What images do you see or hear? What music? Read it.

God goes before us. The earth shakes. Remember the giving of the Law at Sinai? But then what? Was some of the march through the Wilderness a trek through mud? We tend to think of the people going through dry desert, but some of route may not have been. The wadis are water-created. And then we are through into the Land. There is no mention of the Wandering in the Wilderness after the People refused to go into it. Why? Well, maybe we should not dwell on past unfaithfulness, as we can be prone to do. Do not wallow in the past – let alone getting a buzz from recalling past sins. Get on with it! The pouring rain of v. 8 turns into the abundant showers that refresh the inheritance – the Land of v. 9. The people settle, many into farms, and, through them, God provides for the poor.

Then we come to a difficult set of verses. Apparently not all the terms they use are understood. Translations vary greatly. This is a passage I do not understand – like others in the Bible. So I tread lightly. In the NIV vv. 12–13 are in inverted commas. That means that the translators think that these words were the word given by the Lord, v. 11. Some suggest that there is a connection with the Song of Deborah of Judges 5. Suffice it to say that when Deborah was in charge not all the people heeded her call to arms. Maybe they were 'sleeping amid the campfires', v. 13, while the Lord led the faithful. Or maybe, according to the footnote, they slumbered among the saddlebags. Judges 5: 16 speaks of those who stayed among the campfires rather than joining her forces. You could track all that later – tonight there is no time – but Judges 5: 4–5 mirrors Psalm 68: 7–8. Personally I find these verses obscure – to use a neutral term. Who is being addressed? What 'the wings of my dove are sheathed with silver, its feathers with shining gold' means, I do not know.

The text then goes on to speak of the conflicts of the purging of the Land, of how God took Zion as the location of his sanctuary rather than the majestic Mount Bashan. Simply as geology Zion is unimpressive. But with God in residence … vv. 14–18! Let your imagination soar. Marvel! Does this prefigure the Second Coming? Personally I recall some of the paintings of processions in Sixteen and Seventeenth century Venice.

In the next section, vv. 19–31, as before, the section has a superscription before we get to its SELAH. Verse 19 summarises the point being made.

Praise be to the Lord, to God our Saviour, who daily bears our burdens.' SELAH. Our God is a God who saves; from the Sovereign LORD comes escape from death.

Good. Surely we can appreciate that without further comment. God saves. But then things get unpleasant, vv. 21–23.

> Surely God will crush the heads of his enemies, the hairy crowns of those who go on in their sins. The Lord says, 'I will bring them from Bashan; I will bring them from the depths of the sea, that you may plunge your feet in the blood of your foes, while the tongues of your dogs have their share.

I am unsure about this. A bit of me wants to avoid these verses by a joke: to say that v. 21 targets the hairy, so the baldies like me are excluded. But from elsewhere we know that that is sophistry. God does punish those who go on in their sins. That said, the imagery of the people wading in the blood of the enemy, and their dogs lapping their blood, is repellent. There are bits of the Bible I find very difficult. Another is II Sam. 8: 2.

Then in Part 3, vv. 24–27, we get to the procession. This is the Ark coming to Zion. Why are only four of the tribes named? I do not know. But there is this great procession. Note the singers and the musicians. These would be our old friends the Sons of Korah and the Sons of Asaph doing their stuff to the glory of God. Elsewhere we read of their prowess with harps, cymbals and gongs: I Chron. 15: 19–22; 16: 42; I Chron. 25: 1–6 ff. Again let your imagination loose.

I have no idea what v. 30, – 'rebuke the beast, and its bringing silver' – means. Is the beast the Egypt of the next verse? Certainly Egypt and reeds goes together. Remember Moses in the basket. But Egypt was famous for gold, not silver. This Cush was perhaps an area of the west bank of the Red Sea, or of Arabia to its east, or a kingdom down by Ethiopia. It does not matter for us tonight. It is enough to know that God's authority is recognised.

So we come to vv. 32–35. The kings of the earth acknowledge the sovereignty of our God it, as they bring gifts to the temple. And so we end. In the light of all that has gone before, all sing to God.

> Sing to God, O kingdoms of the earth, sing praise to the Lord. [SELAH] Sing to him who rides across the ancient skies above, who thunders with mighty voice.

Remember v. 4. He is the Cloud-Rider, riding across the highest heavens, the ancient heavens, thundering with mighty voice. He is not restricted to his sanctuary or to any temple, vv. 24 and 29.

> Proclaim the power of God, whose majesty is over Israel, whose power is in the skies. You are awesome, O God, in your sanctuary; the God of Israel gives power and strength to his people. Praise be to God!

The God of Israel is majestic. He gives power and strength to his people. He gives strength to us, if we will. Responding, what can we do? We pray and praise.

Gilcomston Prayer Meeting, 22 November 2014.

Psalm 70

In my NIV the superscription to Ps. 70 is: 'For the director of Music. Of David. A petition.' However, if you go to the KJV you read: 'To the chief Musician. A Psalm of David, to bring to remembrance.' In Calvin's commentary the psalm is 'to call to remembrance.' 'A petition' – yes. Ps. 70 is that. But 'to bring to remembrance', 'to call to remembrance' is something else. Today we would say 'bring back to memory' or 'remind'. Only one other psalm has that label – Psalm 38. But whose memory is being jogged? Is it God's? Surely not. Is it David's? Or is it all of us? Some three years ago at our Saturday meeting I quoted an aphorism of the late Yogi Berra of the NY Yankees: 'when you come to a fork in the road – take it!' David and us. This psalm may bring remembrances / memories to each of us. Find your own as we go on.

The psalm itself is a fragment, part of another. As the NIV note points out, it is an almost exact copy of Ps. 40 vv. 13–17. That could be off-putting – what does a recycled chunk of different a poem have to teach us? I was amused to find that Calvin's commentary on Ps. 70 just prints the text. Calvin writes that he discussed these verses before in dealing with Ps. 40. We should just look and see what he said there. He then goes straight on to Ps. 71.

I have never tackled Ps. 40 for the Prayer Meeting, so that avenue was not open to me. But Calvin's swerve did spark a thought. Occasionally we sing Ps. 40. Remember how it starts? 'I waited for the Lord my God, and patiently did bear. At length to me he did incline my voice and cry to hear. He took me from a fearful pit and from the miry clay, and on a rock he set my feet, establishing my way. He put a new song in my mouth, my God to magnify. Many shall see it, and shall fear, and on the Lord rely.' The extract that is Ps. 70 must call Ps. 40 to memory.

But why does Ps. 70 exist as something separate? I came across one intriguing suggestion. According to Wikipedia, a Jewish rabbi, the Malbim, thought that Ps. 40 was written when David was recovering from his struggle with Saul, and that Ps. 70 was the bit of Ps. 40 that he recalled and clung to when he was fleeing from the Absalom rebellion. That could fit. The memory of a previous experience can help with coping with the new. Further, the re-use of the previous psalm answers something that sometimes worries. Repeating previous prayer is ok. God doesn't mind, so long as you're not just gently ambling along a familiar verbal rut, chanting by rote, or intoning ritual phrases. It's the thought that counts. It could well be that David, under pressure in old age, did, for comfort, revive or relive a part of his previous history. His re-use of a previous paean validates us doing the same.[6]

Now, to the psalm itself. It is urgent. It calls on God to 'hasten' (v. 1). It urges Him to come quickly, and, not to delay (v. 5). We have all felt like that. Maybe some more than others, but I doubt whether any of us has been immune. When we need help, we want it without delay. We want it now. However, the urgency is entirely ours. We respond to our situation as we see it. But God does not hurry up at our behest. The timing is His.

We do not know the exact circumstances that provoked this psalm, but tonight it is expedient to follow the Malbim's idea and relate Ps. 70 to the Absalom insurrection. Summoned by Absalom, David's adviser, Ahithophel, deserted David and went over to Absalom's cause (2 Sam. 15: 12; 16: 20–22). Indeed he suggested the immediate pursuit of David with twelve thousand men (2 Sam. 17: 1–2). That was good advice – 2 Sam. 17: 14 says so. But Hushai, running interference for David (if I may use an Americanism), advised delay (2 Sam. 17: 7–14). And in fact that delay allowed David to escape across the Jordan (2 Sam. 17: 22).

Now look at Ps. 70, vv. 2–3. They speak of those that want to kill David and seek his ruin. David prays they are put to shame and confusion, and disgraced (v. 2). And what happened? Well, Ahithophel saw his advice of immediate hot pursuit was not followed. He concluded the insurrection would therefore fail. So he saddled his donkey, went back home to Giloh, put his affairs in order, and committed suicide (2 Sam. 17: 23). And we all know what happened to Absalom (2 Sam. 18: 6–15).

There is another intriguing case. David also speaks of mockers, praying that they are shamed (v. 3). So what about Shimei, Shimei who abused David as he fled from Jerusalem – a mocker indeed. Some would have dealt with him then and there. David restrained them, saying that Shimei was doing what God wanted him to do. He felt the abuse was God's rebuke, but that God just might restore him when he saw how miserable he was (2 Sam. 16: 5–11). And, when David returned Shimei came and made a grovelling

---

6   Cf. Matthew Henry on Ps. 108. See also study of Ps. 108, 18 August 2018.

apology, David was again merciful (2 Sam. 19: 18–23). The whole episode brings to mind Paul's words about blessing and cursing, and coals of fire. Leave vengeance to God (Rom. 12: 19–20). But I did wonder how that fits with David's death-bed instruction to Solomon to see that Shimei did not have a natural death (1 Kings 2: 9). What happened was not immediate. Once he was king, Solomon told Shimei to build a house in Jerusalem, stay there, and not leave the city under pain of death. Shimei did, but three years later, and maybe overconfident, – he had got away with a lot before – he did not ask permission leave the city to go and fetch two absconding slaves. Instead he breached parole, and was executed both for that and for his previous offences (1 Kings 2: 36–46). Ps. 40 echoes once more: 'I waited for the Lord my God, and patiently did bear.... . Many shall see it, and shall fear, and on the Lord rely' (Ps. 40: 1, 3b). It looks to me as if Shimei saw David's restoration and feared, but did not trust. Tested, Shimei's disobedience showed he did not rely on the Lord.

Back to Ps. 70. Verse 4 is the obverse of all that recital of betrayal and mockery in the previous verses. It is an illustration of how to react. David prays: '... may all those who seek you [God] rejoice and be glad in you; may those who long for your saving help always say "The Lord is great"'. Seek God through it all, with rejoicing and gladness, despite being in situations like those sketched in vv. 2–3. Long for God's saving help. It is tempting to relate these verses to the circumstances that we, the church, are in. Certainly the Devil is having a go. But we live in a democratic secular society, and Christians are a minority. The sooner we recognise that the better, and stop looking for some ideal never existent previous age. There are attackers, and there are mockers. But this is not the time or place to enter such matters. I stick to David.

Verse 5. Having handed out the advice of v. 4, and doubtless complying with it himself, David turns back to his own circumstances. He needs help. He knows he needs help. He seeks help. When all is said and done he feels poor and needy. So once again he asks God to come to him and save him, as He has done so often. He knows that God is his help and his deliverer. He has been in the past. David wants help to come without delay – from his point of view. But he does not make a song and dance about it. He does not wallow in a parade of humility. He does not abase himself to persuade God to act. Poor and needy he asks for help, and, as in Ps. 40 v. 1, waits patiently for it to come. And it did.

So, that is the message. David gives it to his people by having the director to set it to music, and sung for them to hear, or even themselves to sing. What message? What message for a time of pandemic, of economic crisis, of political uncertainties national and international? It's a message for each to apply to our own circumstances, but its core is: In need, rely on the God you know, your Saviour. Ask Him for the help you need. Help will come, in His time. For David it brought memories from an awful period of his life. The words from the end of Ps. 70 came back to him as he left Jerusalem, and he saw what happened after that. He brings that memory to the people. For us this psalm can certainly be a petition. May it also bring memories of when our Saviour has helped us. We can also take it as a promise for our future.

I go back to what I drew from Ps. 62 a couple of months ago. Trust God. Ask for help. Then, keep calm and carry on. Help will come, in God's time.

Gilcomston Prayer Meeting, 17 October 2020.

Psalm 72

One of the intriguing and useful things I learned some forty years ago when I was in the Advanced Roman Law class with Peter Stein over in Kings was how to detect when a later editor had changed a text, or inserted his own comment. There is an example in v. 20 of this Psalm: 'This concludes the prayers of David.' In fact we do not know whether this Psalm was written by David or by his son, Solomon, as the superscription to the Psalm might be taken to indicate. Is this psalm by David, v. 18, or is it a Psalm of Solomon – the superscription? I hope that I do not offend anyone by pointing out that it is likely that v. 20 is clearly added by an editor. Are we really to think that David in his old age, about to hand over to Solomon as per I Chron. 28 and 29, or I Kings 1: 28–40, gathered his accumulated manuscripts together, and wrote on this one that it was his last psalm? I think not. It is far more likely that what we have as v. 20 is a note by a copyist or editor, for we are going on to Book III of the Psalms, the Psalms of Asaph. For the editor, copyist or compiler, this psalm meant the end of one set of Psalms, those of David. Calvin suggests rather these words were an addition by an editor, and indeed that the editor may have been Solomon himself. I agree: there was an editor, though we can't be sure whether he was indeed Solomon working on his father's papers. But I would also say that personally I do not think we should worry too much about the biblical texts as we have them. 'What is the real text' problem is a Satanic bog that has drowned many. As C.S. Lewis said somewhere in other language, the tenor of the biblical text is too clear to be bothered about minor matters.

Whatever, this is a psalm about the king. And it fits with I Chron. 28 and 29 to take it as a Psalm of David. If you look back to I Chron. 29: 1 you find David speaking to an assembly of the people. He says 'My son Solomon, the one whom God has chosen, is young and inexperienced. The task is great …' (I Chron. 29: 1). Then remember what is in this Psalm. It is full of hope for the king's reign. So, there is a good argument that our Psalm is indeed David praying for his son Solomon.

To bolster that, look to the preceding chapter, I Chron. 28. David summons the officials of Israel, the mighty men, and speaks of building the temple, which he had wanted to build. But God has said that David's son is to carry out the task, not David himself, (I Chron. 28: 2–3). So, starting at 5b, David charges Solomon in these terms:

[God] said to me, 'Solomon your son is the one who will build my house and my courts, for I have chosen him to be my son, and I will be his father. I will establish his kingdom forever if he is unswerving in carrying out my commands and laws, as it being done at this time.
So now I charge you [Solomon] in the sight of all Israel and of this assembly of the Lord, and in the hearing of our God: Be careful to follow all the commands of the Lord your God, that you may possess this good land and pass it on as an inheritance to your descendants forever.
And you, my son, acknowledge the God of your father, and serve him with wholehearted devotion and with a willing mind, for the Lord searches every heart and understands every motive behind the thoughts. If you seek him he will be found by you: but if you forsake him, he will reject you forever. Consider now, for the Lord has chosen you to build a temple as a sanctuary. Be strong and do the work. (I Chron. 28: 5b–10).

David then hands over the plans of the Temple, and continues: 'Be strong and courageous and do the work. Do not be afraid or discouraged, for the Lord God, my God, is with you. He will not fail you or forsake you until all the work for the service of the temple of the Lord is finished.' (I Chron. 28: 20).

So I submit, in Psalm 72 we have Solomon, the inexperienced, being prayed for most earnestly. But note another phrase in the I Chron. passage. Did it not burst across your mind as it did mine when I saw it? See I Chron. 28: 6b: 'I have chosen him to be my son, and I will be his father.' Does this not resonate through to Matt. 3: 17: 'This is my beloved Son, in whom I am well pleased'? (Cf. Mark 1: 10, Luke 3: 21–22).

That connects with vv. 5 ff of our Psalm. 'He will endure as long as the sun, as long as the moon through all generations.' The succeeding and preceding verses of the Psalm speak of the glories of the king, being like rain on a mown field – can you recall the smell of rain on dry grass, or a mown field after the first cut of spring? He will rule, and all kings will bow before him etc. etc.

But is this not just the overblown language of the Middle East? Do we not see similar language in praise of Saddam Hussein, not to speak of Mao Tse Tung and Stalin? Is it not just standard flattery, hyperbole, not to be taken seriously, though it probably is taken seriously by the potentate to whom it is addressed?

You can think that. Some do. But the question is, how well do you know the person that is being spoken about? Mao and Stalin are, or were, remarkable. They did a lot of good. Both Mao and Stalin achieved much for their countries – I reserve opinion on Saddam Hussein for the evidence is not yet all in. But Mao and Stalin were also monsters.

This king is different. How well do you know him? Yes there is all that about ruling from sea to sea, the desert tribes bowing before him, his enemies licking the dust, and sundry kings bringing tribute (vv. 8–11). It is easy to praise Hitler when he is expanding your lebensraum, your living space.

This king is indeed different. He will judge in righteousness, and the afflicted with justice (v. 2). He will defend the afflicted, and save the children of the needy (vv. 3–4). He will crush the oppressor (v. 4). In his days the righteous will flourish and prosperity will abound, until the moon is no more (v. 7). He will deliver the needy who cry out, the afflicted who have no one to help. He will take pity on the weak and the needy, and save the needy from death. He will rescue them from oppression and violence, for precious is their blood in his sight. (vv. 12–14).

So David spoke in this prayer for Solomon. That was his hope for his son. And it was not fulfilled. Solomon failed. Yes there were the magnificences of his reign, but the warnings of I Chron. 28 were not heeded, and degeneration set in, as we know.

So why are we here tonight looking at this catalogue of hope which we know was not to be fulfilled?

We are here because we appreciate that David was saying more than he knew. That God, in his wisdom allowed this Psalm to become part of Scripture for our comfort and for our instruction.

Some paragraphs ago I pointed to the parallel between God speaking of Solomon, and of Jesus. 'This is my beloved son' (Mark 1: 10, Luke 3: 21–22). 'I have chosen him to be my son, and I will be his father' (I Chron. 28: 6). Surely this psalm speaks far beyond Solomon to our Lord himself. He will endure as long as the sun (v.5), and protects the weak and needy as other parts of the psalm indicate. It is his kingdom that will run from sea to sea, and which will be without end.

And there I could end. But instead, let us read once more the concluding part of the psalm:

Verse 15. Long may he live! May gold from Sheba be given him. May people ever pray for him and bless him all the day long. Let grain abound through the land and on the tops of the hills may it sway. Let its fruit flourish like Lebanon; let it thrive like grass of the field. May his name endure forever; may it continue as long as the sun. All nations will be blessed through him, and they will call him blessed.

Praise be to the Lord God the God of Israel, who alone does marvellous deeds. Praise be to his glorious name forever; may the whole earth be filled with his glory. Amen and Amen.

May the whole earth be filled with his glory – it will be, one day, for everyone to see. It is at present, for those with eyes to see. But, until the earth is filled with his glory even in the eyes of those who would deny it, may we be faithful until that day comes. And one way in which we, together, are faithful, is as we seek to know what God wills, and pray for it to be accomplished.

With that I could indeed now end, but, there is yet something else. So, really finally, I have a thought that intrigues me, but which I can not properly bring out before you. I leave it to grow in your mind and in mine. Maybe here there is some sort of chink in the great high doors of eternity, through which we can perhaps peek or peer. This psalm may be read as David praying for Solomon, his inexperienced son. Beyond that we may read of Jesus our Saviour, as David says more than he knew. But might we, with diffidence, not only substitute Jesus for Solomon, but also for David, substitute God. This is a prayer of a father for his son, and we have thought of the son. Now, think of God, the Father, in eternity, seeing the future of his Son, our Saviour, who was to go through so much in order to save the weak, the needy and the afflicted. The one son was to build the Temple. The other is building his Church. Capture in this Psalm a hint of the father who wants so much for his son.

Gilcomston Prayer Meeting, 20 May 2002.

Psalm 72

'Of Solomon' – not the normal superscription. Previous Psalms say 'Psalm of David. And what about that odd verse at the end. V. 20 says: 'This concludes the prayers of David.' Is David, gathering up his poems in his old age, adding a note that this one was his last? Calvin suggests rather these words were an addition by an editor, and indeed that the editor may have been Solomon himself. I agree: there was an editor, though we can't be sure whether he was indeed Solomon working on his father's papers. In Advanced Roman Law we were shown how to spot when an editor changed a text or put in a comment. This example fits. For the editor, this Psalm is the last of the Psalms of David. The next set is the Psalms of Asaph. And in the head-note the editor also notes that this Psalm, Ps.72, is about Solomon. But really we non-professionals should not worry too much about the biblical text. 'What is the real text' is a Satanic bog that has crippled many and drowned some. As C.S. Lewis said the main tenor of the biblical text is clear.

This is a Psalm about a king. To take it as a Psalm of David about Solomon fits with I Chron. 28 and 29. In I Chron. 28. David has summoned the officials of Israel, the mighty men. He reminds them of his desire to build the temple. But God has said otherwise. At I Chron. 28: 5b, David says to Solomon:

'[God] said to me, 'Solomon your son is the one who will build my house and my courts, for I have chosen him to be my son, and I will be his father. I will establish his kingdom forever if he is unswerving in carrying out my commands and laws, as it being done at this time.

'So now I charge you [Solomon] in the sight of all Israel and of this assembly of the Lord, and in the hearing of our God: Be careful to follow all the commands of the Lord your God, that you may possess this good land and pass it on as an inheritance to your descendants forever.

'And you, my son, acknowledge the God of your father, and serve him with wholehearted devotion and with a willing mind, for the Lord searches every heart and understands every motive behind the thoughts. If you seek him he will be found by you: but if you forsake him, he will reject you forever. Consider now, for the Lord has chosen you to build a temple as a sanctuary. Be strong and do the work ...' (I Chron. 28: 5b – 10).

David then in vv. 11-19 hands Solomon the plans he had for the Temple and its financing, and continues at v. 20: 'Be strong and courageous and do the work. Do not be afraid or discouraged, for the Lord God, my God, is with you. He will not fail you or forsake you until all the work for the service of the temple of the Lord is finished.' (I Chron. 28: 20).

David then turns to the Assembly and in 1 Chron. 29: 1 says: 'My son Solomon the one whom God has chosen, is young and inexperienced. The task is great ...'. Consider that and recall Psalm 72. The Psalm is full of hope for the king's reign. Surely this Psalm is David praying for his son Solomon, the inexperienced. That editor has got it right in putting in the superscription, 'Of Solomon' (v. 1). It's about him, not by him. Solomon is being prayed for most earnestly that he will do as he has been instructed, and that his kingship will prosper. That was David's hope for his son. It was not fulfilled. Solomon failed. Yes, there were magnificences in his reign. The Queen of Sheba sought him out for his wisdom and glory. But the warnings of I Chron. 28 were not heeded. Degeneration set in, as we know.

The middle verses of the Psalm speak of the glories of the king (vv. 8-11), They are 'like rain on a mown field' – can you recall the smell of rain on a mown field – the perfume of the first cut of spring? He will rule, and all kings will bow before him etc. etc. There is all that about ruling from sea to sea, the desert tribes bowing before him, his enemies licking the dust, sundry kings bringing tribute.

Now imagine you did not know these words were written centuries ago, but you come across it fresh and new. You would dismiss it. It's overblown. Is this not just the flowery language of sycophancy? We've read that sort of effusive junk in praise of many of the rulers of former Soviet countries? This is just standard flattery – hyperbole, not to be taken seriously. It's just sycophancy – usually in our reality based on fear and/or self-interest.

The thing about hyperbole is knowing when it is, and when it isn't. That depends on how well you know the person concerned. Take Mao Tse Tung or Stalin. They were remarkable men, praised in their times. Read the histories and biographies. They were also monsters. What about Kim Jong Il? Why are we here tonight looking at a catalogue of hope which we know was not to be fulfilled?

This king is different. Does the language fit anyone you know? Recognise him? How *well* do you know him?

Remember I Chron. 28: 6b. Did that phrase not ring bells: 'I have chosen him to be my son, and I will be his father'. Compare Matt. 3: 17: 'This is my beloved Son, in whom I am well pleased'? [Cf. Mark 1: 10, Luke 3: 21-22].

This king *is* different. Whether David realised it or not, beyond his hopes for the reign of his son, he was prophesying. If you know Modest Mussorgsky's opera, contrast the prayer of the dying *Boris Godunov* for his son. These verses are not hyperbole. The true king *will* judge in righteousness, and with justice (v. 2). He *will* defend the afflicted, and save the children of the needy (vv. 3-4). He *will* crush the oppressor (v. 4). In his days the righteous *will* flourish and prosperity will abound, until the moon is no more (v. 7). He *will* deliver the needy who cry out, and the afflicted who have no-one to help. He *will* take pity on the weak and the needy, and save the needy from death. He *will* rescue them from oppression and violence, for precious is their blood in his sight. (vv. 12–14).

The Psalm goes beyond Solomon. See v. 5. 'He will endure as long as the sun, as long as the moon through all generations.' Back in I Chron. 28: David spoke of Solomon handing the kingdom on to his successors. This king has no successors. There are multiple referents here. Psalm 72 is multifaceted.

We are here because we know that David was saying more than he knew. God has allowed this Psalm to form part of Scripture for our comfort and for our instruction. This Psalm speaks of our Lord. He will endure as long as the sun (v. 5). He protects the weak and needy. It is *his* kingdom that will run from sea to sea, and which will be without end. So, see the concluding part of the Psalm: Verse 15.

'Long may he live! May gold from Sheba be given him. May people ever pray for him and bless him all the day long. Let grain abound through the land and on the tops of the hills may it sway. Let its fruit flourish like Lebanon; let it thrive like grass of the field. May his name endure forever; may it continue as long as the sun. All nations will be blessed through him, and they will call him blessed.

Praise be to the Lord God the God of Israel, who alone does marvellous deeds. Praise be to his glorious name forever; may the whole earth be filled with his glory. Amen and Amen.'

May the whole earth be filled with his glory -- it will be, one day, in the eyes of everyone. It is at present, for those with eyes to see. But, until the earth is filled with his glory even in the eyes of those who would deny it, may we be faithful. And one way in which we, together, are faithful, is as we seek to know what God wills, and pray for it to be accomplished.

With that I could end, but, there is something else. A final thought. Maybe here we can peek through a chink in the great high doors of eternity. You can read this Psalm as David praying for Solomon, his inexperienced son. Beyond that we may also read of Jesus our Saviour. But might we, with diffidence, not only substitute Jesus for Solomon, the king. Can we for David, the writer, substitute God. This is a prayer of a father for his son, and we have thought of the son. Now, think of God, the Father, in eternity, seeing the future of his Son, our Saviour, who was to go through so much to save us. The one son was to build the Temple. The other is building his Church. Capture in this Psalm echoes of a father who wants so much for his child.

Gilcomston Prayer Meeting, 28 January 2012.

Psalm 74

It's intriguing how often the psalms we consider at these meetings chime in with the proximate Sunday message, or with the various seasons of the year. In five days we celebrate Christmas. Tonight we have Psalm 74. Does it fit 20 December 2017? It raises the problem of the Unresponsive God.

Performing a text out loud in different ways can sometimes help to understand it. So how to deliver this one? Frantic, bitter, angry, querulous, bewildered or what?

The Psalm is headed a Maskil of Asaph – a teaching. According to Augustine: this Psalm's title is, "Of the Understanding of Asaph." 'Asaph' in Latin translates as 'congregation', in Greek 'synagogue'. For Augustine the psalm reflects the understanding and concerns of a congregation, a fellowship – a gathering of God's people like us. Articulated by one individual, it outlines what the fellowship was thinking. In short it is not the normal sort of Asaph psalm.

The 'understanding' is certainly is not Davidic. Nor it is of his era. The events it cites – the violation of the sanctuary – did not happen in David's time. There was no sanctuary then. So what would have caused this psalm?

Some think it reflects feelings of desolation after Nebuchadnezzar destroyed the temple and took the people to Babylon. The problem with that is v. 9: 'We are given no signs from God; no prophets are left, and none of us knows how long this will last'. But there were prophets at work in those times – Ezekiel and Daniel come to mind. And Jeremiah had indicated the Captivity would last seventy years. Maybe this fellowship was not well-informed.

We know more about another possibility, the persecution of the Jews by the Seleucid Antiochus IV, Antiochus Epiphanes, which is chronicled in I and II Maccabees. In 313 BC Alexander the Great died. His four principal generals divided up his empire. One, Seleucus I Nicator, got Babylon, Syria and Judaea and founded a dynasty. Some of the Seleucid rulers were sympathetic to the Jews. Antiochus IV was not: rather the reverse. So an uprising started in 174 BC – an *intifada* – led by the Maccabees (cf. Handel's oratorio 'Judas Maccabaeus'). Now Antiochus was in the king-ing business, and, like many a modern businessman decided to take over some competitors – Egypt and Cyprus. He had already made some moves, but was not finished. In 168 BC he led an army south. The story goes that as he approached Alexandria on the road there was a man waiting for him. This was Gaius Popilius Laenas, a Roman emissary. Without comment Popilius handed Antiochus a letter from the Roman Senate instructing him to withdraw. Antiochus said that he would need to consult his advisers. But Popilius drew a circle in the sand round Antiochus' feet and required the king to answer before he stepped out of it. Now as a young man Antiochus had spent ten years in Rome as a hostage. Maybe that explains his reaction. He knew what the Romans were like. He withdrew. Hence the familiar phrase – the 'line in the sand'. (Polybius 29.27.1–8; Livy, *History of Rome*, 45.11)

According to Josephus (Josephus, *Jewish Wars*, I.1.1–2) the episode left Antiochus in very a bad mood. While he was away in the south there had been further trouble in Judea. As a reprisal Antiochus ordered the desecration of the Temple. Many were killed (II Maccabees 5:11–14; 6: 1–12). If that lies behind this psalm, the psalm would be very late. Indeed it would take it off the end of our Old Testament. However, I and II Maccabees are held canonical by the Roman Catholic and the Orthodox churches. But let's not discuss the canon tonight. Suffice it to say that Calvin accepts both possibilities, and refers to both in his commentary on the psalm. I am reminded of the aphorism of the late Yogi Berra (NY Yankees): 'when you come to a fork in the road – take it!'

So what does Psalm 74 say to us? Or rather what do I think it can say to us?

First, despite what the Psalm narrates, the fellowship did not conclude that there is no God – that it is all happenstance, that there is nothing to do other than put up with the accidents of history. Despite all set-backs we should remain faithful.

Second, look at the way the psalm proceeds. God is not a celestial D.J. Trump to be approached in trepidation lest we seem to criticise, or be ungrateful. We don't need to placate with dollops of effusive, even obsequious, flattery. This psalm is how you speak to someone you know and trust. Are you in trouble? Go direct. Pitch straight in. Verse 1: 'Why God have you rejected us forever? Why does your anger smoulder against the sheep of your pasture.' Ask for a change. Verses 2–3: 'Remember the nation you purchased long ago, the people of your inheritance, whom you redeemed

– Mount Zion, where you dwelt. Turn your steps toward these everlasting ruins, all this destruction the enemy has brought on the sanctuary.'

Verses 4–8 narrate what has happened. It is a pretty awful catalogue. Foes triumph in the sanctuary (v. 4), smash costly panelling (v. 6), defile the place, burn it to the ground (v. 7). It gets worse. God has done nothing. Verses 9–11 are a fair old set of charges. Verse 9: 'We are given no signs from God; no prophets are left, and none of us knows how long this will be.' The enemy is mocking and reviling God (v. 10). Is God just keeping his hands tucked in his pockets, rather than striking the enemy down (v. 11)? God is neglecting his people: no signs, no prophets, no promise of an end. So much for God shepherding the sheep of his pasture; no protection. We see just His smouldering anger (v. 1). What is going wrong?

Then things turn 180 degrees. Verse 12: 'But God is my King from long ago; he brings salvation on the earth.' Thereafter the Psalm lists his power (vv. 13–17). God created everything. He made day and night, sun and moon (v. 16). He set the boundaries of the earth and made summer and winter (v. 17). Therefore, given his power, God is asked to not hand over his dove – the people – to beasts. They ask him to remember his covenant with them (v. 20), to protect the poor and needy (v. 21). This fellowship – the congregation this Asaph was writing for – want God to rise up and defend his cause (v. 22). He must not ignore the clamour of his enemies (v. 23).

So, how do you see the tone of this Psalm? Is it frantic, angry, full of complaints, bitter? That might be the easy road to take. I see an alternative. This could be a bewildered fellowship, a fellowship encouraging God to intervene, the God who despite everything they trust. It almost says: 'Come on God: you can do better than this!'

This is a strange psalm to consider in the days before Christmas. We have no idea if, when or how exactly God responded. For what it's worth we know Nebuchadnezzar (possibility 1) had his problems, and the people did return from Babylon. We know that things went awry for Antiochus (possibility 2) in the four years after the desecration of the Temple, for the Parthians (later to be a problem for the Romans) invaded, and he died – accounts vary (see II Maccabees 9, and Wikipedia). No matter. This maskil made its way into the Psalms, to be used in the Temple and in the synagogues (see Ps. 74 in Wikipedia). It has been studied for centuries, and now even by us. Augustine, Calvin, Matthew Henry and many contemporary commentators spend time on it. Why have we landed at it tonight? Tonight we have seen it call for a fellowship to be rescued. But we can take a broader, longer focus. God also draws lines in the sand. A rebellious Devil was ejected from heaven, so in anger he has sought to wreak havoc on God's creation and wreck God's purposes. But God has not been unresponsive. Rescue has happened. Christ has been born. In Him we are saved and safe. A greater enemy than Nebuchadnezzar or Antiochus has been thwarted. That we celebrate.

Now. Try delivering this psalm orally yourself. What do you choose as your tone, pace, inflections? How would you act it out on stage? Are you frantic, bitter, angry, querulous, bewildered or what?

Gilcomston Prayer Meeting, 20 December 2017.

Psalm 76

One of the curious things I have noticed over the years is how the regular progress through the Psalms on these Saturday evenings so often results in an appropriate psalm being scheduled as we come up to particular points in the traditional Church year. So here we are, a week from Christmas, and we are at Psalm 76, and at first sight it is so very far from the Christmas story. What do we make of that timing? The dead bodies of valiant men, v. 5. An angry God, v. 7. Child in the manger, Infant of Mary.

We need to remember who we have to deal with. Our God is God. He is one God. One God in Three Persons, yes. But the point tonight is that he is one God. We do not have several gods, or many gods. When we were in Japan in Kyoto in September we went to see the Temple of the Thousand Buddhas. In what amounted to a long shed were rows and rows of rather dusty figures, slightly smaller than human size. Each was supposed to signify a different aspect of Buddha, and, if you were faithful, each was to be worshipped individually, or you made your own choice from among them.

That is not for us. God is God. He is both the baby and the God of wrath and justice. Jesus is our saviour, and eventual judge of all the earth. He is not just the child, nor the sandaled and bearded, robed, eco-friendly hippie as some present him. This psalm is a corrective for us. Keep the balance – the full view.

Now, look at the psalm. The best suggestion of its trigger is that it refers to the time of Hezekiah and Sennacherib and the Assyrian invasion chronicled in II Kings 18–19, and Isaiah 36–37. (See also the prophecy by Isaiah in Isa. 14: 24–7). You may remember the broad outline of the facts. Sennacherib has taken all the cities of Judah – the northern kingdom, and is coming south. Hezekiah tries to buy him off by emptying the Temple treasury and stripping the gold off the doors and doorposts of the Temple (II Kings 18: 13–16). It does not work. Sennacherib sends his Supreme Commander, the Rabshekah as the AV has it, to demand surrender. In II Kings 18: 32b–35 (Isa. 36: 18–20) the Commander gives the message to a delegation sent out by Hezekiah. Incidentally, note that among the delegation is Joah, son of Asaph the recorder (II Kings 18: 18, 37; Isa. 36: 3, 22). Perhaps that Asaph was later to write the Psalm?? The recorder would be able to write, and a civil servant can be a poet. The Commander also shouts his threats in Hebrew to the people gathered on the walls of Jerusalem to watch. None of the gods of the cities that have already been taken have saved them. But before anything further happens a threat comes from Libnah and Cush, and the Assyrians temporarily withdraw to deal with it. Before heading off to cope with the problem Sennacherib himself sends a message to Hezekiah making the same points: the gods of other nations had not preserved them. This God of Jerusalem would do no better (II Kings 19: 10–13: Isa. 37: 9–13).

Later, having disposed of the threat from Libnah and Cush, Sennacherib himself comes to Jerusalem in charge of his army. They set camp outside Jerusalem. And the angel of the Lord visits the camp, and smites 180 thousand men. In the famous AV translation of II Kings 19: 35: Isa. 37: 36, 'when they arose in the morning, behold, they were all dead men'. Sennacherib broke camp and withdrew to his capital, Nineveh, and stayed there, until assassinated shortly after by two of his sons, perhaps because he had lost his army.

So much for bald facts. But what very important fact have I omitted? Hezekiah had eventually taken the matter to God. He had not done that at first, when he tried to buy Sennacherib off. But when told of the threats of the Commander, then Hezekiah tore his clothes, put on sackcloth and went to the Temple. He also sent his leading people, also in sackcloth, to Isaiah to tell him of the trouble Jerusalem that was in (II Kings 19: 1; Isa. 37: 1). Isaiah replied (II Kings 19: 3–7; Isa. 37: 5–8). It was at that point that the Assyrian army withdrew and Sennacherib sent his letter. Hezekiah took the letter with its contemptuous references to God and the failure of various other gods to protect their cities, to the Temple. He spread the letter before the Lord, and prayed (II Kings 19: 14–19; Isa. 37: 14–20). And Isaiah who, note, seems not to have been sent a message or consulted this time round, sent a long message to Hezekiah – fifteen/sixteen verses (II Kings 19: 20–34; Isa. 37: 21–35). God has been insulted by Sennacherib, and so punishment was coming. And it did.

Now back to Psalm 76. With that history in mind we can ground the psalm in an actual story, which can be helpful.

God did break the flashing arrows, the shields and the weapons of war, v. 3. Valiant men lie dead and sleep their last sleep, v. 5. Note they were valiant men. Being valiant in battle may have nothing to do with the rightness of your cause. And, all this is done by the Lord, resplendent with light, more majestic than mountains rich with game, or as the RSV puts it 'the mountains of prey', v. 4.

This is our God. But there's more to it than that. Reading around and about before writing this text I found that the language of vv. 2 and 4 can be rendered differently from the version in the NIV. God's 'dwelling place in Zion', v. 2, could be translated that his 'lair', or his 'den', is in Zion. And in v. 4 it could be that, rather than being more majestic than the mountains of prey, God leaps on his enemies from the mountains. The imagery is that of the Lion. Horse and chariot are still at his rebuke, and no-one can stand before him when he is angry, (vv.6–7). Given the recently released film of *The Lion, the Witch and the Wardrobe*, we can note that, as Mr. Tumnus says, Aslan is not tame lion.

This is our God. He brings down the arrogant and is to be feared by rulers, v. 12. His anger is not arbitrary, but is directed against sin – in the Assyrian case against the insults hurled against him in the attempts to scare Hezekiah and the leaders of the people. We should remember this at a time that Christ and Christianity are being diminished by political correctness. In the name of not offending others of different views, some suggest that the Christmas festival should be renamed Winterval. We should wish each other Happy Holidays not Merry Christmas, and so on. To airbrush Christ out at Christmas is an insult to be taken to our Lord, just as Hezekiah took the Sennacherib letter and spread it before God.

At this time of year we need to remember that gentle Jesus meek and mild, but the infant of Mary has more to him than ineffective niceness. God is kind. God is gentle. We all have experienced some of that. He is also a God of anger against sin, and of justice in his dealings with men.

The last thing is this. Note v. 11. Make vows and pay them. Not make vows alone. Paying those vows is not a formal exercise. It means keeping in touch with God. Hezekiah's own efforts at bribery were the panicky, pragmatic reaction of a politician: buy off trouble. They did not work. Sennacherib took the money, and kept coming. It was when Hezekiah took the problem to God that salvation came. Yes, I know Hezekiah's later career, and much can be made of that. But at this point in his life it is his turning to God that we should learn from.

So, let us turn to this God. He from whom comes our safety. This God who sent his Son to be born in Bethlehem, to die for our salvation, and who will come to judge the world that holds him in contempt.

Gilcomston Prayer Meeting, 17 December 2005.

Psalm 80

Usually the Psalm near Christmas Day is easy to refer to Christ's birth. This one is not.

This Psalm is picture-rich. The Shepherd of Israel, who leads Israel like a flock, is right there at the start, sitting enthroned between the cherubim. There is the 'shining face' of God. However, tonight we have only time to consider one major image – the vine which takes up much of the poem.

Who wrote this psalm? An Asaph. There seems to have been several of those. When was it written, and why? It does not indicate its origin. But this is one of the Psalms – Ps. 76 is another – that may be rooted in Hezekiah's time and the invasion from the north – see the references to Ephraim, Benjamin and Manasseh in v. 2. II Kings chs. 18–19 and Isaiah chs. 36–37 tell of that invasion by Assyria. The broad outline of the story is that Sennacherib takes the northern kingdom, and heads south. Hezekiah tries to buy him off, emptying the Temple treasury and stripping the gold off the doors and doorposts of the Temple (II Kings 18: 13–16). It doesn't work. Sennacherib sends his Supreme Commander to demand surrender. In II Kings 18: 32b–35 (Isa. 36: 18–20) the Commander meets a delegation from Hezekiah, amongst which is one 'Joah, son of Asaph the recorder' (II Kings 18: 18, 37; Isa. 36: 3, 22). Might Asaph the recorder be the writer of the Psalm? A recorder would be able to write, and even a civil servant can be a poet.

That timing might fit. The Psalm is a cry, seeking rescue, maybe while the Assyrians are still up north. 'Awaken your might: come and save us' (v. 2b). 'Restore us, O God: make your face shine upon us, that we may be saved.' That plea is made three times in a kind of refrain, vv. 3, 7 and 19. But note the increasing intensity. In v. 3 the plea is to 'God', in v. 7 to 'God Almighty' and in v. 19 to 'Lord God Almighty'. Yes, v. 8 goes to Lord God Almighty, and we are coming to that. But the repeated plea/refrain tracks fundamental names of God.

The Psalm is a cry of pain and a demand for relief. Note there is no confession of sin, or, at first at least, no appreciation that God might be justified in withdrawing his protection. Look at vv. 4–6. 'O Lord God

Almighty, how long will your anger smoulder against the prayers of your people? You have fed them with the bread of tears; you have made them drink tears by the bowlful. You have made us a source of contention to our neighbours and our enemies mock us.' It's nae right! Indeed maybe there is even a threat in the text. Look at v. 18. If you save us, 'then we will not turn away from you ...' Chutzpah indeed.

There is an interesting element here. Sometimes God does want you to argue with him: does he get tired of forelock tugging obsequiousness? We can rehearse our unworthiness too often and too much. God wants fellowship with his people, with you and me, as individuals, not as a group. He wants you as a friend, not as a constantly apologetic shrinking violet. Remember the Garden of Eden, and God walking in the cool of the day. He wasn't looking for worship. He wanted a chat. Think of John 14: 23. Jesus said 'If anyone loves me, he will obey my teaching. My Father will love him and we will come and make our home with him.' Home – tea, slippers and a comfortable cardigan with God. Does that echo? But what if we do have divergent ideas? Can there be sharp argument? Extremely, it is said that a rabbinic court in Auschwitz put God on trial for neglecting his people and failing to keep his Covenant with them. That may or may not have actually happened. If it did none of the participants survived: it may only be a rumour. Yes, I know, further into our Psalm, Asaph recognises God's rebuke of the people (v. 16). But recognise the posture of vv. 4–6 of our Psalm. 'You are letting us down.' What happened in the Auschwitz Trial? The verdict was 'guilty'. In the play, one of the rabbis then asks: 'So what do we do now?' Another replies: 'Let us pray.' There's a poignant truth there.[7]

If this psalm was triggered by the Sennacherib threat, its prayer was indeed answered. We have no time to explore the detail. You will find that in II Kings 19 and Isa. 37. Hezekiah came to his senses and took Sennacherib's demands to God. Sennacherib himself came and camped outside Jerusalem. And the angel of the Lord visited the camp, smiting 180 thousand in one night. In the famous AV translation, 'when they arose in the morning,

---

7 Cf. Wikipedia, 'God on Trial' on the Frank Cottrell Boyce TV play 'God on Trial' of September 08. Cf. – http://www.guardian.co.uk/film/2008/aug/19/drama.religion. In *The Trial of God* Elie Weisel says he was in Auschwitz when it took place. Cf. also Wikipedia on Weisel's own play '*The Trial of God (as it was held on February 25, 1649, in Shamgorod)*'. In it the verdict is 'not guilty', following a defence of God by a stranger who is later revealed as the Devil.

behold, they were all dead men' (II Kings 19: 35: Isa. 37: 36). Sennacherib withdrew to his capital, Nineveh, but soon was assassinated by two of his sons, perhaps because he had lost his army.

Now look at that imagery of the vine in this psalm. It takes up vv. 8–16. The people are a vine, which God had brought from Egypt, cleared room for and planted (vv. 8–9). It did well, filling the land, covering the mountains and the cedars (vv. 10–11). Apparently good growing vines can do that. The vine spread from the Mediterranean to the Euphrates (v. 11). Now, however, God has broken down its enclosing walls and every passerby picks its grapes, boars snout their way through it, the beasties of the field feed on it (vv. 12–13). Why, Lord? Why?

The imagery is powerful and acute. It is, of course, taken up elsewhere, often negatively, presenting a view of the Jews as a precious vine that has gone wrong. Perhaps destroying my association of the Psalm with the time of Hezekiah, as written up in Isa. 36–37, there is the earlier text of Isa. 5: 1–2. [It is, of course, possible that Ch. 5 was written after Chs. 36–7]. Isa. 5: 1–2: 'I will sing a song for the one I love, a song about his vineyard. My loved one had a vineyard on a fertile hillside. He dug it up and cleared it of stones and planted it with the choicest of vines. He built a watchtower in it and cut out a wine-press as well. Then he looked for a crop of good grapes, but it yielded only bad fruit.' Isa. 5: 3–6 goes on to prophesy judgement; the walls of the vineyard will be broken and it made a wasteland exactly as the middle of Ps. 80 complains. The indictment of Isa. 5 carries on. Isa. 5: 7: 'The vineyard of the Lord Almighty is the house of Israel, and the men of Judah are the garden of his delight. And he looked for justice, but saw bloodshed; for righteousness, but heard cries of distress.' The chapter goes on to describe what is to come on them. Or what about Jeremiah. 'I had planted you like a choice vine of sound and reliable stock. How then did you turn against me into a corrupt and wild vine?' (Jer. 2: 21). Other prophets speak in similar terms.

And yet elsewhere there is a brighter picture. The spreading vine can be the image of peace and prosperity. Think of Micah 4: 2–4 and the establishment of the mountain of the temple of the Lord. From v. 2: 'Many nations will come and say, "Come let us go up to the mountain of the Lord, to the house of the God of Jacob. He will teach us his ways, so that we may walk in his paths." The law will go out from Zion, the word of the Lord from Jerusalem. He will judge between many peoples, and will settle disputes for strong nations far and wide. They will beat their swords into ploughshares and their spears into pruning hooks. Nation will not take up arms against nation, nor will they train for war any more. Every man will sit under his own vine and under his own fig tree, and no-one will make them afraid, for the Lord Almighty has spoken.' (Micah 4: 2–4). Yet other parts of the Old Testament use vineyard imagery to speak of a restoration. 'Again you will plant vineyards on the hills of Samaria; the farmers will plant them and enjoy their fruit' (Jer. 31: 5). Or Amos: 'I will bring back my exiled people Israel; they will rebuild the ruined cities and live in them. They will plant vineyards and drink their wine; they will make gardens and eat their fruit' (Amos 9:14). The people of Hezekiah's time were to be saved, albeit for only a short time.

How is restoration to come about? That takes us back into Ps. 80, to a verse I detoured round to quote its successor. Look now at Ps. 80: 16ff. 'Your vine is cut down, it is burned with fire; at your rebuke your people perish, Let your hand rest on the man at your right hand, the son of man at your right hand, the son of man you have raised up for yourself.' There is the root of the matter – if I can pun it like that. There is the vine stump from which the Branch is to come (Jer. 23: 5 and 33: 15; Zech. 3: 8 and 6:12).

Let's not hang about. Tonight we can cut straight to John 15: 1: Jesus says: I am the true vine and my Father is the gardener.' Verse 5: 'Remain in me, and I will remain in you. No branch can bear fruit by itself; it must remain in the vine. Neither can you bear fruit unless you remain in me. I am the vine, you are the branches.' You know the passage. It is both a warning and a promise. So from this Psalm let us take both. God and the Son are at home with those they love. That's the basis to talk with them.

Gilcomston Prayer Meeting, 23 December 2009.

Postcript:

As noted, Psalm 80: 12–13 speaks of the wall of the vineyard being breached and wild boars snouting their way through the vines. Some three or four weeks after delivering the study I found that that precise imagery was used by Pope Leo X in the bull *Exsurge Domine* (Arise, O Lord) of 15 June 1520. In his condemnation of forty-one of Luther's ninety-five theses, Leo categorised Luther as just such a wild boar. He therefore required Luther to retract those theses within six months. When Luther did not, the Pope excommunicated him, and his followers, by the bull *Decet Romanum Pontificem* (It pleases the Roman Pontiff) of 3 January 1521. Look the texts up on the Internet! And we know what happened after that.

Psalm 80

It is remarkable that year on year the Psalm for our Prayer Meeting before Christmas Day links to the birth of Christ.

The Psalm is picture-rich. The Shepherd of Israel, leading Israel like a flock, is right there at the start, sitting enthroned between the cherubim, and there is the 'shining face' of God (v. 1). That could evoke much, but I must press on. In this psalm I concentrate on two elements, the plea/complaint and the imagery of the vine.

Who wrote this psalm? An Asaph. We have seen several of those. Which? When was it written, and why? It does not indicate its origin. But this is one of the Psalms – Ps. 76 is another – that could be rooted in the invasion from the north in Hezekiah's time – see the references to Ephraim, Benjamin and Manasseh in v. 2. II Kings chs. 18–19 and Isaiah chs. 36–37 tell of that Assyrian invasion. Sennacherib has taken the northern kingdom and heads south. Hezekiah tries to buy him off. He empties the Temple treasury and strips the gold off the Temple doors and doorposts (II Kings 18: 13–16). It doesn't work. Sennacherib sends his Supreme Commander to meet a deputation from Hezekiah outside the Jerusalem walls (II Kings 18: 32b–35; Isa. 36: 18–20). The Jewish delegation includes one 'Joah, son of Asaph the recorder' (II Kings 18: 18, 37; Isa. 36: 3, 22). Was this Asaph, Asaph the recorder, Joah's father, the writer of this Psalm? A recorder would be able to write, and even a civil servant can be a poet.

If that timing fits, the Psalm is a cry, seeking rescue while the Assyrians were still up north, and before that extra-mural confrontation. 'Awaken your might: come and save us' (v. 2b). 'Restore us, O God: make your face shine upon us, that we may be saved.' The plea is made three times. It's a kind of refrain, vv. 3, 7 and 19. But note the increasing intensity. In v. 3 the plea is to 'God', in vv. 7 and 14 to 'God Almighty', and in v. 19 to 'Lord God Almighty'. Yes, v. 4 addresses the Lord God Almighty, and we will come to that. But the repeated refrain / plea for help tracks fundamental names of God.

The Psalm is a cry of pain. It is also a demand for relief. There is no confession of sin, nor, at first at least, any suggestion that God might be justified in withdrawing his protection. Look at vv. 4–6. 'O Lord God Almighty, how long will your anger smoulder against the prayers of your people? You have fed them with the bread of tears; you have made them drink tears by the bowlful. You have made us a source of derision to our neighbours and our enemies mock us.' Asaph is complaining. It's nae right! Do something about it. Chutzpah indeed.

That is interesting. Asaph is secure enough with God to face up to Him. Sometimes God allows, even expects you to argue with Him: does He get tired of forelock tugging obsequiousness? Those who trust in Christ can rehearse our unworthiness over-much. Accept what Christ has done. Rely on it. Be secure in it. God wants proper fellowship. He wants you as a friend, not as a constantly apologetic shrinking violet. Remember the Garden of Eden, and God walking in the cool of the day? He wasn't looking for worship. He wanted conversation, a chat even. Think of John 14: 23. Jesus said 'If anyone loves me, he will obey my teaching. My Father will love him and we will come and make our home with him.' Home – tea, slippers, a roaring fire, an easy chat with God. Do you ever share a joke with God? Or vice versa? That is real fellowship. Does that echo? Talk about this and that with God. But what if our ideas diverge? Can there be argument? Why not? Moses argued with God over the episode of the Golden Calf, and persuaded God not to destroy the people, though they were punished (Exod. 32: 9–14, 31–35). Abraham argued with the angels over Sodom and Gomorrah. On that authority the Jews were not afraid to argue with God. Think Habakkuk 1. Think C.S. Lewis' *A Grief Observed* (1963, originally as by Nat Whilk, 1961). Written after the death of his wife, in places it is excoriating about God, to the extent that some thought Lewis should not have published it.

Starkly, I am reminded of the story that in Auschwitz a rabbinic court put God on trial charged with neglecting his people and failing to keep his Covenant with them. A play by Frank Cottrell Boyce about it on BBC TV twelve years ago sticks in my memory – I recently managed to get a CD of it. The play may only be based on a rumour. The trial may or may not have actually happened. If it did, none of the participants survived. Yes, I know, further into our Psalm Asaph recognises God is rebuking the people (v. 16). But recognise the initial posture of vv. 4–6 of our Psalm. 'You are letting us down'. What happened in the Auschwitz Trial? The verdict was 'guilty'. Towards the end, as an execution roster is called, one prisoner asks: 'So what do we do now?' Another replies: 'Now we pray.' There's a poignant truth there.[8]

If this psalm was triggered by the Sennacherib threat, its prayer was indeed answered. The detail is in II Kings 19 and Isa. 37. Hezekiah came to his senses and took Sennacherib's demands to God. Sennacherib himself came and camped outside Jerusalem. And the angel of the Lord smote 185 thousand of his soldiers in one night. In the famous AV translation, 'when they arose in the morning, behold, they were all dead men' (II Kings 19: 35: Isa. 37: 36). Sennacherib withdrew to his capital, Nineveh, and soon after two of his sons assassinated him. He had lost his army. He had failed.

What about the imagery of the vine? It takes up vv. 8–16. The people are a vine. God brought it from Egypt, cleared ground, and planted it (vv. 8–9). It did well, filling the land, covering the mountains and the cedars (vv. 10–11). Good growing vines do that. The vine had spread from the Mediterranean to the Euphrates (v. 11). But now God has broken down the vineyard walls. Passers-by help themselves to the grapes, boars snout their way through it, the beasties of the field feed on it (vv. 12–13). That's powerful. Ironically, some twenty-three centuries later, this picture turns up in a papal document. In the first paragraph of the bull *Exsurge Domine* (Arise, O Lord) of 15 June 1520, Pope Leo X speaks of depredations by foxes and wild boars in the vineyard of the church. He goes on to denounce Martin Luther as a wild boar, and requires him to withdraw forty-one of those ninety-five theses. It would seem Leo and his advisers failed to recognise that God was breaking down the walls of the Roman Catholic Church.[9]

The imagery of the vine is powerful. It is, of course, taken up elsewhere, often negatively, presenting the Jews as a precious vine that has gone wrong. Take the text of Isa. 5: 1–7. Isa. 5: 1–2: 'I will sing a song for the one I love, a song about his vineyard. My loved one had a vineyard on a fertile hillside.

---

8 Cf. Wikipedia, 'God on Trial', on the Frank Cottrell Boyce TV play of September 2008. Cf. http://www.guardian.co.uk/film/2008/aug/19/drama. religion. In *The Trial of God* Elie Weisel says he was in Auschwitz when such a trial took place. Cf. also Wikipedia on Weisel's own play '*The Trial of God (as it was held on February 25, 1649, in Shamgorod)*'.

9 When Luther did not retract as ordered, the Pope excommunicated him and his followers by the bull *Decet Romanum Pontificem* (It pleases the Roman Pontiff) of 3 January 1521, which is in very extreme terms, and includes severe other punishments. See: https://www.papalencyclicals.net/leo10/l10exdom. htm and https://www.papalencyclicals.net/leo10/l10decet.htm.

He dug it up and cleared it of stones and planted it with the choicest of vines. He built a watchtower in it and cut out a wine-press as well. Then he looked for a crop of good grapes, but it yielded only bad fruit.' Isa. 5: 3–6 goes on to judgement; the walls of the vineyard will be broken and it made a wasteland exactly as in vv. 11–12 of Ps. 80. The indictment carries on. Isa. 5: 7: 'The vineyard of the Lord Almighty is the house of Israel, and the men of Judah are the garden of his delight. And he looked for justice, but saw bloodshed; for righteousness, but heard cries of distress.' The chapter goes on to describe what is to come as a result. Maybe Asaph had not read Isaiah. What about Jeremiah? 'I had planted you like a choice vine of sound and reliable stock. How then did you turn against me into a corrupt and wild vine?' (Jer. 2: 21). Others speak in similar terms.

Elsewhere, of course, there are brighter pictures. Parts of the Old Testament use vineyard imagery to speak of a restoration. 'Again you will plant vineyards on the hills of Samaria; the farmers will plant them and enjoy their fruit' (Jer. 31: 5). Or Amos: 'I will bring back my exiled people Israel; they will rebuild the ruined cities and live in them. They will plant vineyards and drink their wine; they will make gardens and eat their fruit' (Amos 9: 14). The vine can be the image of peace and prosperity. Think of Micah 4: 2–4 and the mountain of the temple of the Lord. From v. 2:

'Many nations will come and say, "Come let us go up to the mountain of the Lord, to the house of the God of Jacob. He will teach us his ways, so that we may walk in his paths." The law will go out from Zion, the word of the Lord from Jerusalem. He will judge between many peoples, and will settle disputes for strong nations far and wide. They will beat their swords into ploughshares and their spears into pruning hooks. Nation will not take up arms against nation, nor will they train for war any more. Every man will sit under his own vine and under his own fig tree, and no-one will make them afraid, for the Lord Almighty has spoken.' (Micah 4: 2–4).

As we have seen, Hezekiah's people were saved, albeit for only a short time.

How will restoration come about? That takes us back to Ps. 80. Take vv. 14b–16, using the NIV footnote 'branch' instead of 'son': 'Watch over this vine, the root your right hand has planted, the branch you have raised up for yourself. Your vine is cut down, it is burned with fire; at your rebuke your people perish.' There, surely, is the stump from which the Branch is to come

(Jer. 23: 5 and 33: 15; Zech. 3: 8 and 6: 12). That is the root of the matter – if I may put it like that. But then we have v. 17. 'Let your hand rest on the man at your right hand, the son of man you have raised up for yourself.' A 'son of man' on God's right hand, whom God has raised, and on whom his hand rests. So our Asaph, secure enough in his relationship with God to complain to Him, is here given an insight, even if hazily, of a son that saves, an insight, which we can interpret better than Asaph. The 'son of man', who is at God's right hand, has come to save.

Leo X got one thing right. The vine is indeed the church. Leo just had not gone far enough through his Bible for his imagery. Cut to John 15: 1. Jesus says: 'I am the true vine and my Father is the gardener.' Verse 5: 'Remain in me, and I will remain in you. No branch can bear fruit by itself; it must remain in the vine. Neither can you bear fruit unless you remain in me. I am the vine, you are the branches.' That is a warning, and a promise. From this Psalm take both, but at Christmas concentrate on the promise. The son of man fore-seen by Asaph did come. And God and the Son do make themselves at home with those they love. That's our basis for life in and with them. Our chief end is to glorify and enjoy God forever – as the Catechism reminds us. That is why in two days time we are going to celebrate the birth of Christ, our Saviour. To adapt the last verse of the psalm, through his Son, the LORD God Almighty has restored us. He has made his face to shine upon us.

Gilcomston Prayer Meeting, 23 December 2020.

Psalm 82

There are lots of thought-provoking elements in this Psalm. But I begin with one which is not obvious. Look it up in Wikipedia and you find that this Psalm is recited in the Jewish morning prayers every Tuesday. Apparently in Jewish practice every day has a particular Psalm assigned for it, each psalm connected to the days of creation. This psalm is recited as referring to the third day of Creation, the day on which God 'exposed the land with His wisdom, thus preparing the world for His assembly'. What do you make of that?

We do not know what triggered this Psalm, but it is clear that Asaph knew his society. The psalm is book-ended by God. God presides in an Assembly, v. 1. At the end Asaph calls on Him to execute judgment, v. 8. I was in two minds whether the intervening verses are God speaking, or whether the words are Asaph's. For tonight at least I come down on the whole Psalm being Asaph's prophetic vision. For what it's worth, Calvin agrees.

You probably expect me to start with the Assembly and the gods. Instead, first consider the indictment of v. 2. The charge is that the gods have defended the unjust and shown partiality to the wicked. Verses 3–4 elaborate. Justice has failed. Asaph points to injustices done to the weak, the fatherless, the poor and the oppressed. They should have been rescued, saved from the hand of the wicked. This is synecdoche. A part implies the whole. Society should be organised and run justly. As Calvin says, a just and well-regulated government can be identified by its upholding the rights of the poor and the afflicted.

Where are we? We are at *a* Judgment Day, perhaps the very Day of Judgement. God is presiding in the great assembly. What do you see? We have to fill out the view for ourselves. That reminds me of the old joke: 'I prefer radio. It has the best pictures.' What do you see? Some sort of court? The House of Lords at the State Opening of Parliament? Are we in the UN General Assembly, or the Great Hall of the People in Tiananmen Square, both familiar from TV. Do you see Renaissance glories from the Florence Scuola, or the Doges' Palace? Mediaeval visions; the wonderful Hieronymus Bosch? What of the Sistine Chapel Altar Wall?

Who is present? Who are these small-g gods? Are they angels? Are they human beings? Let's stick with angels, first. We do have lots of help in envisioning God in an assembly of angelic beings. Take Job 1: 6–12 where the angels come to present themselves before the Lord, and Satan tags along. Then in Job 2: 1–7, Satan turns up again. His permission to attack Job is extended, and the rest of the book unfolds.

Job affords examples of angelic gatherings. We can go a little further. Think of the morning stars singing together and the angels shouting for joy when God was busy creating (Job 38: 7). Isaiah 14: 12–13 speaks of Satan, the chief rebel among the sons of God, as a 'morning star' who had sought to raise his throne above those of 'the stars of God'. He intended to 'sit enthroned on the mount of assembly, on the utmost heights of Mount Zaphon' – note again the notion of an assembly. What do other angels look like? I dare say wings come to mind, but think of the angel that comes to Daniel. 'On the twenty-fourth day of the first month, as I was standing on the bank of the great river, the Tigris, I looked up and there before me was a man dressed in linen, with a belt of fine gold from Uphaz around his waist. His body was like topaz, his face like lightning, his eyes like flaming torches, his arms and legs like the gleam of burnished bronze, and his voice like the sound of a multitude' (Dan. 12: 4–6). Do note, despite so many depictions of angels in Art, this angel, together with those that came to Abraham and Lot prior to the destruction of Sodom and Gomorrah (Gen. 18 and 19), and the one that came to Gideon's parents (Judges 6: 13–2), do not sport wings.

So, are the gods of v. 1b, angels? Perhaps. They could be spiritual beings that have defaulted, permitting injustice to proliferate. Recall the Song of Moses. Three translations of Deuteronomy 32: 8, but not the NIV or KJV, speak of the High God putting guardians in charge of each nation when he assigned it its place. Daniel's angel said that the prince of Persia had resisted him for three weeks, and that he was going to come back to fight with him (Dan. 10: 13, 20). Now it may be that that angel was speaking of a human prince, but the humans that were with Daniel, though they did not see the angel, were terrified and fled. I doubt whether a human prince of Persia would have resisted. It fits better that such divine beings, small-g gods, each, under the sovereignty of God, guide different peoples. Elsewhere God declares judgment 'on all the gods of Egypt' (Exod. 12: 12) and in Numbers the Lord 'had brought judgment on their gods' (Num. 33: 4). We think of such gods as man-made. Maybe instead they are corrupt guardians originally appointed to a role. That also chimes with Paul in Eph. 6: 12–13: 'For our struggle is not against flesh and blood, but against the rulers, against the authorities, against the powers of this dark world and against the spiritual forces of evil in the heavenly realms.' So in Psalm 82 God, presiding in the council of the elohim (gods), is arraigning them for failing in the duties laid on them (cf. Deut. 32: 8). Look round our world, and see their failures.

But the failures of the spiritual supervisors imply human agency. Does the idea of 'gods' as human beings trouble you? Remember that, when accused of blasphemy, Jesus cites part of v. 6 of our Psalm, John 10: 33–36: 'I said you are gods' (Ps. 82: 6). Note also the genealogy of Jesus in Luke 3: 23–37. It traces Jesus back to 'the son of Adam, the son of God' (v. 37). Whatever our genealogy, we too go back to Adam.

Now look again at the charges levelled in vv. 2–4. Humans do, or don't do, the things that are the fact-bases of the indictment. Justice is not done. The weak, the fatherless, the poor, the needy and the oppressed are not rescued and saved. Instead it is the unjust who have been defended. The wicked have been favoured. Other prophets make similar complaints. Read Malachi and other denunciations of those who fail to shepherd the sheep they are supposed to care for. These are people, not spiritual beings.

So, who are we talking about? Who have failed? The solution is not a state socialism, which seems itself to produce its own set of small-g gods. Commentators have been right to apply these strictures not to institutions but to individuals, who, set in positions of authority, power or influence turn a blind eye to or themselves perpetrate injustice. These are not only over-paid executives, selfish financiers, power and status hungry politicians, or peddlers of religion. Daily the media pull the curtain back on the worlds of entertainment, the arts and music, finance, politics, society life and indeed the ordinary life of many. We see crime, greed, gluttony, neglect, selfishness. Yes, there is much good done. Let's not deny that. But this psalm is going for the dark side. Verses 2–4 can apply to anyone who is in a position of power, even minor power, and abuses it. Remember John's words to so many in Luke 3: 7–14. And the result? The gods, all sorts of gods, walk in darkness and understand nothing, and the foundations of the earth are shaken (Ps. 82: 5). Clamant injustice, selfishness and neglect shake societies. Verses 6–7 are what will happen. These failing gods will die. Yes, that is obviously true of the human gods. It is also true of those spiritual beings, which were supposed to care for the mortals. There is the Lake of Fire of

Revelation chs. 19–21.

So we leave Asaph, shaking with anger as he looks at the society of his time, calling on God, the real God, to rise up and do justice. And us? What about us? It is easy to denounce – look at the Twitter-sphere – but let us also examine ourselves. And let us praise our God, for, as v. 8 says, the world is under his jurisdiction, not these popinjay small-g gods. He will sort them out in His good time.

Gilcomston Prayer Meeting, 17 February 2018.

Psalm 87

This psalm is short but extraordinary in its depth. At first sight it is a celebration of a city, clearly Jerusalem. At second sight it is a celebration of the church. At third sight there is within it something marvellous and a great comfort.

Sons of Korah are responsible for twelve psalms, Psalms 42, 44–49, 84–85, and 87–89. The Sons of Korah were one of the divisions of the Kohathites whose full-time occupation was the twenty-four hour praise in the Temple (1 Chron. 9: 33). According to 2 Chron. 20: 19 they could fairly bellow. Those that could not sing were responsible for Temple security, portering and gate-keeping– you might even say some were the 'bouncers' (1 Chron. 9: 17–23; Ezra 7: 7). Others ran the bakery and prepared the offering bread (1 Chron. 9: 31–32). We do not know whether our author was one of the choristers or was on other duties, and it is good we don't know. Even if you don't sing you will have other important tasks to do. Some can even write wonderful poems. As one of E.E. "Doc' Smith's characters says: 'We can't all be first violinners in the orchestra. Someone has to push air through the trombone!'

Verses 1 and 3 of the psalm make it clear that the subject is the city of God. As Calvin says, there is a double synecdoche in the references in v. 2. Zion is taken as the Jerusalem site and the gates encompass the city.

When and why was this outburst of affection written? We do not know. Some think it was at a high point in the City's history, when it was celebrated as in the days of David and Solomon. Others, including Calvin, think that it was written to encourage when the city was being rebuilt after the Exile. Certainly sons of Korah would have been among the musicians, gate-keepers and temple servants that returned with Ezra (Ezra 2: 41–54; 7: 7). We do not need to come to a conclusion on those questions. The essence remains. This psalm is a celebration, a paean of praise.

How do we get from Jerusalem to the church? That parallel or link was early realised by the Christian church. We will get to New Testament proof of that. But the idea was solid by the time Augustine wrote *On the City of God against the Pagans* early in the Fifth century. Augustine covers much ground, but for tonight just think about that title. Calvin follows suit. For him this psalm points out that God has protected the church of God, while kingdoms have come and gone. God loves Zion. God loves his church. It is entirely appropriate to take this psalm and apply it to the church.

But a city needs a population. Where do they come from? God chooses.

Jerusalem was surrounded by other cities and communities. Verse 4 names some, Rahab, here standing for Egypt, Babylon, Philistia, Tyre and Cush. In fact a list like that was a florid way to speak of the Gentile world. On occasion some could be helpful. That other Rahab from Jericho became an ancestress of Christ. Hiram, King of Tyre, provided timber for a house being built for David (2 Sam. 5: 11; 1 Chron. 14: 1). Later at Solomon's request he sent timber and workmen to help build the Temple (1 Kgs. 12: 11; 2 Chron. 3: 2–18). Indeed, one of those workmen, Huram-Abi, a major artist or a cunning man, as the KJV puts it (2 Chron. 2: 12–13) did much of the Temple decoration (2 Chron. 2: 7, 13–24). Even Cyrus and Darius were helpful in their time (2 Chron. 36: 22–23, Ezra 1: 1–4; Ezra 5: 6–17, 6: 1–13), as was Artaxerxes (Ezra 7: 11–26; Neh. 2: 4–9).

What about remote Cush? That took me to a famous prophecy of Isaiah, Isa. 11, in its time enigmatic.

I quote selectively. Verse 1: 'A shoot will come up from the stump of Jesse; from his roots a Branch will bear fruit.' Verses 10–11: 'In that day the Root of Jesse will stand as a banner for the peoples; the nations will rally to him, and his resting place will be glorious. In that day the Lord will reach out a hand a second time to reclaim the surviving remnant of his people from Assyria, from Lower Egypt, from Upper Egypt, from Cush, from Elam, from Babylonia, from Hamah and from the islands of the Mediterranean' – another listing of the Gentiles. God collects his people, the citizens of Zion, from all over the world. Yes, v. 4 of our psalm indicates that he collects those who acknowledge him, but we know from other bible passages that acknowledging God is not just reciting a formula. At the Second Coming many will claim they have done wonderful things in Jesus' name. He replies 'I never knew you. Depart from me you evildoers' (Matt. 7: 23).

Now, look at our vv. 4–6. Many years ago I did a book on legal imagery in the epistles (*Slaves, Citizens, Sons* (1984)). When I read these verses I recognised what they are all about. This is ancient citizenship law. The text says: 'I will record concerning those who acknowledge me: "This one was born in Zion." Hear this, Rahab and Babylon, and you too, Philistia, Tyre and Cush. Indeed, of Zion it will be said, "This one and that one were born in her, and the Most High himself will establish her." The Lord will write in the register of the peoples: "This one was born in Zion".'

Basically, in those days you were a citizen, a national, of where you were born. Indeed birth is still the simplest way to become a citizen in all countries. Paul was a citizen of Tarsus, no mean city (Acts 21: 39). But back then your natal citizenship was indelible, and there was no such thing as dual-nationality. Yes, there was immigration from town to town – Paul was brought up in Jerusalem (Acts 22: 3) – but you remained tied to where you were born. Mary and Joseph trekked to Bethlehem because of the family connection (Luke 2: 4). If you came from elsewhere you were technically an alien, a stranger without citizenship rights. Paul points out that before the Ephesians knew Christ they were aliens from the commonwealth of Israel. In another translation they were excluded from citizenship in Israel and foreigners to the promises of the covenant (Eph. 2:12). Again Peter sends his epistle to the strangers scattered throughout Pontus, Galatia, Cappadocia, Asia and Bithynia (KJV, 1 Pet. 1: 1). But if you look at the NIV you find 1 Peter being addressed to 'God's elect', to those chosen according to the foreknowledge of God (NIV, 1 Pet. 1: 1–2). Later we read that the elect are 'a chosen people, a royal priesthood, a holy nation, God's special possession' (1 Pet. 2: 9). Formerly they were 'not a people' but now through his mercy they are 'a people of God' (1 Pet. 2: 10). Now they are 'strangers and foreigners' in this world. That can only be because they were citizens of the city of God.

How? Apply all this to vv. 4–6. Those who acknowledge Him, this one and that one, from Egypt, from Babylon, Philistia, Tyre and Cush – even Aberdeen – God says they were born in Zion, and registers them as citizens of Zion. As Jesus told Nicodemus, they have been born again (John 3: 1–8). Their names are written in the Lamb's book of life (Phil. 4: 3; Rev. 3: 5; 21: 27 – contrast Rev. 13: 8; 17: 8; 20: 15). They are listed among the righteous (Ps. 69: 28).

Our psalmist knew more than he knew. He knew a profound truth. He tells us how much God loves Zion, Jerusalem, his city. That is obvious. But he also tells us that those who truly acknowledge God, are the citizens of the City of God. God has chosen them and found them, gathered them from all over the globe. Your citizenship in Zion does not depend on your choice of God, but on his choice of you. Knowing that, surely we can make music and sing, v. 7.

But what does singing 'All my fountains are in you' mean? Remember water was so very important in Zion. God constantly refreshes his city, his people. In Revelation John is shown the river of the water of life in the city of God (Rev. 22: 1–2). What will you sing?? As I was finalising this text Anton Bruckner's wonderful setting of the 'Te Deum', that ancient hymn, came on the radio. It begins: 'We praise thee, O God. We acknowledge thee to be the Lord.'

Bruckner uses lots of trombones.

Gilcomston Prayer Meeting, 13 February 2021.

Psalm 88

There's something funny about the way God works – funny in both senses. It is strange. It can be very amusing. Have you ever thought that God has a wonderful sense of humour? Yesterday afternoon I was asked to take on this psalm because the person scheduled could not get here, and I agreed without looking at it. When I did look at it I found it is a terrible psalm. At first skim through I was appalled. I almost phoned to cancel my acceptance. Who was this Heman the Ezrahite that pours out these bleak phrases as he spirals through despair? It is even bleaker than Ps. 39, where David plumbs the depths. It calls to mind the tribulations of Job. Indeed, Job could have written it, except that it is labelled as by some Heman or other. Augustine spiritualises it as referring to Jesus, and you can see resonances with the Agony in the Garden. But it is better taken as the lamentation and depression of a follower, not of the Master himself.

At first sight it is unrelieved gloom. At second sight it remains gloom. Apparently the very last phrase we have in the NIV could be rearranged. In Hebrew the reading is 'my closest friend is the darkness' – a bleak, bleak ending to bleak, bleak verses. It makes you wonder what it is doing in the Bible. Where is the uplift? Where is the hope? If the Bible were being readied for publication today I am pretty sure Ps. 88 would not have survived the editor's scissors, or the delete key, to be modern.

Had Mike been giving me a choice, as he sometimes does, I would probably have avoided it. What can you make of a psalm like this for edification, instruction and inspiration for prayer? And yet as I looked at it again something clicked, and I hope you will find it useful. Tell me later.

Let's look briefly at the text.

Was the writer ill? He was 'shut up and cannot go out', vv. 8–9. He has no friends around, vv. 8 and 18. He was afflicted from his youth, nervous etc, vv. 15–8. Was he neurasthenic? Even so, notwithstanding his afflictions, he calls on God every day, v. 9. He will call on God every morning, v. 13.

Was the psalm written early or late in life? There might be an argument that it is a bit later on – see the reference to 'from my youth' in v. 15, and to 'friends' in v. 8. And yet these are not compelling as to dating. Once you think about it, this psalm could be written at any point in maturity. You could make a case that this is an old man whose physical disabilities are getting to him. He is shut up, confined and cannot escape, v. 8. He is repulsive to his friends, also v.8. Has he some disease?

And yet. And yet.

I said that as I re–read the psalm, something clicked. The last time I was at this lectern was eight weeks ago. The psalm then was Psalm 80. If you were here then you may remember that it had Asaph and the people complaining to God. They needed protection. The wall of the vineyard that protected the vine, Israel, had been broken down and a wild boar was snouting its way through the vines. Three or four weeks later I found something intriguing. The precise imagery of the snouting boar was used by Pope Leo X in the Papal Bull, *Exsurge Domine* (Arise, O Lord) of 15 June 1520, in which Leo condemned just under half (forty-one) of Luther's Ninety-Five theses, and required their retraction within six months. Luther did not recant, and was excommunicated by the Bull *Decet Romanum Pontificem* (It Pleases the Roman Pontiff) of 3 January 1521. The Reformation followed.[10]

So how does that connect for tonight? What clicked?

After coping with Psalm 80 I read *Out of the Storm: The Life and Legacy of Martin Luther* by Derek Wilson, (London: Hutchison, 2007). It's a magnificent book, much more detailed than Roland Bainton's *Here I Stand* of the 1950s (London: Hodder and Stoughton, 1951, and many later reprints) good though that is.

What clicked was the account of Luther's early life. We tend to think of him as this Great Reformer suddenly emerging to combat the errors of Rome. But he wasn't. He has a history before and after the Ninety-Five Theses. Luther went through such struggles. Depression was a constant companion, particularly in his early years. His health was never very good. He suffered from indigestion and constipation. And apart from that, the rigours he put himself through while he sought certainty in God, wrecked his early health. He might have been a lawyer, but instead he entered the Augustinian Order, and was most sedulous in conforming to the routines that Order prescribed. Why? He complied with all sorts of rules so that

---

10 *Decet Romanum Pontificem* (It pleases the Roman Pontiff) of 3 January 1521, which is in very extreme terms, and includes severe other punishments. See: https://www.papalencyclicals.net/leo10/l10exdom.htm and https://www.papalencyclicals.net/leo10/l10decet.htm.

he would know that he was saved: that he would go to heaven. And yet he lacked confidence in the salvation that the Catholic Church offered. You had to die in a state of grace, which meant, first, that you had been as sinless as possible. Second, in relation to the sins that you had committed, you could get forgiveness from a priest. That meant that you had to have confessed, and been pronounced forgiven for your sins. But how did you know you had remembered everything? Luther was a very considerable bible scholar before he became the reformer. He was the Professor of Biblical Studies at Wittenberg before the furore started. Incidentally, it is little known that George Frederick Handel studied Law at Wittenberg before he became a composer – which may explain 'The Messiah'. But, back to the point: Luther remembered Paul's address to the Areopagus where he spoke of the altar to 'An Unknown God' (Acts 17: 23). What about the Unknown Sin? It was Luther's despair and depression, not unconnected with that fear, that drove him further into the Word of God, where he saw that salvation is a gift, not the result of a form of holiness whether real, feigned or bought. It was (and is) not something that a priest can dispense, or sell. The idea that the Pope, first Julius II and then Leo X, and later, was selling Indulgences to the ignorant to pay for the construction of the new basilica of St Peter's was a major trigger of Luther's reaction. Johannes Tetzel was a consummate snake-oil salesman, but Luther saw through him to the point. You cannot buy your way to heaven by money (end of so much wonderful art), by priests (end of so many priestly foundations), or by being as good as you can be (end of much self-congratulation), so that God just has to let you into heaven.

And even after Luther took his stand, the opposition to him was such that he had many episodes of depression. He was protected, but could not always rely on his protectors. There were gnawing arguments from the constant opponents emanating from the RC Church, for whom he had a fine line in vituperation. Others, he had thought friends, took slightly different positions, which he considered betrayal. His depressions, and his explosive angers when others differed even slightly with him, were avenues the Devil used to get at him.

But I am getting off the point. Or am I?

Who wrote our Psalm? Heman the Ezrahite. Apparently Heman means Faithful. There are ten references to a Heman in the Old Testament. Most of them seem to be the same person, and with one exception they are in

I Chronicles. The exception is 1 Kings 4: 31: 'Solomon was wiser than any other man, including Ethan the Ezrahite – wiser than Heman, Calcol and Darda, the sons of Mahol.' So that Heman was a wise man. But look at that list. Who was the first in the list? Ethan the Ezrahite. Who's he? Look one psalm further on from tonight's. Who wrote Psalm 89? Ethan the Ezrahite – Heman's brother? Was it all in the family? It seems so.

Apart from the Solomonic comparison, the other citations of Heman have to do with the time of David. Heman was a musician. (Cf. I Chron. 2: 6. The sons of Zerah: Zimri, Ethan, Heman, Calcol and Darda —five in all, the last three being in the Solomon comparison list of I Kings 4: 31 above. I Chron. 6: 31ff lists those who David put in charge of the music for the House of the Lord once the Ark was brought to Jerusalem. I Chron. 6:33: 'Here are the men who served, together with their sons: From the Kohathites: Heman, the musician, the son of Joel, the son of Samuel'. And then at v. 39 we find 'Heman's associate Asaph, who served at his right hand: Asaph son of Berekiah, the son of Shimea'. We have been accustomed here at Gilcomston prayer meetings to think of Asaph or the Asaphs, the great writer or writers of Psalms. Maybe Heman, the writer of our terrible Psalm, was someone greater, for Asaph served 'at his right hand'. In I Chron. 15: 15–17 the Levites appoint 'Heman son of Joel; from his brothers, Asaph son of Berekiah; and from their brothers the Merarites, Ethan son of Kushaiah,' to meet David's requirements for 'singers to sing joyful songs, accompanied by musical instruments, lyres, harps and cymbals' as the Ark was brought up to Jerusalem. Heman and his colleagues, Asaph and Ethan, were to sound the bronze cymbals (I Chron. 15: 19). In I Chron. 16 David left Zadok the priest and others in Gibeon to present offerings before the Lord. At v. 41 we find: 'With them were Heman and Jeduthun and the rest of those chosen and designated by name to give thanks to the LORD, "for his love endures forever."' As the Ark approached the city, Heman and Jeduthun were responsible for the sounding of the trumpets and cymbals, and for the playing of the other instruments for sacred song. The sons of Jeduthun were to be stationed at the gate (I Chron. 16: 42).

So much for the music, but turn a few pages further on. In I Chron. 25 Heman and his colleagues have been given new tasks. 1 Chron. 25: 1: 'David, together with the commanders of the army, set apart some of the sons of Asaph, Heman and Jeduthun for the ministry of prophesying, accompanied by harps, lyres and cymbals.' There follows a list of the men who performed this service. And at v. 4 we find: 'As for Heman, from his sons: Bukkiah, Mattaniah, Uzziel, Shubael and Jerimoth; Hananiah, Hanani, Eliathah, Giddalti and Romamti-Ezer; Joshbekashah, Mallothi, Hothir and Mahazioth. All these were sons of Heman the king's seer. They were given to him through the promises of God to exalt him. God gave to Heman fourteen sons and three daughters,'

So Heman, named author of Psalm 88 was quite someone. He was a musician, a wise man, and a seer. I wonder whether his activities as 'seer' exposed him to unwelcome spiritual elementals that encouraged and then fed on his depression? He was a cymbalist. Was he 'heavy metal'?

So where does that leave us. Why is this dismal paean in the Bible?

Simply, it once more confronts us with the Absolute. God is God. We bow to his will. We trust him. Heman still prays to God, though he remonstrates with Him. He is in God's hand. Last time round on Ps. 80 I referred to the TV film, the 'Trial of God'. It was the play about the (query) fictional trial of God by a rabbinic court in Auschwitz in 1944. God was found guilty. Then one rabbi asked 'what do we do now?' Another replied, 'Let us pray'. That is the acceptance that God is God. Just as Job came through to that, so must we. In Jesus God has told us to pray for the extension of the kingdom, whether we understand what He is doing or not: 'Thy kingdom come, thy will be done in heaven and on earth', whether we are depressed or not.

Whether this psalm came from the young Heman, who was later to be so used of God and honoured by David, or whether it was written towards the close of his life after his attainments, is really immaterial. His psalm was recognised as inspired and to be included in the Temple praise despite its terms. Despite his depression, Heman prays on. Look again at v. 9b: 'I call to you, O Lord, every day: I spread out my hands to you.' Verse 13: 'I cry to you for help, O Lord; in the morning my prayer comes before you'. Then look back at the fundamental seed of faith in the psalm in vv. 1–2: 'O Lord, the God who saves me, day and night I cry out before you. May my prayer come before you; turn your ear to my cry.' We don't have it in this Psalm, but I reckon that God responded with love. I remind you of the last verse of tonight's hymn, H. 507. 'Then will He own his servant's name before his Father's face, and in the New Jerusalem appoint my soul a place.'

Gilcomston Prayer Meeting, 28 March 2009.

Psalm 88

At first sight we have unrelieved gloom. At second sight gloom remains. Look at the words at the very end. The very last word is not the NIV's 'friend'. The Hebrew is 'my closest friend is the darkness' – 'darkness', – a bleak ending to bleak verses. It makes you wonder what this Psalm is doing in the Bible. Where is the uplift? Where is the hope? Were the Psalms being readied for publication as a modern set of hymns today I doubt if Psalm 88 would survive the editorial committee. Do you know of any modern hymns or songs that are like this psalm? This glass is not even the proverbial 'half empty'. It is almost empty.

What can you make of a psalm like this for edification, instruction, inspiration for prayer? Augustine spiritualises it and applies it to Jesus – and you can see resonances in the Agony in the Garden and the cry of desolation on the Cross: My God, my God, why has thou forsaken me, Eloi Eloi Lama Sabachthani (Matt. 27: 46; Mark 15: 34). But this psalm is better taken as the lamentation and depression of a follower, not of the Master himself.

Let's start with the author. This is not one of the (Mattel) Masters of the Universe or the He-Man of the later films. Nothing like. Who was Heman the Ezrahite? Heman means Faithful, a good name to have and to live up to, especially given the text we are looking at. There are sixteen references to a Heman in the Old Testament. Most of them seem to be to the same person. All but one are in I Chronicles. The exception is in I Kings 4, the list of Solomon's officials. 1 Kings 4: 31: 'Solomon was wiser than any other man, including Ethan the Ezrahite — wiser than Heman, Calcol and Darda, the sons of Mahol.' So that particular Heman was a wise man. But look who was the first in that list – Ethan the Ezrahite. Who is he? Cast your eyes one psalm further on from this one. Ethan the Ezrahite wrote Ps. 89. Was he Heman's brother? Was it all in the family? Perhaps.

The other citations of a Heman are clearly from the time of David. I Chron. 6: 31–9 lists those who David put in charge of the music for the House of the Lord. They include 'Heman, the musician, the son of Joel, the son of Samuel' (I Chron. 6:33). By the way at I Chron. 6:39 we find 'Heman's associate Asaph, who served at his right hand'. We know Asaph or the Asaphs, as writers of Psalms. Maybe Heman was their tutor. The mighty Asaph served 'at his right hand'.

Further on, in I Chron. 15: 15–17, the Levites appoint 'Heman, son of Joel' among others to meet David's requirements for 'singers to sing joyful songs, accompanied by musical instruments, lyres, harps and cymbals' as the Ark was brought up to Jerusalem. Heman, and his colleagues Asaph and Ethan, are to sound the bronze cymbals (I Chron. 15: 19). In I Chron. 16 David leaves Zadok the priest and others in Gibeon to present offerings before the Lord. At v. 41 we find: 'With them were Heman and Jeduthun and the rest of those chosen and designated by name to give thanks to the LORD, "for his love endures forever."' As the Ark approached the city Heman and Jeduthun were to see to the trumpets and cymbals and for other instruments played for the sacred celebrations (I Chron. 16: 42). A few pages further on in I Chron. 25 Heman and his colleagues have new tasks. I Chron. 25: 1: 'David, together with the commanders of the army, set apart some of the sons of Asaph, Heman and Jeduthun for the ministry of prophesying, accompanied by harps, lyres and cymbals.' There follows a list of those who performed this service. I do not propose to try to get my tongue round I Chron. 25: 4. It ends, 'all these were sons of Heman the king's seer. They were given to him through the promises of God to exalt him. God gave to Heman fourteen sons and three daughters.'

Assuming that all these Hemans were the same person, Heman was quite something. He was a musician, a cymbalist. Was he 'heavy metal'? He was a grandson of Samuel (I Chron. 6: 33). He was known as wise, though not as wise than Solomon. He was a seer. Clearly he was a man of distinction, someone who reached the heights of his profession.

How could someone like that write Psalm 88? The singer of joyful songs, and exponent of the cymbal. Sometimes depths come after heights. Think of Job. Had Heman's activities as a 'seer' exposed him to spiritual elementals that encouraged, and then fed on his depression? (Cf. C.S. Lewis, *The Screwtape Letters*). I look around and would not rule that out. Was Heman ill? He was 'shut up and cannot go out', vv. 8–9 He has no friends visiting him, vv. 8 and 18. He was afflicted from youth – nervous etc, vv. 15–18. Was he neurasthenic? Even so, his afflictions notwithstanding, he calls on God every day, v. 9. He will call on God every morning, v. 13.

Was this Psalm written early in life or late? Maybe it was late. See the reference to 'from my youth' in v. 15, and to 'friends' in v. 8. But these clues are not compelling. When you think about it, this Psalm could be written at any point in maturity. You could make a case that this is an old man whose physical disabilities are getting to him. He is shut up, confined and cannot escape, v. 8.

So where does that leave us. Why is this dismal paean in the Bible?

Simply, it confronts us with the Absolute. God is God. We bow to his will. We trust him. Heman still prays to God. He even remonstrates with Him, vv. 4–12. 'Why LORD am I going through this?' It is possible and sometimes helpful to let rip at God. Heman is secure enough with his God to complain. You don't have to be constantly fore-lock tugging. How well do you know God? Do you know him well enough to have a joke with him? You can, you know. Do you know him well enough to let rip? He understands that bottling things up – being 'brave' – can be corrosive. If you don't like my saying that, I must ask: have you read C.S. Lewis's *A Grief Observed*?

Heman is in God's hand and he knows it. Last time round on Ps. 88 (2009) I mentioned the 2008 TV film, the 'God on Trial' by Frank Cottrell Boyce, which I have previously cited in dealing with Ps. 80.[11] It supposes that in 1944 in Auschwitz Jewish rabbis put God on trial for betraying his people. God is arraigned for abandoning the Jews during the Holocaust, thus failing to keep his Covenant. Surely you can see the point? At the end God is found guilty, though some think there might be grounds for an appeal. After the verdict one rabbi asks: 'What do we do now?' There is silence. Another replies, 'Let us pray'. That is the acceptance that God is God. Just as Job came through to that acceptance, so may we. Jesus told us to pray for the extension of the kingdom, whether we understand what God is doing or not: 'Thy kingdom come, thy will be done in heaven and on earth', whether we are depressed or discouraged or not. And yet, and yet, there is a hope in Heman. For, look again at v.1. 'O LORD, the God who saves me'. In the AV it is 'O Lord, my Saviour'. Despite all the complaint that follows in this psalm, Heman knows he prays to his saviour. God is in control of the troubles affecting him. He can give release.

A couple of Fridays ago Heather was out. I watched a recording of 'Nixon in China'. With regret I found myself wondering whether anyone at

---

11 See Wikipedia on 'Trial of God' as to a play by Elie Weisel, and for the 2008 tv play: 'God on Trial' by Frank C. Boyce. In Weisel's play the verdict is 'not guilty', following a defence of God by a stranger who is later revealed as the Devil.

Gilcomston would respond to the lonely Chou En Lai in the final Aria of the opera:

'I am old and cannot sleep forever like the young, nor hope that death will be a novelty, but endless wakefulness when I put down my work and go to bed. How much of what we did was good? Everything seems to move beyond our remedy. Come heal this wound. At this hour nothing can be done. Just before dawn the warblers begin, the cage-birds answering. To work. Outside this room the chill of grace lies heavy on the morning grass.'

Would that echo with Heman the Ezrahite?? I think so.

Did this Psalm came from a young Heman, later to be so used of God and honoured by David? Was it written towards the close of his life after his attainments were history? Ultimately that is immaterial. This psalm was recognised as inspired and to be included in the Temple praise despite its terms. His depression notwithstanding Heman prays on. Look again at v. 9b – 'I call to you, O LORD, every day: I spread out my hands to you.' Verse 13: 'I cry to you for help, O LORD; in the morning my prayer comes before you'. Then look back at the fundamental seed of faith in the Psalm in vv. 1–2: 'O Lord, the God who saves me, day and night I cry out before you. May my prayer come before you; turn your ear to my cry.' Ultimately Heman knows he is secure in his saviour Lord.

We don't have it in this psalm, but I reckon that God responded with love, otherwise why is this psalm here? If this psalm is 'early Heman', the blessings of his later career would show that. Remember the fourteen sons and three daughters of I Chron. 25: 4. If it is 'late Heman', his answer was still to come. For us that pearl lies in the last verse of an old hymn, (Hy. 507). 'Then will He own his servant's name before his Father's face, and in the New Jerusalem appoint my soul a place.'

Let us pray.

Gilcomston Prayer Meeting, 18 April 2015.

Psalm 91

I wonder how many now remember 'The Good Old Days', that TV recreation of the late Victorian and Edwardian music-hall, transmitted from the Leeds City Variety Theatre? Introducing this Psalm I feel tempted to imitate Leonard Sachs, that doughty exponent of polysyllabic persiflage. There are so many images in it, tumbling over themselves as the Psalmist rejoices in his God. But I don't have a large, gaudy silk handkerchief to wave.

Sometimes it is helpful to link a Psalm with a particular author and/or a particular occasion. I am not sure whether this is one of them. Suffice it to say that various writers have different views about that. Traditional Jewish thinking sees this psalm as following on from Ps. 90, which indicates that it was a song of Moses. Accordingly they, and some modern scholars, consider and interpret the imagery in the light of the Exodus, and you can see that that does fit. The snakes of v. 13 chime with those of Num. 21: 6–9, the punishment for grumbling against Moses, and the cure of the bitten coming through looking on the brazen serpent. The people, all except the faithful spies, dying during the forty years trek after they refused to go into the Land at Kadesh Barnea (Deut. 1: 19) links with the punishing of the wicked (v. 8). And Moses, the friend of God, is pressing on through it all. Others think that the psalm was written, and refers to events during David's reign. Some would put it even later. Yet others think it almost entirely prophetic, the Psalmist seeing into the future, perhaps being premonitory of Jesus, or even seeing through into the days of the Millennium. But for our purposes tonight, I think we should simply luxuriate in it, and take what it may mean for each of us, which may mean different things for different people. It can be a Universal Medicine.

There are basically three elements, vv. 1–2, 3–13, and then 14–16.

The first two verses are an affirmation by the writer. He will dwell in the shelter of the Most High, and rest in the shadow of the Almighty. These are powerful thoughts, particularly if you think of the climate and terrain of Israel. Shelter and shadow – shelter, yes! Shadow? Does God cast a shadow? But you see the writer's point. With a sun beating on you a shadow to rest in is such a blessing. And so the author affirms his faith: 'I will say of the

Lord, "He is my refuge and my fortress, my God, in whom I trust'" (v. 2). But note what has crept in there. 'Shelter and shadow' have become 'refuge and fortress'. This is no protection from natural circumstances. 'Refuge' and 'fortress' have implications of hostile attack, and the need for defence against enemies, whether people or entities, that intend harm. That moves us into the second part, but before we do, there's something else in these first verses that there's no time to go into tonight – it took me a whole Wednesday evening bible-study years ago. In these two verses we have 'the Most High', 'the Almighty', 'LORD', and 'God'. The Names of God are a wonderful study in themselves, revealing different aspects of him.

Verses 3–13 change things. No longer is the author penning his confidence in God. He turns to address us. Only in the second half of v. 9 does he step back and reaffirm his own position. Verse 9 says that if you make the Most High your dwelling – even the LORD, who is '*my* refuge …' will do this and this and this. So in these verses the writer is saying, this is what I have found. Join me.

Then the images rise, one after another. We are saved from the fowler's snare and the deadly pestilence. Like chicks or ducklings, we will be covered by God's feathers, and find refuge under his wings, vv. 5–6. That carries the mind forward to the gospel where our Lord weeps as, on his way to that triumphal entry, Jesus comes into sight of Jerusalem, Luke 19: 41–5. And, by way of contrast with this psalm, remember what Jesus had said not long before, towards the end of that chapter of woes brought about by unfaithfulness. 'O Jerusalem, Jerusalem, you who kill the prophets and stone those sent to you, how often I have longed to gather your children together as a hen gathers her chicks under her wings, but you were not willing' (Matt. 23: 37; cf. Luke 13: 34).

Back to our psalm. God's faithfulness will be your shield and rampart. [Gillian and Andrew's plane lost one of its engines two hours short of Montreal]. Night terrors, the arrow that flies by day, the pestilence that stalks in darkness and the plague that destroys at midday – no antibiotics in those days – you will not fear them. Thousands may die on either side, but you will only observe and see the punishment of the wicked (v. 8).

Then this second part alters. Verse 9 begins with that little word 'if'. If you make the Most High your dwelling – which is what the author has done – 'then no harm will befall you, no disaster will come hear your tent.'

Well now, what about that? Cancer, Alzheimers, heart trouble, car crashes, unemployment – the list is endless. While I was researching for tonight I came across the information that Rick Husband, the Mission Commander of the Shuttle Columbia that broke up over Texas on 1 February 2003, was a Christian. Now I know that Shuttle Mission STS-107 is not likely to have been in our Psalmist's contemplation, but how can it fit tonight? Length of days is mentioned in the last verse of our psalm. But 'length' may be a matter of quality rather than of quantity.

Some would get out of the problems of authorship or dating by saying that this psalm is indeed the song of Moses as he looks back over a long life – see again the reference to length of days down in v. 16 – Moses made it to 120. Moses is looking to his salvation that was to come on Mount Nebo, after God had showed him the Land: Deut. 34: 1–8. Others would get out of the difficulty by saying that our Psalm looks far, far forward into the Millennium of Isaiah chs. 11 and 65, when there will be a new heaven and a new earth. But that does not wash. This Psalm is speaking of treading down, not playing with, lions and serpents.

'If you make the Most High your dwelling' – all will be sweetness and light. Does the phrase carry the inference that if something goes wrong for you, you have failed; your profession is bogus. Or, there is the other temptation. X has problems, you do not. So his/her profession of faith is bogus, and you are ok.

One way through this conundrum is just to butt straight through. All heresies begin by taking a wisp of verses and growing what Prince Charles would call a 'monstrous carbuncle' out of them. I think of the grotesque Christian Scientist Church in Boston, Mass., which extrudes itself from a perfectly traditional Presbyterian church, just as Mary Baker Eddy's doctrines do from her original beliefs.

The Bible does not teach that in this life all will be well for us, as we envisage well-ness. The last verse of our psalm speaks of long life, or in the AV, length of days. And in any event, as to being 'protected': think of Job, or Stephen, all those whom Paul persecuted. Think of Paul himself with his thorn in the flesh (II Cor. 12: 7). Think of Christ.

That takes us to vv. 11 ff: '... he will command his angels concerning you to guard you in all your ways; they will lift you up in their hands so that you will not strike your foot against a stone'. Those are the words that the Devil quotes to Jesus on the heights of the Temple tower in Matt. 4: 5–6. Well no, they are not. The Devil must have been using a defective copy of Ps. 91.

He omits: 'to guard you in all your ways' (Ps. 91: 11b). And that is the point. Make your dwelling in the shadow of the Most High, rest in the shadow of the Almighty, trust in Him as your refuge and your fortress, and all, in the ultimate sense, will be well with you. He will guard you in all your ways. There will be an ultimate serenity of communion with God. What comes to you on the way will come. It will not necessarily be pleasant, or comfortable. It may make our companions uncomfortable, and give them problems.

But look at the last part of the Psalm, vv. 14–16, where it is the LORD that speaks. 'Because he loves me I will rescue him; I will protect him, for he acknowledges my name. He will call on me and I will answer him. I will be with him and honour him. With long life will I satisfy him and show him my salvation.' This is the essence. Close to the Lord, time is irrelevant. Protection and rescue may not mean physical intervention. God being with you in trouble implies that there will be troubles, not immunity from trouble. God honouring his child need not be apparent to others. Indeed it may be that these verses are speaking of things from God's point of view, which may not be obvious to us at the time.

So finally, look again at our Psalmist's start. Like Dvorak's Eighth, it pitches straight in with the major theme. 'He who dwells in the shadow of the Most High will rest in the shadow of the Almighty. I will say of the LORD, "He is my refuge and my fortress, my God, in whom I trust."'

That is for us too to sign up to.

Gilcomston Prayer Meeting, 8 April 2006.

Psalm 93

Sometimes you can link a Psalm with a particular author – David, Asaph, or the Sons of Korah. Sometimes there's a particular occasion or event to look to. Sometimes you get both author and occasion. That can be very useful when you are preparing to take the Prayer Meeting. But, as you can see, this is not one of either group. However, when I started to grub around for tonight I came across a massive help. In some Jewish traditions this Psalm is recited by the congregation at the end of the Friday service, the service of preparation for the Sabbath – the Day of Rest. It is part of greeting the Sabbath. That chimes well with our being here on Saturday evening, to pray just before Sunday. In other Jewish traditions Psalm 93 is recited as part of the Sabbath services themselves. In both instances it first serves to affirm the majesty of God. Secondarily, reciting it reaffirms the faith of the group. It therefore functions in a kind of a way like our recital of the Lord's Prayer in our services. Others recite the Creed. These are the common substrate that binds us. But Ps. 93 is not just a statement of faith. It is celebration of God, our God.

I don't know whether you read much poetry. I don't. I prefer classical music. But music is a variety of poetry as it conjures and moves the emotions, and, if you pay attention, your intellect as well, so I'll mention music along with the parts. The psalm is, of course, poetry. It presents aspects of our God in its three sections, vv. 1–2, 3–4, and 5.

In musical terms we begin with Bruckner 9. 'The Lord reigns, he is robed in majesty; the Lord is robed in majesty and armed with strength.' Robed in majesty: what does that mean? What is 'Majesty'? Its Latin origin simply means 'greatness'. *Maiestas* was the supreme dignity of the Roman Republic. *Lese Maiestatis* was conduct breaching recognition of *maiestas* – a major crime whether by committed by treason or other fundamental disrespect. Enemies committed that crime. Leasing–making, the Scottish common law equivalent, not prosecuted since 1715, was not abolished until 2010 by s. 51(b) of the Criminal Justice and Licensing (Scotland) Act 2010, asp 13. Majesty is the very highest rank: to fail to acknowledge it is treason.

'Clothed in majesty' the Lord is the highest authority that we can know.

All other majesties, including Elizabeth II, Queen of the United Kingdom of Great Britain and Northern Ireland and her other Realms and Territories, are lesser. But what does 'Majesty' mean for us today? Majesty is an odd word, but roughly it involves being invested with both authority and power. Majesty has beauty. It has dignity. It's not overwhelming in a bad sense, but there's something about it that makes you instinctively bow the knee. It is not strident, but it is imposing. Contrast our ceremony of 'Trooping the Colour' with the parades of North Korea. 'Clothed in majesty and power': 'Trooping the Colour' is a good example, but we can take those resonances further. Recall Moses asking to see God in his glory, and God's parading, sheltering Moses with his hand, but allowing him to see his back (Ex. 33: 18–23).

Majesty. You can also get something of what is involved by looking at the recent service in St Paul's in celebration of our Majesty's Jubilee. Dignity and authority was at St Paul's, albeit that in our constitution the real power has gone to the politicians and the legislature. Nonetheless, within our constitution the Crown, whoever is the incumbent, is in law the source of power and authority in the UK. That was clearly recognised in the symbolism of the occasion, if you knew where to see it.

But the Lord is so much more than our Crown. He reigns gloriously, and eternally. The psalm invites us to see this in creation. The world is established, firm and secure – like his throne. I have to say, obviously the writer generalises. There are earthquakes, even back when the psalm was composed. The US Geological Survey instruments registered 6641 earthquakes in the last 30 days, of which 1070 were 2.5 or above on the Richter scale. But the Psalmist makes his point. Indeed earthquakes show God's power. We are surrounded with what the late Ray Bradbury classed as things that invoke the 'Wow' factor. You can perceive the magnificence and power of the Lord in creation. Think of the Milky Way. Have you ever seen it in a truly dark sky? Think of the Hubble pictures of nebulae and galaxies.

On earth, I think of Heather and I going through a narrow corridor in the Volcano House Hotel on Big Island, Hawaii, suddenly finding ourselves standing on the edge of the main crater of Kilauea. Or there's the immensity of the Grand Canyon. At the other end of the scale, think of the wonders of a daisy, the elegance of a butterfly or the bumptious flight of the bumblebee.

The second section of the psalm, vv. 3–4, goes on to the raging waters. Some see this as rebellion against God. Others see it as pointing to his power, which is so much stronger than that of the roiling sea. A storm at sea is terrible, even for modern shipping. For the writer, the sea was something he could not control – scary even. Indeed I suspect he was not a good sailor. As for the power of the seas – well I still have bookmarked on the computer videos of the tsunami hitting Japan on 11 March 2011. That was terrible – a disaster for so many – and yet there was such a solemn power so manifest as the works of man were swept aside. Alternatively, just walk the Beach Promenade when there's a major swell running. The Lord is mightier than many waters. Listen to the opening of Ralph Vaughan Williams' first symphony, the Sea Symphony.

Finally we come to the statutes section, v. 5. As you might expect, I find this magnificent. Bach comes to mind. God's statutes are forever. How does that strike you? Do those words make you apprehensive? 'Statutes' seem to go along with frowns, with prohibition and with punishment. Think 'Ten Commandments'! Are you going to be found out, and punished because you failed to live up to requirements?

It isn't like that. Not at all. Yes, the statutes of the Lord are grandeur, but they are also a promise. There are two kinds of law – two kinds of statutes. There are the ordinary laws – 30 miles an hour, drive on the left, and so on. We can change those. But the statutes of the Lord are more like the laws of physics: fundamental to his creation. They are not menacing. They are simple statements of truth. We live out the laws of physics, taking them for granted. So rephrase the Ten Commandments in your mind. Secure in his love, you will have no other gods but him. You will not set up other idols for yourself. You will not misuse His Name. You will keep the Sabbath holy. You will honour father and mother. You will not murder, commit adultery or steal. You will not give false testimony. You will not covet your neighbours' possessions. This is how you will be: not because you have to be like that, but because it is how you are.

Yes, it takes time to relax and let this happen. But it will happen. It's a bit like swimming. You need to relax. Stiff swimmers sink. Spiritually stiff people are too conscious of 'what they should do' – 'or should be doing'. Relax. The truth of the gospel is that, in the ultimate, through Jesus, this God celebrated in this psalm, is your friend. Talk to him as you friend. Don't live apologetically in the doorway. Enter the majesty of the new kingdom. In Lewis' *The Last Battle* you go through the gate into the new land. We should not be forever bowing and scraping, forelock tugging like some ever so humble Uriah Heap. We are asked to grow up. Be friends with God. Rejoice in his statutes, for, as the psalm concludes, holiness adorns God's house for endless days.

Psalm 93. So much in so little. Let us pray.

Gilcomston Prayer Meeting, 23 June 2012.

Psalm 96

I find the NIV translation of this psalm off-putting. It is too static. We are confronted by words that people just do not use in normal conversation – or should that be 'words that normal people do not use'? Proclaim, declare, ascribe, worthy, equity, rejoice, be jubilant – religious language yes, but the sort of words that you use only in that particular context. They are jargon of a subculture, technical terms, not lacking meaning, but archaic. They make their point coldly. There is a formality present. The NIV reads as a set of instructions.

Is this important? Let me make the point elliptically. As I was preparing for tonight the April 14–20 2018 edition of the *Economist* carried a review of Madeleine Albright's new book, *Fascism: A Warning*. As US Secretary of State from 1997 to 2001 in the second Clinton administration, Albright was responsible for foreign relations. During her time she visited North Korea, then under its 'Dear Leader', Kim Jong Il. In October 2000 seated next to Kim Jong Il in a stadium in Pyongyang, she watched '100,000 North Korean children and adults dance and thrust bayonets in perfect unison'. Kim confided that he had designed the show himself. Now we have all seen those well-choreographed and well-executed North Korea parades and demonstrations of support and joy, but that is precisely not what Ps. 96 is about. It is not a set of choreographic instructions for evangelicals.

The basic Psalm is probably by David, but in our Psalter it just might be a cut and paste job by Asaph. The Psalm is an explosion of joy, genuine joy. It comes from the bringing of the Ark to Jerusalem. Look back to 1 Chron. 15: 25–29. On that occasion David was the choreographer. Indeed, he took part in the parade, dancing with joy (I Chron. 15: 19). Once the Ark had been installed in the tent David had had pitched for it, he appointed Asaph and his associates to praise the Lord (I Chron. 16: 7) and in vv. 8–36 gave them a model to follow. Our I Chron. 16: 23–33 are more or less Psalm 96. We are not here dealing with instructions. We are confronted with celebration, happiness, overflowing emotion. The enthusiasm that swirls round a win at the Cup Final is not a patch on this. We are in the realm of 'Sing aloud to God', the final chorus of Walton's 'Belshazzar's Feast'.

One of the benefits of the electronic age is ready access to a slew of translations. Comparing versions can be helpful. One, useful for Ps. 96 is the paraphrase by Eugene H. Peterson. Yes, Peterson is criticised for taking liberties, but he delivers the punch of Ps. 96 very well.

Eugene H. Peterson, *The Message: The Bible in Contemporary Language.* Psalm 96.

[1-2] Sing GOD a brand-new song! Earth and everyone in it, sing! Sing to GOD —worship GOD! [2-3] Shout the news of his victory from sea to sea, Take the news of his glory to the lost, News of his wonders to one and all! [4-5] For GOD is great, and worth a thousand Hallelujahs. His terrible beauty makes the gods look cheap; Pagan gods are mere tatters and rags. [5-6] GOD made the heavens – Royal splendour radiates from him, A powerful beauty sets him apart. [7] Bravo, GOD, Bravo! Everyone join in the great shout: Encore! In awe before the beauty, in awe before the might. [8-9] bring gifts and celebrate, Bow before the beauty of GOD, Then to your knees – everyone worship! [10] Get out the message – GOD Rules! He put the world on a firm foundation; He treats everyone fair and square. [11] Let's hear it from Sky, with Earth joining in, and a huge round of applause from Sea. [12] Let Wilderness turn cartwheels, Animals, come dance, Put every tree of the forest in the choir. An extravaganza before GOD as he comes, as he comes to set everything right on earth, set everything right, treat everyone fair.

See what I mean? Here is a vitality lacking in the NIV, ebullience in abundance, passion and excitement. So let's look at the Peterson paraphrase version.

'Sing God a brand-new song' (v. 1). I have to say an awful lot of modern hymnology seems to be directed to pleasuring the singer. 'Sing God a new song' is focussed on singing to God. Walton got that right.

Let's go on. Start away out there. Take vv. 5 and 11 together. God made the heavens; a royal splendour, a powerful beauty (v. 5). 'Let's hear it from Sky' (v. 11). Modern city lighting deprives us. Get out into the dark spaces – there are still some – and wonder at the starry night. I have wonderful photos of nebulae taken by the Hubble space telescope. Learn the constellations – yes, they are pagan constructs, but the way to find your way around the stars. Look for the Andromeda Nebula, Messier 31, a galaxy other than our own Milky Way, and 2.5 million light years away. Spot Orion, the Hunter.

See Sirius, the Dog Star, following him. 'Let's hear it from Sky'? Do they indeed praise? In mid-April 2018 University of Birmingham astronomers reported that, using data from the Kepler satellite, they had monitored eight ancient stars and found that their electromagnetic output was oscillating. They were all humming. You can find recordings on the Internet: http://www.iflscience.com/space/the-sky-is-alive-with-the-sound-of-stars. The Cepheid variables pulse. Yes, the stars are singing to God.

'Let's hear it from Sky, with Earth joining in, and a huge round of applause from Sea.' Enjoy, and marvel at the sea. The sea can be scary, but its power reflects that of its creator in storm as well as its occasional tranquillity. 'Let Wilderness turn cartwheels, Animals, come dance.' (vv. 11–12). Rejoice with the creation all around us. Animals dancing? No-one who has seen the nature programmes on the tv, not least those fronted by David Attenborough, can escape from those images. Put every tree of the forest in the choir (v. 12). A choir of trees? Perhaps. Trees pulsate. In a couple of his most mysterious novels my favourite sf author, Clifford D, Simak, envisaged singing trees, and people sitting out of an evening enjoying their concerts. Short of that, here and now, get out, walk among trees, and hear them. You can even speak to them as fellows among creation. Exult with creation as it exults in God.

Now, come closer in. Get to people. 'Earth and everyone in it sing to God – worship God! Shout the news of his victory from sea to sea. Take the news of his glory to the lost. News of his wonders to one and all!' (v. 1–2). 'Get out the message – God Rules! He puts the world on a firm foundation; He treats everyone fair and square (v.10). Why sing and shout? Do the celestial and terrestrial wonders not speak the message well enough? Perhaps not in our present society. But that is why we should join to shout: 'Bravo, God, Bravo!' Celebrate Him (v. 8). Bow before the beauty of God (v. 9). Then to our knees – everyone worship! (v. 9). Prepare that extravaganza before God as he comes, as he comes to set everything right on earth, to set everything right, to treat everyone fairly (v. 13).

Now. Get going!

Gilcomston Prayer Meeting, 26 May 2018.

Psalm 100

A Psalm. For giving grateful praise (NIV): A psalm of praise (AV).

'All people that on earth do dwell, sing to the Lord', to use familiar words from H. 229 – Given covid, this may not the best of times to come to this psalm. I begin by quoting the first two sentences of Calvin's introduction to it. 'The title of this psalm may serve for a summary of its contents. Moreover, its brevity renders a lengthened discourse unnecessary.' An encouraging, not to say enticing, thing to read when you prepare for a gathering such as tonight's. My discourse comes in two parts. First, the importance of songs in praise, and, as you may have expected, of one particular tune. Second, there is the matter of the truths.

As Calvin says, Ps. 100 is short. It is a compressed psalm. I once tagged a different psalm as a Tardis, bigger on the inside than the out (Ps.133, 12 March 2016). This is another. But, cautiously, let me offer an alternative. Tonight was arranged some time ago, so I have been able to mull this psalm over and over. Now, when I was a boy there were things called Gobstoppers. They filled your mouth. They did stop your gob. You enjoyed a gobstopper slowly, different flavours and different colours emerged as you sucked. Looking at this psalm, you really need to take it slowly. Don't rush – though I am going to gallop through it. Savour it bit by bit. Take a phrase. Relax. Let it suffuse you. Take your time. It's a gobstopper.

The hundredth psalm is well known. We don't know who wrote the original, nor why. But we don't need to know that. In Jewish practice it is one of the Songs of Thanksgiving. Different traditions use it in different parts of their services. For them it is thanks to God for the daily miracles around us, for we live in a wonderful world, and constantly are preserved from dangers.

What about that tune? Which tune? Many composers have set Ps. 100. It is the major portion of Part I of Leonard Bernstein's Chichester Psalms. But Bernstein instructs the choir to sing the Hebrew text, so few of us can understand what they sing. That said, Bernstein's setting is wonderful.

One setting is four and a half centuries old. We call it the 'Old Hundredth'. It comes from 1561. That's before Bach! Bach was born in 1685, c. 125 years later. Originally intended for Psalm 134, it later migrated to Psalm 100. The composer was French, Louis Bourgeois, who wrote a number of tunes for the Geneva Psalter. The tune is in long metre, and is stately – unfortunately for many 'stately' means 'slow', even gloomy. You might even think it's a rum tune for a psalm that's about rejoicing. Still, 'The Old Hundredth' is memorable.

It is a simple tune. Calvin, in charge in Geneva, did not care for ornate melodies. Beyond that he wanted everyone to sing the same notes, not to harmonise or descant. Others think differently. Vaughan Williams arranged it for the 1953 Coronation – there is at least one performance available on YouTube. His is sumptuous, resplendent with fanfares, soloists, an organ, and the choir does do harmonies and descants. At the Coronation the Peers Assembled got confused, did not know when to sing, and when not to. And when singing many couldn't get to the end of each line. No matter. Vaughan Williams did a good job. The tune turns up later in all sorts of works, from Bach to Britten. Here's a stray fact: in 1876 Alexander Graham Bell used it in his first public demonstration of a newly-fangled contraption to the American Academy of Arts and Sciences. Any wonder that the telephone became popular?!

The psalm was put into English by William Keithe, or Keith, probably a Scot living in Geneva. Keithe was involved in the 1560 English translation of the Geneva Bible. He also contributed twenty-five psalms including this one, to the Anglo-Genevan Psalter of 1561. They are all in the Scottish Psalter of 1564. It's his version of Ps. 100 we sing to that tune as Hymn 229. Carried by it, his wording sticks. You understand the words; the tune adds emotion / feeling. Pray for those who struggle to translate so that others may grasp and understand. Pray for those who write poems. Pray for composers to create good tunes. Good words, an adhesive melody; a good earworm, can be a gift from God.

So, what about that content?

Verse 1. Who is addressed? 'All people that on earth do dwell' – to use Keithe's words. That looks like everyone. No selectivity. No discrimination. It's 'all ye lands' in the AV, and 'all the earth' in the NIV. However, some have suggested the call is rather to God's people wherever they are. After all v. 3 speaks of 'his people' and v. 4 of entering his gates and his courts. That's irrelevant for tonight. The call certainly is to us.

The Vulgate version begins 'Jubilate Deo omnis terra'. Put the one word

'Jubilate' into Wikipedia and it automatically takes you to Ps. 100. Jubilate God. Praise him enthusiastically. Think of the jubilation on VE day in 1945. Or how some celebrate a football result. Verse 1: 'Shout'. Other translations say 'sing'. It doesn't say sing this psalm. Obviously that's a possibility. But singing leaves things very open. The instruction is to shout or to sing. Maybe there's no need for words. There are many wonderful 'songs without words'. Absent the words the 'Old Hundredth' itself is a rejoicing in God. Making a 'joyful noise to the Lord' is commended in v. 1 in the AV, and elsewhere (Pss. 66: 1; 81: 1; 95: 1 and 2; 98: 4 and 6). No matter. The only restriction on singing is that what you do you do so in a 'cheerful voice' to use the Keithe wording. That is accentuated: I like H 229's 'Him serve with mirth'. The verse speaks of gladness and joy – jubilation. That's an Exocet missile strike on dreary hymn-singing. We should be happy to praise – and there is so much evidence that our God is full of joy. Did God chuckle over the Peers' discomfiture at the Coronation? At least smile with him. Man's chief end is to glorify God and enjoy him forever (Catechism, Answer 1). On the other hand, don't go too far. The instruction is to sing to the Lord. This is not a call to mindless ululation. Don't go hugger mugger. Yes, there can be exhilaration in song, but don't get into this to get yourself high. The focus is not you. 'Sing *to the Lord.*' But this psalm really calls for communal singing. A major downside of lockdown is we cannot yet sing together.

God is gracious. The call is not for unfocussed jubilation. There are reasons to trigger our song. As I said this psalm is a gob stopper. As you let it permeate you there are pointers liberating thought. Fill them with your own images and memories. Colour them, pitch them as you will. Faced with such a call some can be a bit shy. Some are emotionally uptight at the best of times. But think of what God has done for us, and forget whether others find your jubilating off-putting. Covid may constrain, but there is nothing to stop 'jubilating' in private. How about it? Tonight we are on Zoom, and most of you are muted.

Verse 3. He has made us. Be grateful for existing, for being. Things can be tough, but be glad to be. Be glad to be His. We are not a spatter of congealed atoms in a vast universe. We are his people, and he cares. Commissioning the disciples Jesus said: 'even the very hairs on your head are all numbered' (Matt. 10: 30), and from the differently ordered Luke 12: 6-7. 'Are not five sparrows sold for two pennies? Yet not one of them is forgotten by God. Indeed, the very hairs of your head are all numbered. Don't be afraid; you are worth more than many sparrows.'

If you find twittery spugs uncongenial, *passer domesticus* may feel a bit better, but the 'sheep of his pasture' may be more comfortable. That image goes so much beyond the immediate words. We are sheep. We have a shepherd, a good shepherd who has laid down his life for the flock. That's not just rescuing the lost lamb, then, when it wanders off again, saying it's had its chance. Even if it hasn't learned its lesson, it will be sought again. No. Jesus' sacrifice is forever. The wanderer is sought, always.

So verse 4: 'Enter his gates with thanksgiving and his courts with praise; give thanks to him and praise his name.' Let's be couthy about it. Come in aboot and let it oot. Why? Verse 5. The Lord is good. Our God's love endures forever. And it's not the rather passive, praise him. No. We celebrate, we jubilate about our God. He whose faithfulness continues through all generations. So let us just do that. But as we do my mind turns from the Old Hundredth to a hymn twelve centuries older – the 'Te Deum' with its words from the Fourth century, maybe from Ambrose or Augustine. 'We praise thee O God. We acknowledge thee to be the Lord. All the world doth praise thy Name, the Father everlasting.'

Gilcomston Prayer Meeting, 15 May 2021.

Psalm 101

A Psalm of David. From Ps. 95 onwards, we have passed through a sequence of Psalms, each praising God. Shouting for joy at his majesty and his grace. They culminated last week in the Hundredth, one of those magnificent songs that is so ingrained in the spirit of the old Scots Kirk. But which of us could have said what was in Ps. 101 without looking?

Psalm 101 is different. Unlike its immediate predecessors, this one is 'A Psalm of David' and there is no reason to suppose the superscription is not accurate. When it was written, we do not know. It may have been when David came to the throne after the death of Saul – when he was, as it were, setting out at last on his great mission to be the true God-appointed King of the Jews. It may have come later, when he was established. Perhaps it was when he was bringing the Ark up to the Holy City – one of the main peaks of his reign. Different scholars make different suggestions, but it really does not matter.

Ps. 101 is a personal statement. The preceding Psalms are plural, if I can put it like that. They are intended for a group to sing and encourage each other. Psalm 101 is David himself, on his own, singing to God. He sets out his intention in v. 1: 'I will sing of your love and justice; to you, O Lord, I will sing praise.' And he goes on to ask God to respond, to come to him (v. 2).

After that Introduction, there are two main sections. The first is anticipated in v. 2, 'I will be careful to lead a blameless life.' The second has to do with David's outworking of that internal purity. I want to deal with the second part first.

We are in the run-up to elections, the Scottish Parliament and local government in May, and elections for Europe in June. See what David says in vv. 3b to 7.

Consider those words, 'I will not endure' and the list it goes on to specify. The secret slanderer of his neighbour (v. 5a) – the one who leaks, and 'briefs against' his colleagues, to use the modern phrase. Haughty eyes and a proud heart (v. 5b). The deeds of faithless men (v. 3). The deceiver (v. 7). Now, consider our would-be leaders and our actual leaders. Note also that there is nothing here to the effect that a politician's personal life has nothing to do with his ability to do the public job. I wonder whether we need say more than that.

On the other hand, having thought a bit more, there is something else to be said, particularly about the governing to ensure a holy society that comes at the end of the Psalm.

Look at v. 8. 'Every morning I will put to silence all the wicked in the land; I will cut off every evildoer from the city of the Lord.' It would take a bible-study, or several, to explore the application of such a verse in the context of a parliamentary democracy like the one we live in. But something has to be said about the difficulties that verse raises. We cannot construct a complete answer to the problems of Twentieth, or Twenty-first century church and state on the basis of one verse of one Psalm. David lived in a simpler society, where he was the law-giver, and the judge and the administration, and where the population involved was smaller than that of Aberdeen.

This is, in fact, the second major version of my notes for tonight. At this point in my first try I was sidetracked into the difficulties that can emerge with politicians who claim to know the mind of God. But in the second version I scrapped the paragraphs that followed. And inserted the following lines. 'Let me simply say that we must be much in prayer for our leaders. Consider the obverse. What happens when our leaders are anything but god-fearing? Think of Hitler, Stalin, Milosevic.'

In what follows I have restored the omissions.

Surely it is best if, in our legislatures, and in government, we could have morally upright persons, who understand history, economics, foreign affairs and sociology, and who are politically talented. Our lack of such animals, with some or all of these talents, is a mark of the failure of the churches in our century. At this time of constitutional change, we need to pray much about this, praying that God will bring forward leaders from amongst us, men and women who know Him; who are alive to His promptings; who can stand the heat of modern politics; who can resist its temptations; and who know what is really best for our country, even at the threat of the possible expense of their own careers. Maybe He has. I don't know.

Think of David. Think of the programme he sets out in Ps. 101. That would be something if our leadership were that pure. However, having taught constitutional law and human rights, I find myself on an uneasy tight-rope. Surely evil does have to be suppressed. But History is not reassuring as to the abilities to govern of those who claim to be holy and pure. I know this example is from a different religion, but think of the Taleban, or the Ayatollahs. Think of the priests of the Serbian Orthodox Church blessing the troops as they went into Bosnia – I say nothing as to Kosovo. We have no pictures of that. But do I need to say more? Closer to home, think of some leaders of Christian communities of this kingdom, and what is done in the name of religion in the UK. Remember those awful verses of our Lord in Matt. 7: 22–3. 'Many will say to me on that day, 'Lord, Lord, did we not prophesy in your name, and in your name drive out demons and perform many miracles?' Then I will tell them plainly, 'I never knew you. Away from me, you evildoers.'

It is too easy, too simplistic, for a fallen man to claim that God has revealed his will to him and he therefore knows how to govern, how to decide enormously complex matters. Most who make such claims base their conclusions on a very narrow knowledge. To govern a modern society well you need to know and understand history, economics and social forces as well as human nature. As someone has said, politics is the art of the possible, and in a democracy that is true. To know what is what is possible in our society – which means what is achievable starting from where we are – is a talent not given to many, and not given to many of those who think they have it. It is too easy to confuse the mind of God with the power-cravings of the individual. For such to 'serve' may mean to 'rule'.

But that leaves us tonight with a problem. The fact is that in our very fallen civilisation, a deceitful immoral person may nonetheless be better at running democracy than some others whose personal life may be miles better. But surely it is best if we could have in our legislatures, and in government, politically talented morally upright persons. The lack of such animals has been the hall-mark of the failure of the churches. We need to pray much about this, that God will bring forward leaders amongst us who know Him, who are alive to His promptings, who can stand the heat of modern politics, and who can resist its temptations.

But for us here tonight, we, as individuals, not as potential politicians, if we are that. Turn to the start of David's song. There is a key is there for all of us, not just the politicos. Look at vv. 1– 3a: 'I will sing of your love and justice; to you, O Lord, I will sing praise. I will walk in my house with a blameless heart. I will set before my eyes no vile thing.'

The simple fact of the matter is that David loves God. He is intoxicated with him. The whole of his life is based on that love. Yes, we know David was a sinner. He was a bigger sinner than most of us. But notwithstanding his conduct, at least in this song of his intentions he speaks from a full heart. And it is that sort of full heart which we should hope to come to, if we are not there already.

Does love for God burn within you? I don't mean can you work it up, inducing it by something equivalent to the Hare Krishna repetition of Om Mane Padme Om. Simply, is it there? You and I are here tonight. We have come together to pray. That may reassure. We love God, which is why we are here. But we have all some way to go to reach the point David has arrived at.

So I'll end by quoting a paragraph from a science fiction author I happen to like. Terry Pratchett occasionally says things that make you sit up. Take two things from this quotation: One, the way in which the church has effectively silenced itself by undue speculation. The other, what our love of God should be. Or, what it will come to be, as we press on.

Towards the end of his most recent novel, *Carpe Jugulum*. Granny Weatherwax is speaking with Oats, a minister of the Omnian religion. She asks Oats whether anyone has ever seen his God. Oats tells her that no less than 3000 people saw him, on one occasion, some centuries earlier.

[W] – 'But I bet that right now they're arguing about what they actually saw, eh?'
[O] – 'Well, indeed, yes, there are many opinions.'
[W] – 'Right. Right. That's people for you. Now if I'd seen him really there, really alive, it'd be in _me_ like a fever. If _I_ thought there was some god who really did care two hoots about people, who watched them like a father and cared for them like a mother ... well you wouldn't catch me saying things like "There are two sides to every question," and, "We must respect other people's beliefs." You wouldn't find me just being generally nice in the hope that it'll all turn out right in the end, not if that flame was burning in me like an unforgivin' sword. And I did say burnin', Mister Oats, for that's what it'd be. You say that people don't burn folk and sacrifice people any more, but that's what true faith would mean, y'see? Sacrificin' your own life, one day at a time, to the flame, declarin' the truth, workin' for it, breathin' the soul of it. _That's_ religion. Anything else is just ... it's just being _nice_. And a way of keepin' in touch with the neighbours.'

I think David would approve of Granny Weatherwax's point. He knew a God who cared two hoots about him. A God who watched him like a father and cared for him like a mother. That is what burned so eloquently in David. Our Psalm begins: 'I will sing of your love and justice' . Let us do that now.

Gilcomston Prayer Meeting, 10 April 1999.

Psalm 101

A Psalm of David. From Ps. 95 onwards, we have passed through a sequence of Psalms, each praising God. Shouting for joy at his majesty and his grace. That culminated last week in the Hundredth, so ingrained in the spirit of the auld Scots Kirk. But which of us could have said what was in this one without looking it up?

Psalm 101 is different. Unlike its immediate predecessors, the author of this one is indicated. It is 'A Psalm of David'. There is no reason to suppose that is wrong. When it was written, we do not know. Maybe David wrote it just as he came to the throne following the death of Saul – a statement of his intentions as he set out at last on his great mission to be the true God-appointed King of the Jews. Maybe it came later, when he was established as king and he is drawing on his actual experience of governing. It really does not matter. The point is that this Psalm expresses an ideal.

One other preliminary. Some link together the references to his house – vv. 2b 'I will conduct the affairs of my house', and 7a, those who practice 'deceit will not dwell in my house'. They view this psalm as advice on running a domestic establishment rather than how to run a kingdom. That's exegetical desperation, born of a desire to get into print. That said, we should remember what a household meant in those days. Back then David's household would be large, including a number of folk not necessarily blood-related – cooks, cleaners, advisers and friends, hangers-on, free-loaders and useful folk. A wee bit like a congregation. But let's not go down that line of thought.

The Psalm is a <u>personal</u> statement. The preceding Psalms are plural, if I can put it like that. They are intended for the group to sing together. Psalm 101 is singular – David himself, on his own, is speaking to God. 'I will sing of your love and justice; to you, O Lord, I will sing praise.' (v. 1). He affirms. He 'will be careful to live a blameless life' (v. 2a). He goes on to ask God to come to him (v. 2b). These are intertwined. There is no room here for the modern split between private and public life. That is accentuated as we read through the later verses: 'the one whose walk is blameless will minister to me' (v. 6b). I will live a blameless life? Oh, yes, David? Remember Uriah the

Hittite (2 Sam. 11) – David could fall short of his own ideal. But let's look at his principles for governing.

The Lyall archives disclose that this is the second time I have tackled this Psalm. The first attempt was delivered on 10 April 1999. Back then the elections for the new Scottish Parliament were due in less than a month, 6 May to be precise. The campaigns were under way. That produced a wee rant from me. It may happen again, but not tonight. However, there are messages here. Things we need to pray for and against. I note that a Cabinet reshuffle is imminent, to be done, interestingly enough by another David, David Cameron.

Look at the Psalm, beginning at v. 3b. David says: 'I hate what faithless people do; I will have no part in it. The perverse of heart shall be far from me; I will have nothing to do with what is evil. Whoever slanders their neighbour in secret, I will put to silence; whoever has haughty eyes and a proud heart, I will not tolerate.' Jump to v.7: 'No one who practices deceit will dwell in my house; no one who speaks falsely will stand in my presence.' Back to v. 3a: 'I will not look with approval on anything that is vile.'

Look at that list of the vile. Faithless men (v. 3b). Haughty eyes and a proud heart (v. 5b). The secret slanderer (v. 5a) – the one who leaks, and 'briefs against' his colleagues, to use the modern phrase. The deceiver, the false speaker (v. 7). Consider our leaders and our would-be leaders. Consider what's in the newspapers and media almost every day. Read the political histories and memoirs. I was tempted to compile a list – but I have excised it. Make up your own.

Contrast David's avowal (v. 6): 'My eyes will be on the faithful in the land, that they may dwell with me; the one whose walk is blameless will minister to me.' Yes, he made mistakes. We cannot say he brought Absalom up right. As for advisers, well David included the duplicitous Ahitophel (2 Sam. 15: 12, 31–7) [Jewish tradition is that that was not a close relationship. See Wikipedia.] And what about Joab? See 1 Kings 2: 5–6, 29–34. Joab, who had been commander of the army, was executed in accordance with David's death-bed advice to Solomon for his betrayal and unnecessary killings. One way to remove an underling!

In this Psalm at least, David promises well. However, there is something else to be said. What about seeking the holy society that comes at the end of the Psalm. Look at v. 8. 'Every morning I will put to silence all the wicked in the land; I will cut off every evildoer from the city of the Lord.'

It would take several studies to explore such a verse in the context of a parliamentary democracy. But something has to be said about the difficulties the verse raises. We cannot construct a complete answer to the problems of Twenty-first century church and state on the basis of one verse of one Psalm. David lived in a simpler society. He was the law-giver, and the judge and the administration of a population smaller than that of Aberdeen. Preparing for tonight I had a look at Calvin's commentary on the Psalm. It was useful. However, as I have said before, I would not want to have lived in Calvin's Geneva, with its secret police keeping society holy. But, as a sideways comment, have you noticed how many laws now require us to be good. We are not to discriminate on grounds of sex or ethnic origin. We are not to offend, disrespect or hurt people etc: political correctness enforceable by delation by those who claim they have been offended. That's a testimony to a failure of the Christian denominations.

Surely it would be good to have in our legislatures, government and administrations, only morally upright persons, those who lack the defects listed in this psalm. But, that said, I do prefer managerial competency in public affairs to the theologically sound but in practice incompetent. We need to pray for those in any authority – and perhaps rather more for those who want to be in authority – politicians, administrators and public servants. Some should be kept out.

However, that's enough of that. You'll be asking me for names. For tonight – turn back to the start of David's song. There is a key is there for all of us, not just the politicos. Look again at vv. 1–3a: I will sing of your love and justice; to you, LORD, I will sing praise. I will be careful to lead a blameless life – when will you come to me? I will conduct the affairs of my house with a blameless heart.'

The simple fact of the matter is that David loves God. He is intoxicated with him. The whole of his life is based on that love. Yes, David was a sinner. Unless you know things I don't, he was a bigger sinner than most of us. But notwithstanding his later conduct, at least in this song of his intentions he speaks from a full heart. That sort of full heart is where we should hope to come to, if we are not there already.

Let us therefore pray.

Gilcomston Prayer Meeting, 18 August 2012.

Psalm 103

The last time I was at this part of the Hall we looked at Psalm 88, a Psalm full of woe and depression. Last week, Ps. 102 was the prayer of an afflicted man. Tonight's Psalm is very different.

I have a butterfly mind. It flitters about, making all sorts of connections. Tonight is no different. This outpouring of joy in God brings to mind so many things. So it is something of a relief that the Psalm does have sections. That imposes some degree of discipline on my thought. Roughly speaking it divides thus: vv. 1–5 the psalmist's own testimony. Vv. 6–14 elaborates the general beneficence of the Lord. It looks more carefully at Man in vv. 15–18, and concludes with another paean of praise of the Lord in vv. 19–22.

Take the start, particularly vv.1–2: 'Praise the Lord, O my soul, all my inmost being, praise his holy name. Praise the Lord O my soul, and forget not all his benefits.' It's like the start of Mahler 8, the 'Symphony of a Thousand'. There is the organ pedal note – at least a thirty-two foot base E flat – then a massive orchestral E flat major chord, and then the choir explodes into 'Veni, Creator Spiritus' – 'Come, Creator Spirit' – a ninth century hymn of faith, possibly by Rabanus Maurus, (780–856 AD) the then Archbishop of Mainz in Germany. If it is properly done Mahler 8 has a choir of seven hundred and fifty and an orchestra of two hundred plus. Magnificent. Yes, other orchestral pieces come to mind, – Vaughan Williams' *A Sea Symphony* for example – but only Mahler 8, Part I, meets the glory of Psalm 103. 'Praise the Lord, O my soul.'

Vv. 3–5 then list God's goodness to David. God forgives sins and heals diseases (v. 3). He redeems from the pit and crowns with love and compassion (v. 4). He satisfies with good things and renews youth (v. 5). And there I stall: can this be that David who wrote those other psalms, the lamenting psalms, the complaining psalms? Is this a young man's Psalm, written before major sins were committed and major flaws exploited by the Enemy? Think of certain of the psalms of David's old age. They can be terrible. And yet this psalm is freely – ecstatically, even – rejoicing in God's goodness.

As to the timing of this psalm, no-one knows. But we can say this: notwithstanding age, aches and pains, the gloomeries of an occasional gut infection, seasonal affective disorder, setbacks and other downers, there are times when all that clears away and we rejoice just as David does here. You can just love the Lord – not the vacuous evangelical mantra, 'Praise the Lord', but rather a welling up of deepest love. This psalm is an outpouring of innocent emotion. It puts me in mind of Abigail – my newest granddaughter for those that don't know – staggering towards me, smiling, grinning indeed, with absolute innocent pleasure and trust. Others here may also have seen this from her. It's the same here. David really does love his Lord. He's completely innocent about it. He's not out to praise so he'll get a reward – some sort of spiritual sweetie, or something else that he wants. The words spill out, almost spontaneously – although this is a worked-on poem. It's that way round. It's not an incantation to prove to the Lord – or worse to others – that David loves the Lord. These words come from the heart – even in a sense not from the head.

The next chunk, vv. 6–14, speaks of the goodness of the Lord to all mankind and particularly to Israel, though it has a more sombre strain running through it. My mind-pictures here include many from the Hubble Space Telescope, the aurora borealis as seen towards the end of that recent wonderful TV programme with Joanna Lumley, almost anything by Anton Bruckner, that simple, devout genius – but particularly his Ninth Symphony.

Jump to v. 14. The Lord knows how we are formed. He remembers that we are dust. Our days are like grass, and we flourish like a flower of the field (v. 15). The wind blows, and it is gone. Its place remembers it no more (v. 16). Yes, there are exceptions – here we are tonight re-thinking thoughts penned by David who lived thirty-five centuries ago. But the point is generally true. Who here knows anything about James Bryce, Robert Alexander Mitchell, Robert Forgan? They were all ministers of Gilcomston. What of Walter Macgilvray the minister who built these buildings? You walk past a memorial plaque for him to the right of the window in the vestibule every Sunday morning.

Yet it is precisely because God knows we are dust, soon to perish and be forgotten by men, that the Lord as a father has compassion on those that fear him (v.13). A father. I used to have problems with these ideas. As some know my father was killed in the War. I did not really know what being a father was until I was a father myself. This Father is compassionate and gracious, slow to anger, abounding in love (v. 8). That means a lot to me now. Particularly he cares for those that love him. He 'does not treat us as our sins deserve, or repay us according to our iniquities' (v. 10). Why? Because 'as high as the heavens are above the earth, so great is his love for those that fear him; as far as the east is from the west, so far he has removed our transgression from us.' (vv. 11–12).

As said, all flesh is grass (to use the AV version of v. 15ff). But 'from everlasting to everlasting the Lord's love is with those who fear him, and his righteousness with their children's children – with those who keep his covenant and remember to obey his precepts' (vv.17–18).

'Remember to obey.' 'Those that fear him.' Does this not run counter to what I was saying about David's explosion of love? Not at all. Note the distinction in v. 7: 'He made known his ways to Moses, his deeds to the people of Israel'. Moses was the friend of God. He obeyed because God was God and he loved him. The same was true of David. It can be true of us as well. Is God your friend, as well as being the Creator of the Universe? Remember God walking in the Garden in the cool of the day (Gen. 3: 8). Does he ever come and have a friendly visit with you? Think of Jesus speaking of he and his Father making their home with you (John 14: 23). Or is your fear more akin to terror? Are you scared of an unpredictable tyrant? Do you obey because 'it's the rules', or because it's the only way to be? Do you see the Ten Commandments as rules, or a statement of how you behave? Is obedience conscious, or is it automatic – part of your autonomic spiritual nervous system? Your autonomic nervous system works without you thinking about it – that's how you breathe. Spiritually you should be complying with the Commandments unthinkingly, not because you know them by heart. That is how it should be because you love him and you are friends. This God cares for you and for me.

The final section is vv. 19–22. The Lord is on his throne (v. 19). All praise him, angels, the mighty beings that do his bidding (v. 20), the heavenly host, the servants that do his will (v. 21). 'Praise the Lord, all his works everywhere in his dominion' (v. 22). Then David, having zoomed out to take in the angels and all creation, comes right back to where he started, his own response to God. 'Praise the Lord, O my soul' (v. 22).

In grandeur this is Yosemite Valley with El Capitan, The Half Dome, the Bridal Veil Falls. It is the end of Mahler 2. It is Dali's 'Christ of St John of the Cross' swinging out over you. But more graspably – the end of this Psalm evokes a set of memories of smaller things. 'All flesh is grass' (v. 15) – 'Praise the Lord, O my soul' (v. 22). I remember walking through a field back of Slains Castle some years ago. I remember walking beside a field a couple of weeks ago out at Gill's. It's sunny. A breeze ruffles the grass – all flesh is grass (v. 15). And the air? The air is full of larks, singing their hearts out. 'Praise the Lord, O my soul' (v. 22). Wind, warmth, the smell of fresh grass, and larks, larks, and more larks. The collective noun for larks is 'an exultation'. That fits exactly. Wee birdies. Powerful voices praising, exulting in God. Let us do the same.

Gilcomston Prayer Meeting, 18 July 2009.

Psalm 104

Two weeks ago Psalm 102 was the prayer of the afflicted. Last week was an outpouring of joy in God, his goodness to David and to all mankind. This one turns to creation – without which we would not be. We don't know whether it is one of David's – Pss. 103 and 105 are – or whether a few hands were involved in making it, but that's not important.

This is a long psalm. Thirty-five verses. Did you read through it before coming tonight? Even if you did I cannot assume that you know it well. I didn't. Maybe I still don't. However, there are two groups that would know it. One group is observant Jews. They recite it every day during morning service. The other group would be within the Eastern Orthodox Church. I am going to take a little time to explain the latter. The Eastern Orthodox Church nurtures its flock through symbolism, magnificent music, art and emotion. Its ceremonials impart the idea of God, Jesus and salvation. You grasp and surrender to fundamental truths through what is going on. An Orthodox Church building is laid out like the Temple in Jerusalem. Its nave, where the congregation is, is the Holy Place, the sanctuary. Beyond it is the Holy of Holies. There is a screen, a wall, between the two. That is the iconostasis, often golden and always covered with icons and holy paintings. There's something similar, though far less, in most Episcopal cathedrals. In the middle of the iconostasis are the Holy Doors, the access from the nave to the Holy of Holies. So how do devout Orthodox know this Psalm better than we do? On Sundays and major feast-days Psalm 104 is sung (sometimes only in part and usually by a choir) at the start of the Great Vespers. The officiating priest or priests stand outside the Holy Doors, facing the congregation. The Doors are shut. High symbolism. Completely anachronistically for the Orthodox, as set in the Great Vespers Psalm 104 is thought of as sung or chanted by Adam as he stands outside the doors of Eden – doors now closed and barred to him (Gen. 3). Then come the litanies and prayers asking for access to the Holy of Holies. The Doors are opened and the priests enter the Holy of Holies. To a Presbyterian it's an odd notion, but think about that. Adam outside Eden, clinging to faith in his Creator, manifest through creation. The Doors open to the Holy of Holies.

That's why the Orthodox _know_ this Psalm. If you have heard Tchaikovsky's, or better Rachmaninov's magnificent setting of the All Night Vigil, which includes the Great Vespers, you have some idea of the resonances of Orthodoxy.

Now read it. What is it all about? I said that Adam was clinging on to faith in his Creator. And that is what this Psalm is about. Creation and God, the Creator. It starts with the glory of God (v. 1) but swiftly passes to the manifestation of his power in creation: light and the heavens, v. 2; the clouds and wind vv. 3–4. The foundations of the earth are laid v. 5. The waters of both rivers and seas are organised, vv. 6–13. Verses 14–18 are about vegetation and animal life – though birds and donkeys are mentioned in relation to the waters. Then there is the sun and the moon and day and night (vv. 19–24). It culminates in v. 24 with God in his wisdom making many creatures. Leviathan is in the sea (v. 26). Verses 27–30 stress the dependence of all on God. Without him all vanishes. Verses 31–32 pray that the glory of God will endure as the creator rejoices in what he has done and is doing. Then the writer of the psalm speaks for himself. All his life he will sing to the Lord (v. 33) and he hopes that his meditations will be acceptable (v. 34). Then oddly, given what has gone before, he prays for the destruction of sinners and the wicked (v. 35). The Psalm ends with the repeated 'Praise the Lord'.

What can I say about this? The Psalm comes to us in cold print. We read words, which you must allow to conjure images and feelings. My reaction is that it is something really for music, and, of course it is a song of praise. But I have no idea how it was sung in Jewish worship. What happens in synagogues now? Or is it just chanted? What music would we put to it? Modern hymnology is inadequate. It needs a symphony – or many of them. Emeritus Pope Benedict XVI was right when he recently praised music as leading the receptive to God.

Alternatively go explore creation. Enjoy God in his handiworks. Man's chief end is to 'glorify God and enjoy him forever' (Cat. 1). Marvel at creation. Wander the forests. Hug a tree. Hill-walk. Prowl the beaches. Enjoy a rainstorm. Take binoculars into a garden. Sit ten feet from the flower-bed, and use them to look at what's there.

That said, some of this Psalm does read oddly. On the face of things v. 2 is bizarre – 'the Lord … stretches out the heavens as a tent and lays the beams of his upper chambers on their waters'. Verse 13 has God watering the mountains from those upper chambers. You have to understand that through your imagination, through myth. You cannot take it as reality. It expresses understanding, not fact. The earth is set on its foundations and can never be moved (v. 5), though it can tremble and mountains smoke (v. 32). Such reflects the scientific knowledge of the time. What of plate tectonics? Have you ever wondered whether David, or other writers of the Psalms, thought the Earth was flat? Or, that the Sun went round the Earth? Or, that the Earth was the centre of the Universe? We know different now – though some time ago now I was startled to be asked in all seriousness by a Gilc. attendee whose name you would recognise, if the stars are further away than the planets. But how would the writers of the Psalms react to the New Horizons probe's pictures from Pluto? What of the revelations of Hubble, Spitzer and the other Space Telescopes? The writers of these songs to God might take some time to get their heads around modern knowledge, but certainly it would not disturb their knowledge that there is one creator, one God.

That there is just one God was not a common notion in Near-East religions. Akkad, Sumer, Babylon and Egypt each had a set of gods. Some were creators, all usually feuding with their fellows. But that said, we must acknowledge that the Pharaoh Akhenaten was mono-theist. Indeed Psalm 104 has many parallels with his 'Hymn to the Sun' of c. 1350 BC. Akhenaten tried to change the Egyptian state religion to mono-theism, worshipping the Sun, or a power behind the Sun, as the fount of all being. He did not succeed. Some have thought that someone who knew Akhenaten's effort wrote tonight's Psalm. That brings an intriguing thought. Rabbinic Judaism dates Moses to c. 1391–1271 BC, which straddles Akhenaten's dates. Had Akhenaten imbibed monotheism from the Jews? Did Moses know the 'Hymn to the Sun'? Did the descendants of someone who trekked from Egypt carry it down the centuries to the Psalmists? Who knows?

Speculation. That's the sort of thing that ambitious theologs trot out to make their reputations. Let's leave all that and join the Psalmist's intoxication with God, our creator, our sustainer. Our God, who is also our saviour. Paul says, 'As in Adam all die, so in Christ all will be made alive' (I Cor. 15: 22). He has opened the Doors of the Holiest of Holies for us. Let us go in.

Gilcomston Prayer Meeting, 8 August 2015.

Psalm 108

This is a solemn but triumphal psalm. It is also an oddity. Is it a cut-and-paste job? Vv. 1–5 are more or less vv. 7–11 of Ps. 57, and vv. 6–13 are more or less vv. 5–12 of Ps. 60. Both of those are by David. They are 'miktams', whatever that is, and are written for the Director of Music. Ps. 57 is specified to be sung to the tune of 'Do not destroy', and is noted as written after David had 'fled from Saul into the cave'. Ps. 60 is to be sung to the tune of "The Lily of the Covenant.' Its occasion is 'when he fought Aram Naharaim and Aram Zobah', – both peoples of Mesopotamia and Syria – and 'when Joab returned and struck down twelve thousand Edomites in the Valley of Salt'. It is specifically said to be 'for teaching'. So the sources of Ps. 108 have military connections or connotations.

As usual I looked to see what Augustine and Calvin had made of our psalm. The result was surprising. Both say that they have covered what is important in it in their comments on Pss. 57 and 60. Augustine notes a variation in name of God in the two texts, but says little about that, and really adds nothing. Calvin just says 'see what I said earlier'. Not very helpful.

But is Ps. 108 a cut-and-paste job? Ps. 108 is designated as a psalm of David, and is 'a song'. I have not done the scholarly legwork, but as I read and re-read Ps. 108 I began to wonder. The fact that Ps. 108 comes a long way after Pss. 57 and 60 does not prove that it was compiled from them. I found myself wondering whether Ps. 108 might have been composed early in David's life, and that later he pasted parts of it into Pss. 57 and 60. I now think I think so. Remember it was the reputation of the young David as a songster and harpist that led to his being recruited to lift the afflicted Saul's spirits (1 Sam. 16: 14–23).

'Cut and paste' raises a question, whichever way round it happened. The fact that there is duplication between these psalms in our Scriptures shows that it is possible to take wisps of the Bible, chunks indeed, and use them to illuminate, guide and instruct for other situations. All three of these psalms are part of Scripture. Matthew Henry accepts Ps. 108 as derivative from the others but says that its example teaches us:

that we may in prayer use the same words that we have formerly used, provided it be with new affections. It intimates likewise that it is not only allowable, but sometimes convenient, to gather some verses out of one psalm and some out of another, and to put them together, to be sung to the glory of God. In singing this psalm we must give glory to God and take comfort to ourselves.

An example of doing precisely that is the modern use of Matt. 18: 20 – the 'two or three gathered together' passage. Jesus' words are actually said in the immediate context of dealing with a sinning fellow-believer (Matt: 18: 15–20). Two or three are determining the matter, and Jesus says he will be there. He participates in their decisions. But it cannot be wrong to broaden out the phrase (v. 19–20) to other applications. Many have found that helpful.

With some justification Spurgeon calls Psalm 108 'The Warrior's Morning Song'. Those bits turn up in those military-related psalms as indicated, but there is more to the point than that. To make sense the 'warrior' writing thus must be young and fit. These are not the words of a retired veteran. This is a young man at the start of adult life, thinking about God and the future.

Now, what about content?

Look at vv. 1–2. Some translations say my heart is 'fixed'; others that my heart is 'steadfast'. Whatever, David is going to praise. He is going to sing. He is going to use the harp and the lyre. And it's not going to be a tone-perfect, smooth, refined, understated performance. He is not going to intone material from an officially approved Book of Common Prayer, lovely though Evensong can be. He is going to sing his heart out: he is going to awaken the dawn. He's stirred to the depths.

There is one musical setting that does this justice. You would recognise tunes from Leonard Bernstein's 'West Side Story' or 'On the Town'. He also wrote some wonderful religious-based music including the 'Chichester Psalms' of 1965. Pss. 100, 2, 23, 131 and 133, are set in that order, some in whole and some in part. But a wisp from Ps. 108: 2 begins it all. The choir's first words are: 'Awake, harp and lyre! I will awaken the dawn' (NIV), or in the KJV 'Awake, psaltery and harp: I will rouse the dawn!' You wouldn't know that just by listening for Bernstein requires the choir to sing in Hebrew. The choir sings *maestoso* double forte. It is solemn and majestic. Verse 1b said the psalmist is going to sing and make music with all his soul. Bernstein responds admirably.[12]

But apart from rousing the dawn, the psalmist is going to put everyone in the picture. V. 3: he will praise the Lord among the nations, and sing of Him among the peoples. He's not just praising God as an act of worship; he's going to share about Him.

Share what? David is going to sing of God's love, a love higher than the heavens, and a faithfulness that reaches the skies, v. 4. God is to be exalted above the heavens; his glory is over all the earth, v. 5. But David is not setting down the words he is going to use. He's stating his purpose, what he is going to tell others about. He's not going to go around saying 'God is wonderful; God is marvellous', and expect people to accept what he says *simpliciter*. He is going to show that God is wonderful, loving and faithful. That's an important principle. 'Show, don't tell' is the way to communicate. 'Show'. Don't instruct how to react. People need to be convinced, not hectored into a submissive silence.

At this point David changes tack. He looks around and sees how things are. Vv. 6–13 are about the God of vv. 1–5. God has rejected the people and no longer goes out with their armies (v. 11). So David prays for help and salvation (v. 6). He calls on God to deliver those whom God loves (v. 7). If this psalm was composed when David was young that makes sense. Things were less than perfect in the later parts of Saul's forty-two-year reign (1 Sam. 13:1). But note two things here. First, God loves his people. That is basic. Second, the rejection spoken of in v. 11 is not incompatible with the love spoken of in vv. 4 and 7. Rejection can be disciplinary, not necessarily final, as the rest of the psalm shows. Remember 'the naughty step'.

In vv. 7–10 David envisages God speaking, asserting his power. Vv. 7–9: Shechem, Succoth and Gilead are his, as are the lands of Manasseh, Ephraim and Judah. So are Moab and Edom. He will triumph over Philistia. These are all territories, which the young David would have known. They bordered on where he was. Then a perhaps unknowingly prophetic David goes on. Which is the fortified city of v. 10? Could it be Jebus, later to become the City of David? Certainly God was later to lead him to march on Edom (v. 10) – see the occasion of Ps. 60. He asks for God's aid against the enemies because human aid is worthless (v. 12). With God victory will come (v. 13).

---

12 See the Wikipedia article on the 'Chichester Psalms' and https:// leonardbernstein.com/works/view/14/chichester-psalms, which includes Bernstein's own account of how he came to write it.

All that is a future programme, dimly foreseen by a man on the brink of maturity. And it all hinges on the initial verses of the psalm. This psalm is by someone entranced, almost intoxicated, by his love of the God he knew. No wonder he was going to sing his socks off. No wonder that he was going to awake the dawn.

Can we, shall we, do the same?

Gilcomston Prayer Meeting, 18 August 2018.

Psalm 109

I have been in two minds how to proceed tonight. Do you read ahead? Do you have some idea of what we are coming to before our meetings? Usually I read the Psalm in the minutes before the meeting starts, but what have you done about Ps. 109? It's a bosker! I am minded to slide us in gently, to dilute its impact by a wee old story.

There was a Minister and his Beadle. The Beadle was a man that bore grudges, and the Minister had remonstrated with him time and again. One day the Beadle had yet another grumble about a member or other of the congregation. The Minister tried again. 'Forgive him, Alexander,' he said. 'Forgive him. And, as the Bible says, you will be heaping coals of fire on his head.' The Beadle looked at the Minister from under bushy eyebrows for a minute. Then, to the Minister's surprise, he smiled. 'Aye, Minister,' he replied. Then, after a pause he added 'Aye, Minister. That's right. Burn the brute.'

This is an extraordinary Psalm. It is one of the so-called 'imprecatory' Psalms. Indeed it's the worst of them all. There are six including this one, Pss. 35, 58, 69, 83, 109 and 137. An imprecation is the calling down of a curse or ill-fortune on someone. This one certainly does that. Indeed some think it is so extravagant and 'un-Christian' that it should not be in the Bible at all. The redoubtable German Gerhard Kittel of 'Kittel and Friedrich' was of that view. What about the Sermon on the Mount? What about turning the other cheek (Matt. 5: 39: Luke 6: 29)? What about loving your enemies (Matt. 5: 43–45)? What about blessing those that curse us (Luke 6: 28)? What about praying for those who persecute or mistreat us (Matt 5: 44; Luke 6: 28)?

Some try to get out of the problem this way. Look at vv. 1–5. There David is speaking in the plural – of 'they' – the people that hate him, 'wicked and deceitful men [who] have opened their mouths against [him] and spoken with lying tongues', those who 'surround' him with 'words of hatred' and attack him 'without cause', repaying evil for good, hating his friendship. 'They' have it in for him. But then vv. 6–19 goes over to the singular. 'Appoint an evil man to oppose him ...' etc etc. So the suggestion is made that this is not David calling down these curses, but rather David is quoting the curses called down by someone else on him, David. They are what someone else wants to happen to David.

An interesting suggestion, but it is undercut by v. 20, where it is really quite clear that the psalmist wants these things to happen to his foe: 'May this be the Lord's payment to my accusers, to those who speak evil of me.' Of course, in the Bible there are examples of evil being turned back on plotters: Haman hanged on the gallows he had built for Mordecai (Esth. 7: 9–10). Daniel's accusers are thrown into the lions' den (Dan. 6: 24). But the language of vv. 6–19 that is invoked by v. 20 is too vehement for that. To excuse David that way goes too far. For me at least it is too difficult to see the argument that David is quoting an enemy and hoping the enemy's curses will be turned back on him as anything other than a well-intentioned effort to save God's face, by saving David's face – pretending that this man of God couldn't possibly think like that.

Personally, I am glad this Psalm is here – and I am glad that Mike asked me to deal with it tonight – to face up to it.

I think that David was so frustrated that he lost the heid [sc. had a loss of judgement]. Not only that, but he lost the heid and wallowed in it for a bit before he came to his senses. And it is good for us to see that. Why do I say he wallowed in it? Well, remember that this is a psalm. It's a poem written in the Jewish style, odd to us though that style is. Oh, I suppose, it might have 'just come to him', fully formed. He was a poet, and some say that the more poems you write the easier it can become. But David must have worked on it, considered its order, the words, what it was saying, the repeated thoughts that are the hallmark of Jewish poetry. He must have gone over it. And David wrote it down. He wrote it out. He did not tear it up on the grounds that it contained unworthy thoughts. And it's in our Bible.

So what is there in it for us? Why am I glad that we have it, that it is part of Scripture?

It shows that you can be overwhelmed. I don't know if you have been through that. I have. Sheer frustration and anger at unjustified opposition, undermining comment, deliberate misrepresentation and the like, can boil over. I have been a Dean of Law. I have sat, pencil in hand, thinking about a particular person. I've done it more than once. I have snapped the pencil. In a sense it is therapeutic. It lances the boil. It gets rid of it. I don't know about you, but when I start to get an upset stomach, as I did quite often when I was young, I can stick my finger down my throat, make myself sick, and get rid of the problem. I still can. The same can be done spiritually. Yes there is the Sermon on the Mount. That is how we must behave. But what about the inside? Bottle it up and hope it goes away? Suppressing emotions can really screw you up. And surely here is an emotional reaction.

But notice two things. First, David is clear that his accusers and detractors are in the wrong. David knows that they are inventing things – that there is no justification for their words or plots. We cannot take any comfort from such a Psalm if we are in the wrong. That needs other steps – corrective steps.

Second, see what David is doing in this Psalm. He does not directly upbraid the evildoers, or that specific person of vv. 6–19. David goes to God. He confesses all his frustrations and feelings to God. I hope I do not offend if I put it this way: David vomits out his bile to God – and God cleans it up.

Look at it happening in the Psalm.

Verses 1–5 set the scene. David is being maligned, undermined, plotted against, without cause. But note v. 4b: 'but I am a man of prayer'. He has justified complaints, but he takes it to God. 'Take it to the Lord in prayer' can be awfully trite. Indeed, it can contribute to that feeling when you're overwrought about something, that the very being overwrought is in itself wrong. You are not 'turning the other cheek', or whatever. You have sinned by still having these feelings.

Come to the reality of the Psalm. In vv. 6–19 David lets rip. What a catalogue! And among it there is v. 8 – 'may another take his place of leadership'. Peter quotes that verse in Acts 1: 20, in justifying the election to replace Judas as an Apostle. Based on that, some, troubled by the vehemence in the psalm, have suggested that really this was David foreseeing Judas, not David himself reacting to his own problems. Some will do anything rather than see what is there, including, I found, St. Augustine.

But see where David goes after the catalogue, and the wish that it would all happen to his accusers (v. 20). Vv. 22–5: David has been shattered by it all. He's fading away like an evening shadow, shaken off like a locust. His knees are giving way. He is thin and gaunt. He is an object of scorn. Those who see him shake their heads in scorn. Yes. Things have gotten to him, physically as well as mentally. Maybe they should'nt have. But they have. He has bottled things up, and he has paid an emotional, and indeed a physical, penalty. He vomits out those curses, a catalogue reflecting his pain. This is the anguish of the Third Movement of Dimitri Shostakovich's First Violin Concerto and the Stalin referents. This is Francis Bacon's 'Three Figures at the Base of a Crucifixion' – the 1944 version, though to a lesser degree the 1988 version has the same effect. Does anyone know what I am talking about?

Back to more familiar territory. Where does David go? He goes to his Sovereign Lord. Verse 21: 'But you, O Sovereign Lord, deal well with me for your name's sake; out of the goodness of your love deliver me.' I'll repeat that: it is: 'out of the goodness of your love deliver me'. Not out of the goodness of God's heart – but out of the goodness of God's love. That's quite different. You can do something out the goodness of your heart, can't you? But doing something out of love ... ? Well, I hope you know the difference.

So David snuggles in to God. Maybe he should have done so earlier. But he does it now. 'Help me, O Lord my God, save me in accordance with your love' (v. 26). Oh, yes, he has backward glances. The enemies are to know that God has done it (v. 27). They may curse, but God will bless (v. 28). They will be put to shame (v. 29).

We don't know what triggered this Psalm. Some say the time of the treason of Absalom, including the invective of Shimei as David fled Jerusalem (1 Sam 15–18). Others look to Nabal, then the husband of Abigail, cursing David when he was in flight from Saul (1 Sam. 25). But we don't need to know what caused the Psalm. And we don't need to know how or even whether God fulfilled David's prayer. The answer may have been 'Yes', or it may have been 'No'. After all we don't know God's purposes with David's enemy. Think of what God did with Paul, who certainly was an enemy of Christ and Christians before his conversion.

What we do need to know, and make our own, is the end of this Psalm. For we can all get overwrought. Look at it: David has gone past his fury and complaints. Vv. 30–31: 'With my mouth I will greatly extol the Lord. In the great throng I will praise him. For he stands at the right hand of the needy one, to save his life from those who condemn him.'

David – once again in a Davidic mess – has seen where his salvation lies.

Gilcomston Prayer Meeting, 12 August 2006.

Psalm 109

This is an extraordinary Psalm. It is one of the so-called 'imprecatory' Psalms. An imprecation is the calling down of curse or ill-fortune on someone. This one certainly does that. There are six imprecatory Psalms, Pss. 35, 58, 69, 83, 109 and 137. It's the worst of them all. Indeed some think it is so extravagant and 'un-Christian' that it should not be in the Bible at all. The redoubtable German Gerhard Kittel of 'Kittel and Friedrich' was of that view. Would the editor of a modern Christian song-book would include something like this? What about the Sermon on the Mount? About turning the other cheek (Matt. 5: 39: Luke 6: 29)? What about loving your enemies (Matt. 5: 43–45)? What about blessing those that curse you (Luke 6: 28)? What about praying for those who persecute or mistreat you (Matt 5: 44, Luke 6: 28)? What about Jesus weeping over Jerusalem (Matt. 23: 37–39; Luke 19: 41–44)? Curiously, that latter passage is always treated as a sad lament, though it could be read as anger.

Some try to get out of the problem this way. If you look at vv. 1–5, David speaks in the plural – of 'they' – the people that hate him, 'wicked and deceitful men [who] have opened their mouths against [him] and spoken with lying tongues', those who 'surround' him with 'words of hatred' and attack him 'without cause', repaying evil for good, hating his friendship. 'They' have it in for him. But then vv. 6–19 goes over to the singular. 'Appoint an evil man to oppose him … etc, etc'. So the suggestion is that David is not calling down these curses, but rather that he is quoting curses called down on him by someone else. They are what someone else wants to happen to David.

Interesting, but undercut by v. 20, where it is clear that the Psalmist wants these things to happen to his foes: 'May this be the Lord's payment to my accusers, to those who speak evil of me.'

Of course, there are examples of evil being turned back on plotters: Haman hanged on the gallows he built for Mordecai (Esth. 7: 9–10). Daniel's accusers thrown into the lions' den (Dan. 6: 24). But the language of vv. 6–19 that is invoked by v. 20 is too vehement for that. To excuse David that way goes too far. The argument that David is quoting an enemy and hoping the enemy's curses will be turned back on him is too difficult accept as anything other than a well-intentioned effort to save God's face, by saving David's face – pretending that this man of God couldn't possibly think like that.

Personally, I am glad this Psalm is here. We need to face up to it.

I think that David was so frustrated that he lost the heid [sc. had a loss of judgement]. Not only that, but he lost the heid and wallowed in it for a bit before he came to his senses. And it is good for us to see that. Why do I say he wallowed in it? Well, remember that this is a psalm. It's a poem written in the Jewish style, odd though that style is. Oh, I suppose, it might have 'just come to him', fully formed. He was a poet, and they say that the more poems you write the easier it can become. David must have worked on it, considered its order, the words, what it was saying, the repeated thoughts that are the hallmark of Jewish poetry. He must have gone over it. And David wrote it down. He wrote it out. He did not tear it up on the grounds that it contained unworthy thoughts. And it's in our Bible.

So what is there in it for us? Why am I glad that we have it, that it is part of Scripture?

It shows that you can be overwhelmed. I don't know if you have been through that. I have. Sheer frustration and anger at unjustified opposition, undermining comment, deliberate misrepresentation and the like, can boil over. I have twice been Dean of Law. First time round as the hand-over my predecessor gave me some advice. 'Frank', he said. 'Just remember that the Dean is the tree for the Faculty dogs.' Very true. I have sat, pencil in hand, thinking about particular persons. More than once I have snapped the pencil. In a sense it is therapeutic. It lances the boil. It gets rid of it. I don't know about you, but when I start to get an upset stomach, as I did quite often when I was young, I can stick my finger down my throat, make myself sick. I still can. It gets rid of the problem. The same can be done spiritually. Yes there is the Sermon on the Mount and those other passages. That is how we must behave. But what about the inside? Bottle it up and hope it goes away? Suppressing emotions can really screw you up. And surely here is an emotional reaction.

But notice two things. First, David is clear that his accusers and detractors are in the wrong. David knows that they are inventing things – that there is no justification for their words or plots. We cannot take any comfort from such a Psalm if we are in the wrong. That needs other steps – corrective steps.

Second, see what David is doing in this Psalm. He does not upbraid the evildoers, or that specific person of vv. 6–19. David goes to God. He confesses all his frustrations and feelings to God. I hope I do not offend if I put it this way: David vomits out his bile in front of God – and God cleans it up.

Look at it happening in the Psalm.

Verses 1–5 set the scene. David is being maligned, undermined, plotted against, without cause. But note v. 4b: 'but I am a man of prayer'. He has justified complaints, but he takes it to God. 'Take it to the Lord in prayer' can be awfully trite. Indeed, it can contribute to that feeling when you're overwrought about something, that the very being overwrought is itself wrong. You are not 'turning the other cheek', or whatever. You have sinned by still having these feelings.

But come to the reality of the Psalm. In vv. 6–19 David lets rip. What a catalogue! And among it there is v. 8 – 'may another take his place of leadership'. Peter quotes that verse in Acts 1: 20, in justifying the replacing of Judas as an Apostle. Based on that, some folk, troubled by the vehemence in the psalm, have suggested that really this was David foreseeing Judas, not David himself reacting to his own problems. Some will do anything rather than see what is there, including, I found, St. Augustine.

After the catalogue, and the wish that it would all happen to his accusers (v. 20), see where David goes. Vv. 22–5: David has been shattered by it all. He's fading away like an evening shadow, shaken off like a locust. His knees are giving way. He is thin and gaunt. He is an object of scorn. Those who see him shake their heads in scorn. Yes. Things have gotten to him, physically as well as mentally. Maybe they should'nt have. But they have. He has bottled things up, and he has paid an emotional, and indeed a physical, penalty. He vomits out those curses, a catalogue reflecting his pain. This is the anguish of the Third Movement of Dimitri Shostakovich's First Violin Concerto with its Stalin referents. This is Francis Bacon's 'Three Figures at the Base of a Crucifixion' – the 1944 version, though to a lesser degree the 1988 version has the same effect. Does anyone know what I am talking about?

Back to more familiar territory. Where does David go? He goes to his Sovereign Lord. Verse 21: 'But you, O Sovereign Lord, deal well with me for your name's sake; out of the goodness of your love deliver me.' I'll repeat that: it is: 'out of the goodness of your love deliver me'. Not out of the goodness of God's heart – but out of the goodness of God's love. That's quite different. You can do something out the goodness of your heart, can't you? But doing something out of love … ? Well, I hope you know the difference.

So David snuggles in to God. Maybe he should have done so earlier. But he does it now. 'Help me, O Lord my God, save me in accordance with your love' (v. 26). Oh, yes, he has backward glances. The enemies are to know that God has done it (v. 27). They may curse, but God will bless (v. 28). They will be put to shame (v. 29).

We don't know what triggered this psalm. Some say the time of the treason of Absalom, including the invective of Shimei as David fled Jerusalem (1 Sam 15–18). Others look to Nabal, then the husband of Abigail, cursing David when he was in flight from Saul (1 Sam. 25). But we don't need to know what caused the Psalm. And we don't need to know how or even whether God fulfilled David's prayer. The answer may have been 'Yes', or it may have been 'No'. After all we don't know God's purposes with David's enemy. Think of what God did with Paul, who certainly was an enemy of Christians before his conversion.

What we do need to know, and make our own, is the end of this Psalm. For we can all get overwrought. Look at it: David has gone past his fury and complaints. Vv. 30–31: 'With my mouth I will greatly extol the Lord. In the great throng I will praise him. For he stands at the right hand of the needy one, to save his life from those who condemn him.'

David – once again in a Davidic mess – has seen where his salvation lies.

Gilcomston Prayer Meeting, 25 August 2018.

Psalm 110

My normal practice when doing these studies is to try to establish who may have penned the psalm, and why it may have been written. There are many scholarly views as to the writer and purpose of this one, and intriguing they are too. But tonight we will go with the biblical answer. Jesus tells us that David was speaking by the Holy Spirit (Mark 12: 36). So we know authoritatively who wrote the psalm. Why was it written? The Holy Spirit told him to. Why? So that these centuries later we may know more of our Saviour.

Now I hope you will not misunderstand when I say this. To me this psalm is a simple matter of fact. It is not assertive. It is not precatory. It is not rejoicing. It is not grieving. It is not reflective. It is not praising. It is just a calm statement of facts. If you consider the first seven psalms of Book Five of the psalms, Pss.107–109 look to God for salvation. Pss. 111–113 give thanks for salvation given. Ps.110 shows us the bridging between these two, the person, the Messiah who is both King and Priest, who in that dual capacity brings salvation about.

Ps. 110 is said to be the psalm most quoted in the New Testament. Two snatches from it make it familiar. There is v. 1, with which Jesus confounded some Jews. There is v. 4, the 'priest forever, in the order of Melchizedek'. But then it becomes a bit of an enigma with v.7 – the drinking from a brook and the head held high. So: three parts.

'The LORD says to my lord, sit at my right hand'. Jesus quotes the verse possibly twice – the Gospels are not entirely clear as to circumstances. In Matt. 23: 41–45 Jesus asks the Pharisees who had come to try to trip him up: 'What do you think about the Messiah? Whose son is he?'. In Mark 12: 35–37 and Luke 20: 41–44 we know that Jesus asks the question while he is teaching in the Temple. 'While Jesus was teaching in the Temple courts he asked, "Why do the teachers of the law say the Messiah is the son of David? David himself, speaking by the Holy Spirit declared: The Lord said to my Lord; sit at my right hand until I put your enemies under your feet.' How can David's son be his lord??' In all the reports the Pharisees have no answer, and in Mark the people were listening with delight. The Pharisees problem is this. They do have the idea that there is a messiah to come, but instead of seeing Jesus properly they fail to connect the dots. They had seen his miracles, wonders and signs but viewed him as a threat.

Peter teases it out for the folk mystified by the apostles who were speaking of the wonders of God on the day of Pentecost. Parthians, Medes and Elamites, residents of Mesopotamia, Judea and Cappadocia, Pontus and Asia, Phrygia and Pamphylia, Egypt, the parts of Libya near Cyrene; visitors from Rome, Cretans and Arabs, all heard their own languages, not the Galilean they expected from Galileans, as Luke reports (Acts 2: 1–12). Peter explains what is going on – why his fellows are so enthused. He takes David's confident affirmation in Ps. 16: 6–11 that his Lord would not abandon him or let his holy one see decay and points out that David was long dead. So Ps. 16 was prophetic about the Messiah, and not about David's own future. Peter then quotes Ps. 110: 1 and affirms that the resurrection proves that Jesus is the long-promised Messiah, the Christ, he of whom David had spoken. He is the Lord to whom the Lord makes the promises of Ps. 110.

Now, before moving on there is one other point to see. This Lord will rule among his enemies before subduing them. And he will have a willing army, volunteers in his battles (vv. 2b–3). How willing are we?

Verse 4 takes us to mystery. This Lord is a priest forever after, or in the order of, Melchizedek. Melchizedek is someone of whom we know little or nothing. The name is generally understood to mean 'king of righteousness'. He was king of Salem – later to become Jerusalem, but at this time it was only a small place, of no particular note. Abram encounters him in Gen. 14. After Abram has helped defeat the kings who had kidnapped Lot, (Gen 14: 12–16), he meets the king of Sodom and the king of Salem. And the king of Salem, Melchizedek, brought bread and wine, and blessed Abram in these words: 'Blessed be Abram by God Most High, Creator of heaven and earth: And blessed be God Most High, who delivered your enemies into your hand. And Abram gave him tithes' (Gen. 14: 19b–20 NIV).

I assume that 'bread and wine' will have echoed in your mind. But we must press on. Melchizedek was a priest of the Most High God, and as a priest was able to bless. Now we know that Abram not a priest, although he could sacrifice to God and did so. But the point is that in Bible times the priest was intermediary between man and deity. And there were many priests of many different gods. Extraordinarily Melchizedek was a priest of the Most High God, Abram's God, as Abram immediately makes clear to the king of Sodom (Gen. 14: 22). Now we also know that later on no king of the Jews was or could be a priest. The king was not to intrude into the office of priest. Uzziah, previously a good king, was stricken with leprosy when he became arrogant and tried to offer incense in the Temple (2 Chron. 28: 16–21: 2 Kgs. 15: 5).

But Melchizedek was both king and priest. How come? Well, it is the Lord, the Most High God, who selects his intermediaries and he had chosen Melchizedek to be one of them. By the way, that raises a question. Were there other king/priests of the Most High God around elsewhere? There's a thought. Will we encounter them and their fellow worshippers in heaven? No matter. Abram knew Melchizedek as a priest of the Most High God. That is why he gave him a tenth of everything – tithes (Gen. 14: 20b). That fits. Isn't it true that worshippers of the true God recognise and salute each other?

So the Most High God of Ps. 110: 1, as we may transpose the terminologies, has decreed that the Lord spoken of as David's Lord is a 'priest forever after the order of Melchizedek'. Why? And so what? That is explained for us in the Epistle to the Hebrews. Going through that would take hours, which we have not got tonight. Suffice it to note that Heb. 1: 13 quotes v. 1 of our psalm as part of the argument. In the book the writer demonstrates that Jesus, is the great High Priest designated as such by God. He has gone into the Holy of Holies as our intermediary. And there, as our priest he has presented a sacrifice for us. And that sacrifice is himself. He is the sacrifice for the sins of all who believe in Him.

So, in Ps. 110 we have David's Lord as King and Priest. But what about verse 7. It's a puzzle given the preceding verses. 'He will drink from a brook along the way, and so he will lift his head high.' Why did David write that? What does it have to do with the rest of the psalm? Some translations footnote that scholars are uncertain as to what it means, so it is not surprising that many have speculated about it.

Tonight I go along with Calvin and others who link it to Gideon in Judges 6–7. The story is long. I leave out much detail. Suffice it to say that because the Israelites had sinned, Midianites had occupied much of the land displacing the Israelites for some seven years until eventually they cried to the LORD (Judges 6: 1–6). Gideon gathered an army of thirty thousand (Judges 6: 33–35). But God told him how to whittle them down to a number acceptable to God. After two thirds went home Gideon took the rest to water and watched how they drank. Some got down on their knees. Others lapped from their hands. The latter were selected. The result was an army of three hundred, and, through the power of God, that minuscule force routed the Midianites.

Gideon's story has many many lessons – he needed God to give him an awful lot of reassurance and encouragement – but that's not for tonight. What I take from it is this. The Midianites had not yet been dealt with. Those that went down on their knees had only thirst in their minds. Those selected, the lappers, remained watchful for danger. Now transfer that to Ps. 110 v.7. The picture is that this Lord will always be alert, *en garde* – ready to protect and defend his people. That is reassuring, isn't it? Our King, our Priest is our perpetual protector.

The psalm does not rejoice in that or in anything else it contains. It remains a simple, plain assertion of facts. Facts for us to accept and live by. I remind those who will understand the language, and apologise to others, that 'facts are chiels that winnna ding, an downa be disputed' (Rabbie Burns, 'A Dream', 1786). They are like the unalterable laws of physics, which we automatically obey and take account of in life. These are the rocks that are the foundation of our faith. David reports without comment. But we know what it all means, and we can rejoice.

Gilcomston Prayer Meeting 24 July 2021.

Postscript

The day after that this was delivered, it occurred to me that the King and Priest elements come together in a way that can be thought of in musical terms as counterpoint. In counterpoint two or more separate themes or tunes are played simultaneously to produce the overall effect.

I have also discovered that its Latin text is set as Part 2 of Monteverdi's Vespers of 1610.

Psalm 115

We do not know when or why this Psalm was composed. Something or other may have triggered it, but we do not know what that was. Alternatively it may have no single source, but it is a mature consideration of things. It refers to surrounding nations (v. 2). That might indicate it was written before the Exile and the Jews reduction to vassal status, but we just do not know. For tonight its occasion is irrelevant. Suffice it to say it is one of the six 'Hallel' psalms – Psalms 113–118 – recited as a unit on joyous occasions such as the Passover and the Harvest. What is important is that it is an affirmation of faith.

The second thing to say is that it is a song or a chant. It was to be sung or chanted by at least two choirs. It is not a theological disquisition. Its truths are there to be seen as you go through it. They are there to be thought about. But it is written for participation, not analysis.

Why do I say it is a song? Well, look at vv. 9–11. 'All you Israelites, trust in the Lord – he is their help and shield. House of Aaron, trust in the Lord – he is their help and shield. You who fear him, trust in the Lord – he is their help and shield.' The first half of each of these verses calls on an audience – 'All you Israelites ... House of Aaron ... You who fear him ...'. The second half of each verse goes into a third person statement of what or who the Lord is. Isn't that odd? It is if you look at it cold, but if you envisage one group singing the first bit, and the response coming antiphonally from another group, it makes sense.

Now go back. Think of v. 1 as being for every-one, the part sung in unison. Thereafter it is easy to split the verses, one choir singing the first bit and another singing the other bit. Yes, we could debate how to divide some of the other verses, but that is not important. I am not writing a technical paper. Where the choirs might come together towards the end is not clear. But certainly if I were staging a performance I would at least have v. 18 sung by all: 'It is we who extol the Lord both now and evermore. Praise the Lord'. It is intriguing to think what Thomas Tallis or Claudio Monteverdi would have made of it. What might Guiseppe Verdi or Charles Ives have produced? What do you think??

We have a song, not an expository disquisition. So what?

First it is an affirmation of faith. The people are in distress, and yet their hope must be in the Lord their God. 'Not unto us' ... (v. 1). What exactly they want is not clear, but their hope lies in God out of his regard for his glory. They are dependent on him. That has something to teach us. We pray, but we should pray that God will glorify himself in this way and that: that is a core message.

Verse 3 is important. God does what he pleases. That could lead you to think of God as arbitrary, swinging erratically from this to that depending on our prayers. How arrogant! Look at the world. There's all sorts of things going on to make you wonder whether there is a God at all, and if He is what is he playing at. It can be very personal. Remember C.S. Lewis' period after his wife died, when he wrote of God the Vivisectionist in *A Grief Observed* (1961). Think of Gilcomston today. But while God is doing what pleases him, there is ultimately a moral basis to it, even though it may not be apparent to us. The trap lies in that word 'pleases'. What pleases carries with it no departure from morality, from God's intrinsic nature. 'What is moral is, of course, just a point of view' – is a point of view. Your view is your view. We are in a Postmodernism climate. Moral relativism is rampant, isn't it?

But that would be a wrong interpretation of v. 3. Donald Mackinnon, then Professor of Moral Philosophy at Aberdeen, took me through such thought back in 1961. At that time a possible criminal sentence was to be 'detained during Her Majesty's pleasure'. That was an indefinite sentence of imprisonment for the protection of the community. The terms may have been sanitised since then. But Mackinnon's point was that it had to do with the will of the monarch, not with her emotional state. Criminal law and procedures still operate on that basis. And that is not wrong. But we must recognise that what might strike us as unreasonable occurrences do happen not only by God's permission, but by his will. Calvin points out that if God does whatever pleases him, we cannot ask why does he permit what he does not wish? Why does he not restrain the Devil and those who oppose his will?

Is God to be thought of as suspended between possibilities, allowing what he does not want, tolerating what he does not wish, and somehow as an unconcerned spectator in heaven? No. He governs what happens, and what happens is his will, including our recent weeks. His permissions are for the best, puzzling and uncomfortable though we may find them. There is a time to hunker down, seek his face, and wait prayerfully. We may come to understanding: we may not. We may be pained; we may not. It is His will.

The rest of the psalm shows the way through all this – through to the affirmation at the end. This is not 'whistling in the dark to keep your spirits up'. It is how the people of God react to the uncertainties that come to any rational Christian. But note I insert that adjective, 'rational'. Irrational Christians do exist. The singers of Psalm 115 were not such. Reliant on their God, the choirs performing this psalm are not on some sort of an emotional binge. Their faith is anchored in his Word. He speaks to his people.

The contrast is in the next verses. See vv. 4 ff about the 'other gods'. They are manufactured, v. 4. Oh they could be lovely objects, made out of silver and gold, v. 4. Go look at the rather wonderful statues from Akkad in the Louvre – Marduk, Ishtar (Inanna) and the others. But they cannot speak, v. 5a. They do not see, v. 5b. They do not hear, v. 6a. They do not smell, v. 6b. They have hands but cannot feel, v. 7a. They have feet but cannot walk, v. 7b. They cannot utter a sound, v. 7c. They are useless. And yet, and yet. Terrible as it is we must recognise that this is how things are. We are set in a community where people look askance at us and ask 'where is their God?', v. 2. We are in a community where other gods guide people's lives and are implicitly worshipped. Not idols, but more pernicious eidolons than that. And we are scrutinised. Our response can on occasion at least, be derision at the idols that govern some lives, whether money, the local football team, or whatever. But that is enough of that. We must pray for these others, not crow, not vaunting some sort of superiority, for such were some of us. Are we still?

Come to the rest of our psalm. See the repeated 'trust in the Lord' of vv. 9–11, and the promises of blessing of vv. 12–13. See the confidence of the choirs. His people will flourish, v. 14. Then the Psalm ends affirming belief.

None of that conclusion negates what I said earlier about God doing what pleases him. None of that ignores the history of his people. None of that shuts our eyes to the news that so distresses us. But tonight, see v. 18: 'It is we who extol the Lord, both now and evermore. Praise the Lord.'

Gilcomston Prayer Meeting, 24 October 2015.

Postcript

The domestic reference to Gilcomston is that our minister had recently re-signed.

Psalm 117

This is the shortest of the Psalms. When I was allocated it I looked it up and found myself wondering what it was doing in the Psalter. It is very similar to what we sing during services as part of the 'ritual'. At first sight it is more akin to 'Praise God from whom all blessings flow' which we sometimes sing at the end of our communion services than it is to the other psalms we consider in these Saturday evening gatherings.

Often when preparing for these meetings I have a look at Augustine's and Calvin's commentaries on the Psalms. On this one both are much terser than their usual. Yet both identify what we are coming to – especially in this instance, Calvin. It is a remarkable Psalm. The more you look at it the more it grows. The more it grows, the more it glows. [Poohs and Piglets are allowed to subvocalise the appropriate 'tiddly-poms']. But let me slide us in with a couple of images.

First, round about now walking the grove at Hazlehead Park that runs down to the garden centre you find lots of beechnuts on the path. Take one of those curious spiky triangular seeds in your hand and then look up at the tree from which it has fallen. Further on in the woods pick up an open pine cone and shake out the winged seeds – much smaller than a beech nut. Look at one of them – and then consider the magnificent pines. Small seeds have great potential.

Second, I ask a question. Do you ever use binoculars? Probably. Have you ever used binoculars to look at a flower? On a country walk, or even in your garden, try using binoculars. Not for far away objects, but to look at things that are near. Stand six to ten feet or so back and use them to look at a flower-head, say a spray of vetch. Watch the efforts of a bee on a single bramble flower. Using binoculars you see things that you don't normally see. You see detail. The binoculars concentrate the attention. They cut down how much you see round about. They also shorten the depth of your focus, and magnify the object itself. It's the same with this Psalm. Yes, it is short, but that constrains our thought within its boundaries. We're not being bombarded with a variety of images. It's saying only a few things, but very particular things.

Vv. 1–2: Praise the LORD, all you nations; extol him, all you peoples. For great is his love toward us, and the faithfulness of the LORD endures forever. Praise the LORD.

The first thing to grasp is the phrase at the beginning and the end – 'Praise the LORD'. This is not a command, although it is both a call, and in itself a praising. It is not 'praise God – or else'. There is a difference. Think of the recent choreographed celebrations of the sixtieth anniversary of the Communist regime in China, or of the parades that celebrate the birthdays of Kim Il Sung or Kim Jong Il. Think of the Nuremberg rallies. 'Praise the LORD' is not that. Nor is it the theological equivalent of the Zhdanov Doctrine – an indication of a line to take – celebrate Communism, and, incidentally the role of Stalin in guiding the nation. Failure to conform to that Doctrine ran you into difficulties, and potentially into the Gulag. No. This 'praise' is a spontaneous overflow of true emotion and/or a call to let that emotion spill out. It is real. It is neither synthetic nor feigned. It is not a form of words to be uttered (convincingly or not) with one eye on whoever may be watching. It is simply and soberly 'Praise the LORD'.

Second, this 'LORD' is in those squat capitals that the NIV and some other translations use to indicate that this is Jehovah. Jehovah is the strong name of God, the God revealed to Moses at the Burning Bush (Exod. 3).

Third, note to whom the call comes. 'Praise the LORD, all you nations; extol him, all you peoples.' That is important. It is not a call just to Jews. It is not a call just to believers. It is not a call just to Christians. It is a call to all nations and all peoples. Yes, the call may be ignored, but the call is to all. It connects directly with Jesus' instruction: 'Go and make disciples of all nations' (Matt. 28: 19).

Paul, of course, did not have the Gospel of Matthew at hand to quote. But he makes use of our Psalm. Look at Romans 15 when he is setting out the basis of his ministry. There would be no point in his straveiging round the Roman Empire unless it was God's intention to gather his people from all nations. Writing to what was largely a Gentile church, the church in Rome, he exhorts them: Rom. 15: 7 –11:

Accept one another … just as Christ accepted you in order to give praise to God. For I tell you that Christ has become a servant of the Jews on behalf of God's truth, to confirm the promises made to the patriarchs so that the Gentiles may glorify God for his mercy, as it is written`:

"Therefore I will praise you among the Gentiles; I will sing hymns to your name." [2 Sam. 22: 50; Ps. 18: 49]. Again it says, "Rejoice, O Gentiles, with his people." [Deut. 32: 43]. And again – now we come to our Psalm, but with the shift to show that it refers to Gentiles as part of the 'all nations' – "Praise the Lord, all you Gentiles, sing praises to him, all you peoples." And again, Isaiah says, "The root of Jesse will spring up, one who will arise to rule over the nations; the Gentiles will hope in him."

'Praise the LORD all nations, all peoples.' He has his people everywhere. That's why we are here.

Praise the LORD. But why? The Psalm answers that question for any who need it to be answered. Praise the LORD 'For great is his love toward us, and the faithfulness of the LORD endures forever' (v. 2).

Great is his love. We exist, the world exists because of his love. We can take the world, the entire Universe indeed, too much for granted. I am reminded of one of Piet Hein's *Grooks*, which makes the point of the wonder of it all. 'We glibly talk of nature's laws; but do things have a natural cause? Black earth into yellow crocus is undiluted hocus-pocus.' But his love has gone further than mere creation. Our Psalmist did not know this as he wrote, though surely now he does. The LORD has given his Son for our salvation. He is loving. He is faithful. He restores us to our true place within his purpose.

'Praise the LORD'. Take this tiny seed of a Psalm. See its immensity.

Gilcomston Prayer Meeting, 24 October 2009.

Psalm 121

This is one of the Psalms that is ingrained in the mentality of the Scottish Kirk – or at least it was. Conventicles meeting out in the snow come to mind. If you don't feel its deep cadences echoing deep down, it's time you did. Yes, the tune helps – unlike so many modern ones – but even without the traditional tune it speaks to the marrow. With all due respect to the newer translations, there is a speaking majesty in the words of the Authorised Version, and, as an old AV man, I will slush about from the NIV to the AV.

This is a transparent Psalm. By that I don't mean you can see through it: rather the reverse. It is one through which the light of God passes unhindered. Truth is here. Let it strike home. I recently heard an interview with Stephen Hawking. He was asked about that famous throw-away comment in *A Brief History of Time*, about knowing 'the mind of God.' He explained that for him if anything God is behind the mathematics that dictate how the Universe works. This god is detached, uninvolved, and you cannot have a personal relationship with him. Olaf Stapledon's *Star Maker* (1938) comes to mind.

This Psalm contradicts Hawking. God cares for us. He does intervene. We can be friends.

As the heading says, this is one of Psalms of Ascent. It is one of fifteen such psalms, and belongs in their first group, where what is being thought of is the impending journey. Where are we going? We are going up to Jerusalem.

Most of us don't think that way. I almost said '*we* don't think that way', but perhaps that is too sweeping. For the Jew of the time the psalm was written, going up to Jerusalem was so very special. In fact, three times a year the Jews went up to Jerusalem for the sacrifices and offerings. But if you could not afford the time or the expense of the regular journeys, 'going to Jerusalem' was that much more special when you did manage it. And that always opened up the danger that the going – that the experience itself – might bulk too large. The very God in whose Temple the pilgrim was going to worship, might get forgotten in the thrill of 'being there'. It can happen today. Going to Westminster Chapel, to All Souls, to St Peter's, going to

Gilc. – or even going to Jerusalem – can overwhelm to the extent that God is upstaged. But for others it was indeed the presence of God that was sought. Remember Isaiah's experience (Isa. 6: 1–3). Remember Simon and Anna, going day after day to the Temple, and one day being able to greet the infant Christ (Luke 2: 22–38). God is our aim.

But this Psalm is about that journey, the journey up to Jerusalem, getting there. And we are apprehensive, fearful indeed.

'I to the hills will lift mine eyes. From whence doth come mine aid?' (v. 1).

Or is it, 'I to the hills will lift mine eyes from whence doth come mine aid?' – in which version the aid will come from the hills.

Ink has been spilt on that question of punctuation. Tonight I take it in the sense that there is a threat, and it comes from the hills. Use your mind. Here is the group walking along the track – no motorways then. As you go to Jerusalem from any direction you end up going through narrow defiles, areas where attack would be easy. Remember that in those days the Land was well forested. Yes, today there is barrenness, bare rock and arid expanses. But they are there because Titus obeyed the orders of his father, Vespasian. As Josephus recounts in his contemporary *History of the Jewish War* the rebellion of 70 AD resulted in the felling of the forests of Palestine, and they have never recovered. But when our author was writing the orchards and forests of the historical books such as the Kings and the Chronicles, those of other Psalms and of the Song of Solomon, are still there – with, potentially, brigands and worse lurking in their fastnesses.

'Our safety cometh from the Lord' (v. 2a). Do you know that as a general truth? Probably. Do you know it as a personal experience? Cars overturn, jet engines fail – to take two examples I know to have occurred among the fellowship. And then, as Donald Rumsfeld famously observed, there are the 'known unknowns.' We just do not know how often, or where, we have been preserved. And, staying with Rumsfeld, there are the 'unknown unknowns.' His list is not as silly as silly commentators presented it.

Where does our help come from? It comes from the Lord. Of course in minor terms it may come through a human agent who may speak a word, or provide physical help. But such are agents – physical angels as it were. Ultimately our help comes from 'the Lord, the Maker of Heaven and Earth' (v. 2a).

Then the Psalm shifts focus. In vv.1–2 we have the individual fearful and asking the question – 'who is going to help me'? Now the speaker shifts.

Now the words are either of a teacher, or the chant of the group you are travelling with.

Verses 3–8 are wonderful, verses to stick deep into your psyche – verses to draw on. Because in one way, the feared attack of v. 1 *may* happen. In another way, it *will* happen.

The promises of vv. 3–8 show that the slipping foot is possible, that there is the threat of sunstroke, or whatever is symbolised by the moon strike – lunacy?? The Lord will protect.

And yet, is all this not simply propaganda? Is the Psalmist whistling in the dark to keep our spirits up? Joseph Goebbels said, say a thing often enough with enough conviction and you will be believed. Chant this Psalm to preserve your delusion. What about the world we see around us? Does the Lord watch over us (v. 7a)? Yes, we may agree to that. But does he keep from all harm also (v. 7b)? Some of us have lost jobs. Some have deadly illnesses. All of us are getting old.

Well, as C.E.M. Joad (an articulate agnostic, who, incidentally, became a Christian late in life) famously used to say on *The Brains Trust*, 'it all depends what you mean by … '. And it all depends on whether you pick isolated texts and passages out of the Bible, and erect them into general propositions. Do not do that. You have to take the Bible as a whole. Even when this Psalm was being written there was a backlog of knowledge that, thanks to sin, life could be hard and difficult.

So, what I am led to say is threefold.

First, for many of us this Psalm is evidently true. The Lord has protected and will protect. We know that by experience. We are here, now.

Second, I remain convinced that the Lord does not lead us through unnecessary difficulties. I know in a way that downplays the element of sin, and our choosing to go astray. But I think it is true. In due course we will look back and see his care carrying us through where we had to go to be what we are when we get to heaven. Despite C.S. Lewis's feeling expressed for much of *A Grief Observed*, God is not a sadist. Lewis came through to see that.

Third, I must make a detour.

The last time before tonight that I sang this Psalm was at the funeral of a colleague, Sandy Mather, Professor of Geography at Aberdeen. He was 5% younger than me. An elder at the Free Church, he asked for it to be sung at his funeral on 22 November just three weeks ago.

We are on a journey – to the New Jerusalem. Some of us have been going for years. Others for much less. Some of us have indeed stumbled. Some have neglected his care. But he does care.

It was right to sing this Psalm at Sandy's funeral. Verse 7: The Lord will … watch over your life.' He will watch over our going out and coming in forevermore. We are going to go out of this world, and will come in to the place he has prepared for us. In the meantime, verse 2: 'my safety cometh from the Lord, who heaven and earth hath made.'

Gilcomston Prayer Meeting, 9 December 2006.

Psalm 122

Fifteen Psalms, Psalms 120–134, are known as the 'Psalms of Ascent', their common superscription denoting precisely that purpose. They are also known as 'Songs of Degrees', 'Songs of Steps' or as 'Pilgrim Songs'. One, Ps. 127, says it was by Solomon. Four, Pss 122, 124, 131 and 133, indicate they are by David. Even so commentators and academics discuss who wrote them, why they were written, and when they were performed in the Temple ritual. Their later liturgical use varies both within Judaism and in Christianity. Were they songs to sing while people were going to Jerusalem for the three principal feasts? Or had they to do with the actual Temple worship? Were some written for particular occasions? We do not know.

Many have thought that Ps.120 was a pilgrim setting off, Ps.121 was him on the way, and that in Ps.122 he had arrived. I think we have not got there yet, in absolute terms at least.

Calvin takes the view that this psalm was written by David to celebrate the final stage of bringing the Ark to Jerusalem (2 Sam. 6: 12–17; 1 Chron. 15: 128). He concentrates on that. Others think that David is celebrating his capital city once it was established. Matthew Henry treats the psalm as to be sung by pilgrims on their way to a feast at Jerusalem, and it may have been. All well and good, but all a bit flat-footed. Augustine has it better. He ignores such matters and uses it to glory in the Church of Christ.

Fourteen weeks ago on 18 August we looked at Ps. 108, that possible 'cut and paste' job. I then noted that, wherever its bits came from, it showed it is valid to use chunks of Scripture for teaching and for help in prayer in contexts quite different from their origin. I take the same view tonight. Considerations of Ps.122's 'occasion' are irrelevant. We have this psalm now. It can benefit us. So I am going to follow the Augustine line and consider Jerusalem as a type of Christ's church.

This psalm is a celebration. C.H. Parry caught its thrust. He set an abridged version in his Anthem for the Coronation of Edward VII in 1902. 'I was glad, glad when they said unto me . . . .' The choir soars. Parry captures a dignified solemnity that is important. An analogue comes from Italy. In Pisa, Florence or Padua go into the baptistery beside the main cathedral – they are all separate buildings. Give your eyes time to get accustomed to the reduced light – outside is always bright in Italy. Then look up. Gazing down from the dome above are ranks and ranks of saints – the Church – gathered there to welcome the child. This is the real Jerusalem.

But what of Jerusalem as the Church of Christ? In Rev. 21: 9–14 we read of the New Jerusalem, decked as the Bride of the Lamb. How far does history of the City of David match that idea? Bluntly, it doesn't. There are more similarities with the earthly city than the ideal, both physically and in social history. The story of Jerusalem parallels the disasters and misadventures of the Church Visible.

Physically Jerusalem has a chequered history. In vv. 3 and 7 David writes of a city, compactly built, with gates, walls and citadels. Later it was in ruins. Rebuilt by Ezra and Nehemiah, it was again to be destroyed. I and II Maccabees chronicle civil war and troubles, in particular with Antiochus Epiphanes. We know what the Romans did to it. The inside of the Arch of Titus in the Roman Forum shows the spoils of the Temple being carried off. Yes, Jerusalem has walls now, contributed by Crusaders and the Ottomans beginning with Suleiman the Magnificent. But it's nothing like the city John saw in Rev. 21. It is now a place of tension. Soldiers patrol with their guns at the ready, and there is that new Wall.

Look at the social history of the Church Visible. Be clear-sighted. It is so very different in different places. I recall a simple communion in a hut out on the Hungarian puszta, and sung Eucharist in St Paul's in London. You will have had similar experiences. But some variants do seem bizarre.

And apart from variation there is an appalling history. The centuries have seen religious hostility, hostility between professing Christians, hostility to the point of warfare. In Matt. 23: 37 Christ castigates the Jerusalem of his time as the killer of the prophets. There are the many many splits. Last month the Moscow patriarchate withdrew recognition of the status in Orthodoxy of the Ecumenical Patriarchate of Constantinople. That was for political, not doctrinal reasons. The Ecumenical Patriarchate has said it will give separate standing within Orthodoxy to the Ukrainian Orthodox church, which has broken from the jurisdiction of the Moscow patriarchate because of the events in the Crimea and the eastern Ukraine.[13]

---

13 Formally Metropolitan Epiphanus, the head of the Ukraine Orthodox Church and the Patriarch of Constantinople, Bartholomew I, signed the 'tomos', the decree of autocephaly at a ceremony in Istanbul on 5 January 2019, and the Ukrainian Church received it the next day.

Closer to home, what of the history of the Church in Scotland?

True, sometimes separation is necessary. Paul warns against those who love to debate genealogies, arguments and quarrels about the law (e.g. Tit. 3: 9; 1 Tim. 1: 4). Of course there can be a stand on principle. But some splits are down to clash of personalities, people whose minds really are set on earthly things (Rom. 16: 17–19; Phil. 3: 19), grabbing or intent on preserving power. Take a local example from the past, so as not to stir current affairs. Two hundred and fifty years ago in Aberdeen there was a major spat between the Rev. Sir William Dunbar and the Rev William Skinner, Scottish Episcopal Bishop of Aberdeen. It covers many pages of the Court of Session Reports of the time. Defamation and other matters were alleged, but it was power that was at stake. Remember that, from the point of view of the authorities, Jesus was crucified because he was a threat, political as much as theological. Over the centuries generations of leaders have failed. Seeking position, power, prestige, a following and corresponding emoluments, based on their claim to speak for God, they have been imitating the Devil, who, quintessentially, is after the top spot. It's all laid out in that speech transcribed for us by C.S. Lewis in 'Screwtape Proposes a Toast' (1969). Or think of Sinclair Lewis's novel 'Elmer Gantry', now 90 years old, still relevant to the contemporary scene. God is sickened by high days and holidays *ex facie* held to honour him, but really held to bolster their organisers and give shallow pleasure to their acolytes. Many Old Testament passages show God seeking love rather than feasts and sacrifices (e.g. Isa. 1: 11; Jer. 6: 20; 7: 21–26). The point of festivals can get lost. Think of the modern Christmas-tide.

Yet, as we look at history, and the many variant churches, there is a sub-stratum, a commonality of faith. The rituals and ceremonials of the Orthodox churches are suffused with the Gospel. Pope Francis' pastoral letter 'Evangelii Gaudium', of 24 November 2013 – 'The Joy of the Gospel' – contains much good as it calls on us to get to know Jesus. We sing hymns by Cardinal Newman and by Frederick William Faber. Both Calvin and William Still could contemplate a renewed Roman Catholic Church.[14]

So, as we are mindful of those common underpinnings, this Psalm invites

---

14 S. M. Manetsch, 'Is the Reformation Over? John Calvin, Roman Catholicism, and Contemporary Ecumenical Conversations', (2011) 35 *Themelios* 185–202; http://themelios.thegospelcoalition.org/article/is-the-reformation-over-john-calvin-roman-catholicism-and-contemporary-ecum. W. Still, *The Work of the Pastor*, (Christian Focus, 2010), 117.

us to see beyond the current mess to the coming Kingdom, to Jerusalem the bride of Christ. It also allows us, in miniature, to see our own gathering as mirroring, however defectively, the Jerusalem David saw and foresaw in Ps.122. Take it as an encouragement to keep going. We're not there, but we're going to be. Read it to yourself, but be sure to read it out loud, putting as much into it as you can manage.

> I rejoiced with those who said to me, "Let us go to the house of the LORD." Our feet are standing in your gates, Jerusalem. Jerusalem is built like a city that is closely compacted together. That is where the tribes go up – the tribes of the LORD – to praise the name of the LORD according to the statute given to Israel. There stand the thrones for judgment, the thrones of the house of David. Pray for the peace of Jerusalem: "May those who love you be secure. May there be peace within your walls and security within your citadels." For the sake of my family and friends, I will say, "Peace be within you." For the sake of the house of the LORD our God, I will seek your prosperity.

Tonight we can rejoice. Let us enter the house of the Lord. Let us pray for the true Jerusalem, the real Church, the real essence of those minor churches. May those who love it be secure. May there be peace within it. May there be security for the sake of our family and friends; those we know, brought to us in tonight's news, and our fellows who we don't yet know.

Gilcomston Prayer Meeting, 24 November 2018.

[The Latin text of Ps. 122 is set as Part 4 of Monteverdi's Vespers of 1610.]

Psalm 123

We generally call Psalms 120–134 the 'Psalms of Ascent'. Some call them the 'Songs of the Steps'. The New English Translation of the Septuagint[15] calls each 'An Ode of the Steps'. Now an Ode is a lyric poem, so that casts a light on how Jews thought of them. They were not written as a unit. Rather various people composed them at various times. In biblical times Jews would sing or chant them on their visits to Jerusalem for the major festivals. As we have them they do form groups, Psalms 120–122 being preparation for the journey. Psalm 123 is the fourth of the sequence. We are on the way.

The label 'Steps' makes perfect sense for this one. Apparently the Hebrew of this psalm is unique. It rhymes. Most of the pilgrims would be on foot. I don't know Hebrew, but rhyming could fit a walking gait – left right, left right, left right mile after mile. But be aware of something else. Speak it. Sing it. Chant it. How would you voice these words? Would you be slogging on? Would you be marching on? The Psalm has a different tone and impact depending on the cadence, speed and inflection you give it. Are you trudging, close to your limit, just managing to put one foot after the other? Have you a heavy load but you are yomping? – some may recall the word from the Falklands War. Are you marching? Maybe we should schedule auditions.

Psalm 123 is short. It has been spoken of as a sigh. It is a prayer – a short prayer. We can be so verbose when addressing God. The Lord's Prayer is short but its simple words cover everything (Matt. 6: 9–13 or Luke 11: 2–4). Spurgeon cites Luther to the effect that the force of a prayer does not depend on length, but in fervency of spirit. You can cover weighty matters in a few words, particularly if there is no time for long prayer – precisely the sort of praying we should do later tonight.

Who wrote this particular psalm? Why? When? We do not know. We do not need to know. Enough that generations of pilgrims recited it or sang it on the way to Jerusalem. In due course the compilers of the Book of Psalms recognised it as inspired. And so it has come down through the centuries to us tonight.

---

15 The electronic version of the New English Translation of the Septuagint (OUP, 2009) is at http://ccat.sas.upenn.edu/nets/edition/.

Verse 1 says a lot in a few words. 'I lift up my eyes to you, to you who sit enthroned in heaven.' That's the NIV. Other translations are different. The English version of the Tanakh, (the Masoretic text of the Hebrew Bible[16]) reads: 'To You, (capital Y) enthroned in Heaven, I turn my eyes.' The NET rendering of the Septuagint is: 'To you I lifted up my eyes, (past tense) you who reside in the sky.' Both put the 'I' in second place. The familiarity, the intimacy, that directness of approach is amazing. No need for passwords. No security questions. No placatory verbiage. To You, up in heaven. 'LORD our God' does not come until well into v. 2. See the parallel with the directness of the Lord's Prayer also addressed to someone in heaven. Though in it, of course, there is a degree of intimacy that goes one beyond v. 1 of our Psalm. Jesus invites us to pray to Our Father. To me that is very special. My father was killed in the War when I was barely one. But irrespective of that v. 1 of our psalm indicates the writer has direct access to God. He calls God simply 'you' – extraordinary! To you I lift my eyes.

Come now to vv. 3–4. The psalm asks for mercy, for help. Contempt and ridicule rain down from the arrogant and the proud. The cry is for relief. Contempt and ridicule comes to all who throw in their lot with Jesus. Jesus himself warns: 'Blessed are ye when men shall revile you, and persecute you, and say all manner of evil against you falsely, for my sake' (Matt. 5: 11 AV). You won't like it unless you've got other psychological problems, but it is going to happen. Paul speaks of himself as an appointed herald, apostle and teacher, then adds: 'That is why I am suffering as I am' (2 Tim. 1: 12: cf. 2 Tim. 2: 8b–9). Later he writes: 'In fact, everyone who wants to live a godly life in Christ Jesus will be persecuted' (2 Tim. 3: 12; cf. 1 Pet. 4: 4). You don't provoke it (2 Tim. 2: 24–26), but even the most emollient will get hit (Matt. 5: 11).

Now you may have noticed that I have jumped over v. 2: 'As the eyes of slaves look to the hand of their master, as the eyes of a female slave look to the hand of her mistress, so our eyes look to the LORD our God, till he shows us his mercy.'

Slavery is something that we today recoil from, I hope. The recent history of slavery – say the last 300 years – is repellent, but of course Britain got rich on it and its cotton and sugar product. There was the US Civil War (1861–1865) turning precisely on slavery, and there are still residual US problems

---

16 The electronic version of the English translation of the Tanakh, (the Hebrew Bible, Masoretic Text) is at https://www.sefaria.org/texts/Tanakh.

traceable to that history. Modern slavery exists. Wikipedia on 'Slavery in the 21st Century' will tell you that there are 38 to 46 million in slavery of one kind and another. Various national laws and international treaties try to combat it, but it is still out there. In the UK we have the Modern Slavery Act, 2015 c. 30, but there are still reports of forced labour and exploitation.

However we are looking at Ps. 123 v. 2. Discard your modern repugnance. When this psalm was written slavery was an unquestioned part of life. It is there throughout the Old and New Testaments. Do a search for 'slave' on an electronic version of the NIV and you will get 179 verses to look at. Slaves were a part of society throughout biblical times. Despite Egypt, the Jews kept slaves. So far as I can see there's not much detail known about slavery in Judaism at the time this psalm was written, but slaves were a normal part of a well-off Jewish household (Wikipedia, 'Jewish views on slavery'). Modern translations tend to use the term 'servant' but that is cosmetic. There were rules protective of slaves; excessive punishment could lead to liberation (e.g. Exod. 21: 20–21, 26–27) and a slave always got the Sabbath off (Exod. 23: 12). But slaves were there. Intriguingly Eliezer of Damascus, who would have been Abram's heir in the absence of an heir born in wedlock, may have been a slave (Gen. 15: 2–4). The Septuagint calls him the son of Masek, a female homebred servant, which would make him a slave. The child of a slave is a slave. The Tanakh calls him 'Dammasek Eliezer', Abram's steward.

Slavery crops up in the New Testament. Paul uses the civil laws of his times to drive home his message. Many years ago I explored that in a book on legal metaphors in the epistles.[17] Rom. 6: 15–23 makes illuminating use of slavery metaphors. Or go to 1 Corinthians: 'Were you a slave when you were called? Do not let it trouble you, although if you can gain your freedom do so. For the one who was a slave when called to faith in Christ is the Lord's freedman. Similarly one who was free when called is Christ's slave' (1 Cor. 7: 21–22). If you know your Roman law that contrast – slave/freedman, free/slave – is exquisite. Christian slaves are to serve their earthly masters wholeheartedly and obey them 'as slaves of Christ' (Eph. 6: 5–8). Paul does not tell Christian masters to free their slaves, but to treat their slaves well and to never threaten them for they are both under the same Master in heaven (Eph. 6: 9). That said I would love to know whether Philemon freed Onesimus (Philemon 15–16). Of course now some berate Paul for

---

17 *Slaves, Citizens, Sons: Legal Metaphors in the New Testament Epistles* (Grand Rapids: Academie Press / Zondervans, 1984).

not condemning slavery, but that is quite anachronic. In Paul's time slavery was common. You have to live in the society you are in. So Psalm 123 v. 2 says to us wherever we are we are to look for mercy to the hand of our heavenly Master. As slaves of Christ we look to him for mercy, protection and instructions for we are to do his will.

So, finally, a picture. Imagine a stocky, bald, hook-nosed, beetle-browed, bandy-legged figure striding up a road, as it happens the road to Iconium. That's a vignette from the apocryphal but very early 'Acts of Paul and Thecla', which just may be a glimpse of the actual Paul (*Acts of Paul and Thecla*, 3). An awful lot of Paul's missionary journeys were done on foot. No doubt some of the time he talked with his companions, but surely we can imagine him occasionally going over and over this psalm, sometimes as he trudged, sometimes as he marched, always doing his Master's will. 'I lift up my eyes to you, to you who sit enthroned in heaven'. Let's do that now.

Gilcomston Prayer Meeting, 23 October 2021.

Psalm 124

Psalm 124 is another in the series of the Psalms of Ascent. Psalm 124 looks back. It considers past events. Next week Psalm 125 looks forward. So we come to these two appropriately at the turn of the year.

I start with a clarification, maybe a warning. This Psalm is a retrospection. It recalls trials, and deliverances. At tomorrow's morning service the new interim arrangements for the strategic leadership in Gilcomston are to be – what is an appropriate word? – inaugurated. Gilcomston has had its troubles. But I am not linking this Psalm to recent history, and exhort you to avoid the temptation so to do. Too often the history of churches ends in repetitive self-justification, and the loss of commitment to the spread of the Gospel. We are here to get to know Jesus better, not relentlessly to dig up and analyse the past.

Now, a cultural point: I am not sure whether you all can or will follow me here. Gilc-ites are, bluntly, a mixed crew. Many of us do not know Scots history. For those who do, this Psalm reverberates. Through the centuries it has spoken to our forebears. Remember the Covenanters fleeing the persecutions of those times. There were the conventicles. Let those who know summon those dark days to help them grasp this Psalm. Let those who do not, turn to the histories. 'If not the LORD had been on our side' Scotland, Scottish politics and Scottish society would be different.

Now, irrespective of the headnote, we do not know whether it was David that composed it. If he did, what triggered this Psalm? Was it a response to a particular event? It may have been. In this company I need not cite occasions when the Lord saved David, and of others when he saved the People under David. Or was what started off as a response to one scary event broadened out as David's life went on. Is this psalm as it now is because he is looking back on many events? I think it probably is. The images of the snared bird and the waters flooding don't fit as speaking of a single event. What do you think?

If David did not write it, whoever did could think of so many other occasions when the LORD had saved his People. Remember this Psalm was chanted or sung on the pilgrimage road up to Jerusalem. Imagine you are after the Return from Babylon, and you are heading up to Jerusalem. These words make it only natural to think in personal terms. You have been protected and have returned to the Promised Land. Take that forward to tonight. Can you look back and see resonances of when the LORD's hand has protected and delivered you? I can.

And note it is the LORD that protects. The word is in those block capitals in the NIV. That means it is translating the highest name of God, Jehovah. The most expressive name of God that we can appreciate.

Now, turn to the imagery. Vv. 2–3: 'if the Lord had not been on our side when people attacked us, they would have swallowed us alive when their anger flared against us.'

Attack is clear enough. We know what that means. We know flaring anger. Have you not known it rise in your heart? Have you been on the receiving end? If that raises ill memories, think of the rants that occasionally crop up on the TV, whether in plays or in the news. Then there is that uncertain image – 'swallowed alive'. People don't swallow people. There are few animals that fit the imagery that swallow their prey whole, but none in the Middle-East, except maybe crocodiles. The local wild animals would have torn their prey prior to consumption and we get to the 'torn into pieces' metaphor down in v. 6. We use the phrase today. Feel with the Psalmist as he recalls the unreasoning hatred of his enemies, their envy, their malevolence. Think of the venom of the Internet trolls. Images of the prey of lions if you are pretentious, or jackals if you are not, flesh out these words. As you slog on with your sights set on Jerusalem, to the left and the right there are the curs, lurking, envious, antagonistic, wanting you to fail, waiting, longing to feast on the fragments of your hopes. And, irrespective of how you feel today, there are all those occasions in your past. But the LORD has defended you. He is on your side. He is on our side. Slog on in the light of deliverances past.

Now look at vv. 4–5, which makes such immediate sense for us today. If the Lord had not been on our side, 'the flood would have engulfed us, the torrent would have swept over us, the raging waters would have swept us away.' Think of the TV news these last weeks, those floods in Cumbria and Lancashire, the Dee, Don and Ythan this week. Two elements are here, the devastation wrought by floods and the raging waters.

Take raging torrents first. Did you see the Ballater caravan being swept down to crash into the bridge? Think of Abergeldie Castle, threatened by the

Dee in spate, thanks to Storm Frank. All those usually reasonably tranquil flows transformed into roiling brown violence. Think flash floods, Boscastle in 2004. Two or three of us here tonight might think of Lynemouth in 1952.

But there can be a different kind of flood. Think of the Japanese tsunami of March 2011. I still have bookmarked on my computer two versions of that disaster. Do you remember the TV pictures? The relatively slow inundation as it deepens and deepens, and gets nearer and nearer. Inexorable. That can be just as frightening. There may be something to think of here. What about living with the prospect of redundancy, waiting for the decisions of others. What about health worries?

That latter thought was prompted by Matthew Henry on Psalm 124, or more possibly a mis-transcription of his words as reported on the Internet. I think there has been a typographic error. You are allowed to laugh. On the Internet version Matthew Henry writes:

> David penned this psalm (we suppose) upon occasion of some great deliverance which God wrought for him and his people from some very threatening danger, which was likely to have involved them all in ruin, whether by foreign invasion, or intestine insurrection, is not certain.

Intestine insurrection? It could be a misprint, but remember how you feel when your health goes wrong. The devil can use a gut infection. There may be slower, longer problems. And yet through it all, the LORD protects – maybe not your job, maybe not your body, but the 'you' he knows so well.

That takes us to vv. 6–7. The Psalmist rejoices: 'Praise be to the LORD, who has not let us be torn by their teeth. We have escaped like a bird from the fowler's snare; the snare has been broken, and we have escaped.' The enemies have been thwarted. That wonderful picture of the bird escaping a broken snare.

Come. Flap your wings, and soar. As the Psalm says in v. 8: 'Our help is in the name of the LORD, the Maker of heaven and earth.'

Let us seek his face as we head towards Jerusalem.

Gilcomston Prayer Meeting, 9 January 2015.

Psalm 126

The fifteen Psalms numbered 120–134 form a distinct group within the Book of Psalms. As others have said these Saturday evenings, they are the 'Songs of Ascent', 'Songs of Degrees'. Much ink has been spilled and a certain amount of thought has been devoted to them. Clearly they were not all written at the same time, or indeed by the same person. Nor were they written for the same purpose within the liturgy of the Temple. Various books and articles try to tease out that end of things. But, however they were used within the Temple ceremonial, it is accepted by most that they also were psalms frequently used by pilgrims as they made their way to Jerusalem for one or other of the great Jewish festivals. The Song of Ascent concentrated the mind as the individual made his or her way to Jerusalem. And tonight, our psalm should help concentrate our minds as we turn to prayer.

It is also accepted that the fifteen Songs of Ascent come in groups of three. Last week John Fraser dealt with the sixth in the chain. Our psalm tonight, Ps. 126, begins a more general set, where a broader view is taken. 'I' is the frequent note in the first four psalms. Pss. 124 and 125 move from a dark view in which the terrors of the past are present, to a still somewhat in-turned view where the poet is entreating against evil. Ps. 126 takes us further.

It has two sections, as the paragraphing in the NIV indicates. The first verses reflect on the Lord's goodness to his people, and the second half on life in the Land.

Commentators link this psalm with the return from Babylon, and that connection is obvious. There may be other events that this psalm can be linked to but tonight we will stay with that major Return. The Lord has 'brought back the captives to Zion' – a clear reference to a Return, and most obviously probably the Return from Babylon. And, when the Lord brought back the captives to Zion, 'we were like men who dreamed.'

What a contrast is represented by v. 1! Have you had the experience where things were pretty awful – and then everything went right, the problem was solved. Things came good. Have you ever become accustomed to living under the cloud of whatever it was, and then almost out of the blue the awfulness was lifted?

Think of the Jews in Babylon. Turn a few pages further on to Ps. 137. I prefer the RSV – and remember also the shimmering choral setting in Walton's *Belshazzar's Feast*.

By the waters of Babylon, there we sat down and wept, when we remembered Zion. On the willows there we hung up our lyres. For there our captors required of us songs, and our tormentors' mirth, saying, 'Sing us one of the songs of Zion'. How shall we sing the Lord's songs in a foreign land?

But they were there seventy years.

There were also some left in Zion, who too suffered through that period. Whether these were people who had actually been left behind, or whether, as the King James Version indicates, some had escaped from Babylon and gone home (Neh. 1: 2) is not entirely clear, but for our purposes this is not really important. There were some in the Land, who had that continuing sorrow, blunted a little as it may have been by time. You can get used to anything. Then Hanani brought some men from Jerusalem to Susa, the capital of Babylon, to a man called Nehemiah, who apparently had no idea how things really were back in Judea. Maybe this visit came as a surprise to Nehemiah. Maybe he had asked for them to come and see him. We don't know. Now Nehemiah was highly placed. A Jew, living reasonably contentedly, though, we must assume, with some pain in not being in his home-land. But things were personally ok for him. He was the cupbearer to the King, a high and important position. This comfortable Nehemiah was appalled at what he heard of life back in Jerusalem. And he prayed, and fasted for some days (Neh. 1: 4–11), and, given the opportunity (which only came some four months later (Neh. 2: 1; cf. Neh. 1: 1)), when invited to he shared his concerns with King Artaxerxes. You know the story after that, but note his diplomacy in waiting.

So who wrote this psalm? Was it someone who went with Hanani to Susa, rejoicing when the captives came home? Might it have been Hanani himself? Or was it someone who came from Babylon to Jerusalem? Could it be Nehemiah? We don't know. Spend some time thinking of it as penned by those different potential authors, for you can get different aspects or nuances out of this psalm depending on who you think wrote it.

Think of Hanani, the man who in a sort of way started it all off, and how he would react to the captives coming home. Think of Nehemiah, troubled and praying, and the swift grant of his request to the King (Neh. 2: 4 and 6). Then think of Nehemiah later seeing those folk return from Babylon.

We do usually think of Nehemiah and the Return. But think now of those others, the returnees named in the genealogies of Nehemiah and Ezra. They were children of the Exile, who had settled down in that foreign land. Like Nehemiah they had been just getting on with their lives, living with the dull pain of not being in their home-land, but accepting that sorrow. Then the news came that they were to go home. Think of their stunned delight. Think of them trekking to their spiritual home. Read v. 1 of our psalm again. 'When the Lord brought back the captives to Zion, we were like those who dreamed.'

God does act like that. Mouths are filled with laughter, and there are shouts of joy. It becomes difficult not to go about with a silly grin on your face.

And the nations see it, and, note, see it accurately. 'The Lord has done great things for them.' (v. 2b). The Lord has done great things for us, and we are filled with joy.' (v. 3). Don't bottle it up. Be glad when the Lord does great things for his people anywhere. Be glad when the Lord does great things for you.

But then there is the other half of the psalm. Some say that it is the writer recognising there still were others back in Babylon who had not yet made it back home. Verse 4 has alternative readings. One is 'Bring back our captives, O Lord, like streams in the Negev' – a fascinating picture of streams of people wending their way through the desert to Jerusalem. It is cinematic, like those pictures you sometimes see of men trekking through a desert, or worse, through the Russian winter. Or perhaps what the poet was thinking of was the way in which the freshets gush when there is rain in the Negev, and the dry wadi suddenly becomes a swirling river. Maybe the prayer is 'send back our remaining exiles like a flood'.

But there is also in the verse a hint of problem, that of water. Others say that in the second half of the psalm the poet is seeing that there is a future that has to be coped with. Water problems, food problems. There is perhaps some disillusionment here. Maybe the joyfulness had gone too far, and this is the poet voicing a very normal let down.

The reality of what the returning exiles came back to is present in these verses. The land had been spoiled and neglected. Irrigation systems had lapsed into disrepair, and fields had not been cultivated. The watercourses needed careful re-building. The fields needed weeding and ploughing. Huge works would be required to bring things back to what a returning people would need for their supplies. And it had to be done.

Or think of Nehemiah, joyful at the start of the Return, and then the difficulties he had in getting things done, not to forget the opposition of Sanballat and Tobiah (Neh. 4). There was the hard grind of keeping the returnees going and keeping them faithful to the necessary tasks indeed, as the books of Nehemiah, Ezra and Haggai show.

Do not too quickly and easily – even facilely – spiritualise the message of this half of the Psalm. Work was needed. A trite evangelical use of v. 6 can mislead. 'He that goes forth weeping, bearing the seed for sowing, shall come home with shouts of joy, bearing his sheaves with him.' V. 5; 'May those who sow in tears reap with shouts of joy'. Many spiritual exhortations have been hung on these words. And we are encouraged to weep and lament. Oh, we are told to go out to spread the word, but it is the weeping that is the attraction for some. The formal traditional phrases lovingly declaimed, are really emptied of their meaning by familiarity. We can enjoy the weeping bit, and think less of the sowing and the ploughing that goes before it. [Vv. 5–6 are set in the second part of the first movement of Brahms German Requiem].

Pay attention to what is being said. It is not the weeping and the tears that produce the harvests. It is the seed, sown in a well-irrigated and well-cultivated field. Yes, there are parallels to be drawn here with the parable of the Sower (Luke 8: 5–15) as well. But remember a prayer for our generation is not more sure of reply if it is couched in a lament and in tears. The weeping and tears of Ps. 126: 4–6 relate to the heavy labour, the shifting of stones, and the ploughing of land that had been neglected for seven decades. The people who were going to have to weed and till, and build and repair canals and irrigation schemes to cope with the spates coming down in the Negev. Remember they had been town-dwellers in Babylon. It was a whole new experience for them – a steep learning-curve, to use a horrible modern expression but one not un-useful in this connection. 'Steep' gets at your legs, doesn't it? The weeping and tears are a by-product of the work, not the work itself. Think, if you had to go out and cultivate a neglected farm to get your food, rather than pop down to the super-market. How many among us would or could wield a spade?

So, as we turn to pray, for our congregation, our parish, our city and nation, for the growth of Christ's church throughout the world, let us remember this psalm. As generation upon generation made their way to Zion with this Song of Ascent on their lips, they remembered what the Lord had done for them, which was so good, and so unexpected that they thought they were dreaming. They also remembered that a lot of solid work was involved, not merely the adoption of some liturgy, a particular form of declaiming words and an ability to weep on demand. We at Gilcomston may have to learn to do things we've not done in the past. We will have a new parish to care for, and in that respect we really are like the town-dwelling exiles of Babylon called now to farm.

But then, as God's work is done, there are the shouts of joy when the harvest comes.

Gilcomston Prayer Meeting, 8 April 2000.

Postscript

The domestic reference at the end of the text is that in 2001 the Gilcomston parish was added to by half the parish, consequent on the closure of Langstane Church, which lay just across Union Street,. Previously the Gilcomston parish was very small, and not a 'normal' parish.

Psalm 129

The fifteen Psalms numbered 120–134 in our version of the Old Testament form a distinct group within the Book of Psalms. They are the 'Songs of Ascent', the 'Songs of Degrees'. Much ink has been spilled and indeed a certain amount of thought has been devoted to them over the centuries. Clearly they were not all written at the same time, nor indeed by the same person. Nor were they written for the same purpose within the liturgy of the Temple. Various books and articles try to tease out that end of things. But, however they were used within the ceremonial of the Temple, most consider that they also were psalms sung by pilgrims as they made their way to Jerusalem for one or other of the great Jewish festivals. The Song of Ascent concentrated the mind as the individual made his or her way to Jerusalem. Thereafter they were used in the ceremonial of the Temple while it was functional. Tonight, our Psalm should help concentrate our minds as we turn to prayer.

Most commentators consider that the fifteen Songs of Ascent come in groups of three. The movement of these is first where we are, and then on towards Zion in number three. Psalm 129 is the first of another triplet.

I was in two minds whether to accept Mike's invitation to tackle tonight's Psalm. My mind was changed when John Fraser was dealing with Ps. 126 three weeks ago. Some may have noticed I don't usually bring a Bible to these meetings, nor do I pick up a church Bible. Instead I use the Metrical Psalms version.

If you look up Ps. 129 in the hymnbook we use you will find Psalms 126 and 129 are printed opposite each other. As I waited for the start of the meeting three weeks ago I naturally looked across from 126 to 129. And something stood out: the contrast between them. Psalm 126 has those that sow in tears reaping in joy (Ps. 126: 5), and returning bringing their sheaves with them (Ps. 126: 6). In Ps. 129: 7 the hand of the reaper is empty, the gleaner has found nothing to gather. That intrigued.

This one is a problem. How do you see it as you read it? Is it an 'I'm all right, Jack?' psalm. Is it a precursor of the parable of the Pharisee and the Tax Collector (Luke 18: 9–14). Is the writer inviting its singers to say –

'You persecuted us. But the Lord has turned all that back. You were wrong. And you are going to get hammered. All your life is to turn to dust and be without reward or lasting result. But see us?? We're the lads. Nya! Nya! Nya!' Such an attitude can go worse than that. In Iran if you oppose the government you may be damned as fighting against God. Some theological discussion I have read can get close to that. Not to come up to date, some of Luther is extraordinary.

Before Christmas there was an article in (I think, *The Times*) by Dominic Lawson, the journalist, son of Nigel, the Chancellor of the Exchequer and brother of Nigella. Lawson, a practising Jew, referred to a problem which Jews have at Christmas. Judaism, in its various manifestations, is not an evangelical or proselytising religion. Christianity is. For him Christianity is pushy.

It is true that Judaism does not seek converts. Indeed it makes it difficult to become a member of the Jewish religion – you cannot become a Jew. You can be a convert but normally conversion is discouraged. What a departure that is from the idea that the Jews would show forth the Glory of God for the conversion of the Gentiles! But that could be consonant with a 'nya nya nya: we're nae like you' interpretation of the Psalm.

That I cannot accept. This Psalm has more to teach us than contempt for those who do not share our views. And, that is why I will not attempt to relate this Psalm to current events. What this Psalm does teach is to be clear-sighted. To tell it like it is.

What of the context or relevance of the Psalm? Both Calvin and Augustine relate it directly to the Church, but we should go further back. The first half of the psalm speaks of Israel being oppressed, but the oppressors have not gained victory. Ploughmen have ploughed Israel's back, but the Lord has cut Israel free.

One possible context must be the return from the Exile. Israel has been kicked around, but God has ripped up the chains that had been put on them. Cyrus sent the Jews back to rebuild the Temple. And what happens? Those who hated Israel get to work. The local high-and-mighty try to stop the rebuilding of Jerusalem. They complain to Artaxerxes himself, and the work is indeed stopped (Ezra 4). But then the Jews appeal to Darius, and the work is restarted. Indeed Tattenai, the governor of Trans-Euphrates is ordered to help. Ezra comes from Babylon on the instruction of another Artaxerxes, and comes with authority to set up a civil administration in Jerusalem (Ezra

7). But things stall. Nehemiah is sent to be governor. Rebuilding starts again, including the wall. And Sanballat, Tobias and the others, the local high-and-mighty, try to stop it. That was opposition from outside. But note in Neh. 6: 14 Nehemiah calls on God to remember not only Sanballat and Tobias for their actions, but also the prophetess Nodiah and 'the rest of the prophets who have been trying to intimidate me'. Foes of the spiritual Israel can come from within it.

Let's look at another, a later instance. Consider the Gospels. Christ is born to a couple who were of David's line. Jesus grows, traditionally the apparent son of a carpenter. But when his ministry begins, he is opposed by the institutional church. Opposed? He is got rid of. His execution is choreographed by the leaders of Israel – another set of the high and mighty.

That takes us to the second half of the Psalm. What is all this about grass on the housetops? We can see clearly enough the tenor of v. 5, a prayer that they who hate Israel be turned back in shame. But grass?? This is the contrast with Psalm 126. There the reaper returns with songs of joy carrying his sheaves (Ps. 126: 6). Here in Ps. 129 there is no crop. Housetops were flat, or nearly so. The place the seed lands would be warm, but water would be intermittent and the soil shallow. The result? Immediate sprouting, then a swift withering. It's the parable of the seed and the sower with the seed falling on stony ground (Mark 4: 3–20). The reaper cannot fill his hands nor the gatherer fill his arms from this grass. There is nothing to harvest: nothing to be proud of.

Those who oppose. The high, the mighty, as they thought themselves, are left high and dry, without anything to show for their lives. They are gone swiftly. We know of Sanballat, Tobias, Noadiah and her acolytes who opposed Nehemiah (Neh. 6: 14), Annas, Caiaphas. But we know of them not because of their fame, their distinction, but because of their opposition to Israel and ultimately to Jesus. Opposition that failed, but so much of it coming from 'religious' folk. Recall Jesus being criticised for healing on the Sabbath (Luke 13: 10–17). This the area of Matt. 7: 21–23, regarding knowing a tree by its fruit, which ends with Jesus sending away those who had claimed to prophesy and work marvels in his name. 'I never knew you. Away from me, you evildoers' (Matt. 7: 23).

What of the end of the Psalm? It puzzled me. What is the author thinking of? How does it link with the earlier verses? Augustine clarified it for me. Customarily when you were passing a neighbour who was working his field you would greet him. 'The blessing of the Lord be upon you'. But when you pass by those who are high-and-mighty but who are not doing the work of the Lord, when you pass by those who are not tending or harvesting the crop of the Lord, but rather are snooty, exalted, making on how hard they are working for him but who are not in fact doing his work, you will not congratulate them. See them as they are, and behave accordingly. You don't attack them. You don't despise them to exalt yourself. Remember that Matt: 7 from which I just quoted begins with a warning against judging others. But Matt. 7 does go on to the passages about thorn-bushes not producing grapes, and thistles not producing figs. There is a difference between judgement and recognition / discernment. We must be careful in how we react. Where there are questions, you cannot have a free and easy relationship. Remember also there is the realm of the parable of the wheat and the tares, when the angels of the Lord come and sift the field, casting the tares into the fire. We are at Matt. 13: 24–30, and with Christ's explanation of it at vv. 36–43. We don't head in and pull up the weeds ourselves – leave that to God. But while perhaps sometimes tares need to be told they are tares, at least we should not pretend they are wheat.

So as we come to prayer, let us be clear-sighted. Let us be sensitive to reality. Let God show us what to pray for, and what to pray against.

Gilcomston Prayer Meeting, 16 January 2010.

Psalm 133

This psalm is a real Tardis. It looks small, but once you open its door and step inside it is so much bigger than it looks. Its sentiments are so beguiling! A thanksgiving for concord among the brethren. An exhortation to keep it going. 'Behold, how good and how pleasant is it, that brethren should dwell together in unity' – to use a different translation of v. 1. Is that all? This capsule of truth is difficult to crack open. Once you cut into it, this diamond has many facets. I begin with helpful history.

In his commentary Augustine says (para 5) that v. 1 is the basis of the word 'monk', stemming from 'monos' – one. Apparently in the Greek that is the last word of v. 1. Put v.1 together with Acts 4: 32 – 'the brethren were of one heart and mind and had all things in common' – and you get the monastic life. Simple living, together, at one, in harmony. Life stripped down to its essentials in order to worship and serve God. In Augustine's time there were many monasteries, often small – 3 to 6 members was usual. The Desert Fathers, living up the Nile valley from the mid-second century on, were famous.[18] But how should such a group run its affairs, particularly if it is large? About 400 AD Augustine wrote a Rule, a model for how monastic life should be organised. He wasn't the first. Others set out their ideas. Through the witness of living together in unity, the later monastic Orders helped spread the Gospel. We don't know the detail of the Christianisation of Aberdeen, but we can be sure they nourished our city. We have the same task. Black Friars, Grey Friars and the Carmelites show up in our street names down beside the railway station. What about the White Friars? Aberdeen did not escape them. The White Friars are the just mentioned Carmelites. Respectively they followed – and still follow – the Rules of St Dominic (Black Friars/Cistercians), of St Francis (Grey Friars) and of St Albert (White Friars/ Carmelites). The Rule of St Albert is short, and worth a look. It is in Wikipedia. All the Rules are more evangelical than you probably expect.

---

18 *The Lives of the Desert Fathers: The Historia Monachorum in Aegypto*, trans. N. Russell trans., Intro. B. Ward, (London: Mobray, 1981).

Yes, there came to be much corruption and falling away from high ideals. The gluttonous, libidinous monk did become a figure of fun, and contempt. Remember Carl Orff's *Carmina Burana*? Notwithstanding, we should recognise that the monastic impulse was (and for some still is) the desire to live life in harmony with others – an application of v. 1. Let's not knock the purity of intention of many who over the centuries sought to implement it. But in his commentary on this Psalm Augustine does also write of 'false monks' and false men among the clergy and the faithful even in his time. That has modern resonances. I can think of some, as 'orthodox' as one would wish, but who are duplicitous, manipulative and self-seeking. Some are after acolytes. Others look for control, influence, power, fame or money or any combination thereof. Their commitment to 'unity' is self-serving. Of course you can see that not just in religion but also in politics or day-to-day relations. I have seen it in academe.

But to stick with religion, I have found dissecting this Psalm difficult. Today we view so many differentiations. There can be such hostility, overt, more often disguised, smiles and handshakes followed by off-screen disparagement. In a congregation there can be snide remarks, avoidance, cutting dead. History has seen wars and persecutions based on religious difference. Not just Roman Catholic versus Protestant, but also among Protestants – see the Switzerland of the early Sixteenth century, though nationalism and ordinary politics were well into the mix as well. A bit later there is Westminster Confession Chapter 25.6 (1646) and its condemnation of Roman Catholicism, with the Pope identified as Anti-Christ. That reflects its time rather than theological truth. In contrast consider modern Catholicism. Some time ago I circulated to the eldership a link to Pope Francis's *Evangelium Gaudi* – the Joy of the Gospel (2013) – as of interest. None have commented. Given what he says at the end of *The Work of the Pastor* (Christian Focus, Fearn, 2013) William Still would have been intrigued by the *Evangelium Gaudi*. And would you believe that in his commentary on this psalm John Calvin says there will be a duty to welcome the Papists should they return to the Lord.

That said, we face the modern scene. It is not reassuring. Some of you know that I have a book coming out shortly on church and state in Scotland. To get it done I have read through a fair amount of material on church history, including many court cases. They do not sit well with this psalm. Nor does recent history at Gilcomston.

'Behold, how good and how pleasant is it, that brethren should dwell together in unity.'

When did David write these words? Is it just a 'blessed thought'? Matthew Henry points out that David had many children. Was it written for their instruction? David's home life had its problems. Was it a plea amidst family turmoil? Handsome son Absalom murdered Amnon his half-brother, David's eldest son. Absalom hated Amnon because he had raped Tamar, Absalom's favourite sister. The story is in II Sam. 13. Did that trigger a desperate prayer to God that David's sons, the brethren, would live together in harmony? Later we have Absalom's return to Jerusalem. Then II Sam. 14–15 tells of his undermining of his father's authority and his final rebellion. Might that fit with our psalm? Or is the psalm David's grateful response to tranquillity after a period of problems among the general population? Does it express gratitude for peace?

But I need to go further. Let me take this in two ways. First, I note that throughout the centuries Christians have had problems in getting along. The monastic orders quarrelled. The Devil aggravates difference whenever he can. Offence taken and over-reaction can start pernicious cancers. Pride and jealousy, envy and rivalry are potent ingredients, chilli-like in their effects. Remember Paul writing of those preaching Christ out of selfish ambition, envy and rivalry and trying to cause trouble for him (Phil. 1:15, 17). Recall his reference to selfish ambition and vain conceit in Phil. 2: 3, and to division, smooth talk and flattery in Rom. 16: 17–18. Again, think of Phil. 4: 2–3, where Paul entreats Euodia and Syntche to be of one mind. What caused that spat? What had got into those two wifies, they who, contending for the gospel had stood as Paul's co-workers? We don't know. What was the point at issue? Was it just a clash of personalities? Personalities can be toxic. So remember Psalm 133: 1.

Second, note the language. What I am going to say depends on linguistics, and I don't know Hebrew, but, comparing various translations, the last word of v. 1 is 'unity'. It is not 'uniformity'. To me that implies the richness of polyphony, Tallis, Monteverdi, Bach. 'Concert' means playing together, but the members of a symphony orchestra do not all play the same note. Instruments have different timbres, and in a concert each has its own contribution to make. A character in an old SF novel said, 'we can't all be first violin-ers: someone has to push the wind through the trombone.' Or to stay with the music metaphor, some sing a descant. There needs to be tolerance and room for difference while all are devoted to the same end. There should be no pressure to conform in inessentials. But it doesn't always work like that. Some of us still carry a touch of leprosy as a result of being inadequately enthusiastic in leaving the Church of Scotland. And of course there have been later events.

Uniformity raises the question of limits. But where do limits lie? So often opinion divides, and the Gospel is made unattractive. See how these Christians love one another: see how Christians can't get along. Church planting is one thing. Splits – setting up on your own – are something else. One group thinks something absolutely essential. Others do not. Sometimes it is really a matter of culture rather than fundamental difference – church government. What is essential? When can we not dwell together in unity? When should we not live as one together? When should we form separate groups? There are many potential points of disunity, of separation. Having previously mentioned Paul's entreating of those Philippian women, I must also note, with emphasis added, his earlier written words to the Romans: '*If it is possible*, as far as it depends on you, live at peace with everybody' (Rom. 12: 18).

Dissension has damaged the cause of Christ. Recently re-reading *The Pilgrim's Regress* I found C.S. Lewis quoting George Bernard Shaw in the Introduction to Book 3. Shaw wrote: 'The more ignorant men are, the more convinced are they that their little parish and their little chapel is the apex to which civilisation and philosophy has painfully struggled up.' Tenacity is remarkable, and praiseworthy when well founded. But court and other reports contain many examples of small mindedness, personality clashes, jealousies and rivalries, usually masked as a 'stand on principle'. II Cor. 6: 17 – 'come out from among them and be separate' – can be seductive. But actually it is just an instruction not to be unequally yoked with unbelievers and to flee from idolatry. It is not an encouragement to break the unity of the brethren and set up your own shop to pander to your own predilections and presuppositions. Peter and the others were wrong to eat separately from the Gentile brethren (Gal. 2: 12–13). And then look at history after secessions. The awful thing is that so often splitters and schismatics later spend so much time and energy justifying their stance rather than getting on with spreading the Gospel – wee groupies hugging together to keep warm. They're like the Dwarfs at the end of Lewis' *The Last Battle* (except Poggin).

Yet this is one of the last of the Psalms of Ascent. Its facets are proof that Scripture can have many applications. So in closing think of those, united in pilgrimage, singing this Psalm as they slog through the final miles. Think of those friars, working together, as we should, to spread the Word even in Aberdeen. This Psalm encourages. Verse 3b leaves the promise that where there is unity among the brethren God does bless. Unity is a precious oil. Unity is as dew on thirsty ground. We need that lesson. But be careful of this Psalm. Yes, it is a consolation. It is also a warning.

Gilcomston Prayer Meeting, 12 March 2016.

Psalm 134

Praise the LORD, all you servants of the LORD who minister by night in the house of the LORD. Lift up your hands in the sanctuary and praise the LORD. May the LORD bless you from Zion, he who is the Maker of heaven and earth. (NIV).

Behold, bless ye the LORD, all ye servants of the LORD, which by night stand in the house of the LORD. Lift up your hands in the sanctuary, and bless the LORD. The LORD that made heaven and earth bless thee out of Zion. (KJV).

Ps.134 is the last of the 'Psalms of Ascent', or the 'Psalms of Degrees'. They have occupied us for fifteen Saturday evenings. It can help to think of them as chronicling progress on the way to one of the feasts in Jerusalem. The travellers begin a fair distance away, and then close in on the Holy City, singing or chanting these Psalms as they go.

This one is different. Matthew Henry and others suggest that the pilgrims have got there. He thought the time to sing this song as being when, having done your duty, you left the Temple buildings. I could go along with that. Spurgeon goes further. For him the pilgrims are leaving Jerusalem. They are going home, departing very early in the morning so as to get the best of the daylight for their journey. As they go they see lights in the temple area, so they commend those who serve the Temple, particularly those doing the night watch.

If you think of the original use of the Psalm in that way you can split it up between different voices. The first part, vv. 1–2, would be the pilgrims, and v. 3 the response of the priests. Indeed, Calvin says precisely that. For him v. 3 is definitely by the priests. He points out that 'the LORD bless you from Zion, he who is the Maker of heaven and earth' (NIV), or 'The LORD that made heaven and earth bless thee out of Zion' (KJV), was a standard form of priestly blessing.

Maybe Spurgeon takes things too far. But whatever you think about the use of the Psalm when there was a Temple, the fact is that it remains part of Jewish liturgy. Jews recite it before starting to study the Torah, and vv. 1–2 are part of the penitential prayers before major festivals. In Catholicism and Anglicanism it forms part of Compline, the service at the end of the working day. Presbyterians use it. In short it has benefitted the church down through the ages.

The point is that the Temple always had priests and Levites on watch. 'Praise the LORD, all you … who minister by night in the house of the LORD…' Yes, others might stay overnight in the Temple. Remember the aged Anna of Luke 2: 36–38, so overjoyed when Mary and Joseph brought Jesus to the Temple. She 'never left the temple, but worshipped night and day, fasting and praying'. But there were also priests and Levites whose duty was to staff the Temple at night, and to praise the Lord while doing so.

From here we can take two routes that share a common focus. The focus is the personnel, the priests and Levites engaged in the service of the Lord. In modern terms we can think of them as those called into a particular ministry of whatever kind. These are those who: 'who minister by night in the house of the LORD'. They 'lift up [their] hands in the sanctuary and praise the LORD'.

Route 1 is benign. We know so many ministers and others who are full-time missionaries. Tonight surely we will pray for those.

Route 2 is not so simple. When we began I read to you two versions of the psalm. The language is similar, but did you notice the difference? The KJV began 'Behold'. So does our Psalter, and the texts used by Augustine and Calvin. This makes 'behold' a clarion, a wake-up call. What's my point? The point is that this psalm could be a pointed exhortation to the night shift to do their job properly.

Calvin says that the priests and Levites are being reminded what their duties fundamentally are and mean. There is a tendency, common to all who perform ceremonies repetitively, just to go through the motions. The watchers are warned not to succumb to it. Yes, it could be a chore to be in the Temple at night when others are in their beds, but praising God and keeping watch are duties, valueless unless done with true devotion. Standing idly, or passing the time chatting or gossiping, would be to fail properly to worship God – which is what they were there for. Bring that forward. And do remember that there is a Devil running interference, to borrow a term from American football.

All religions offer opportunities for those who claim to stand between believers and a deity, whatever they call themselves. Run alphabetically the gamut of religions from Shinto-ism to Scientology – clericalism has many facets. What of Christianity? Do ministers and others do their duty? History is not reassuring. Today some get submerged in social work. Even the most thoroughly orthodox may in practice be self-serving – prestige, a quiet life, an indoor job with no heavy lifting – you name it. This very weekend the Pope is presiding over a conference on child abuse by priests. There are Gehazis (2 Kings 5: 20–27). Religious-based relief organisations with 'charitable status' provide large salaries for those who run them. I have cited *Elmer Gantry* (1926) here before now. Sinclair Lewis' novel is within ten years of its centenary: it could have been written today. See how often the TV evangelists tout for funds. Look at the dynastic theological empires, with TV programmes, some with universities, and some now embroiled with Donald Trump. There are the peddlers of the 'Prosperity Gospel'. There is commerciality. There is the evangelical/ fundamentalist circuit, analogous to the Pop festivals. Read *Crazy for God*, (New York, Carroll & Graf, 2007), the autobiography of Frank Schaeffer, son of Francis Schaeffer, the founder of L'Abri. There are the itinerants, moving from campaign to campaign, conference to conference, and making their living on it. They preach, but do not minister. Did you see the appeal by a 'minister of God' for $300 million, so that he could upgrade the plane that flies him round the world evangelising?

Some weeks ago Esther prayed cogently along that line. Yes, we should pray for those we know who devotedly do their duty. We should also pray for, and sometimes against, those who do not. There are those who, at ordination or commissioning, affirm beliefs which they do not, or do not now, hold. Yet they take their comforts and their money.

So, what does this psalm teach? It teaches us to pray for those whose duty it is to minister. But there is something else. The psalm is not necessarily directed to prayer for the abstract or for named others elsewhere. We are all priests. Peter wrote: '…You also, as living stones, are being built up a spiritual house, a holy priesthood, to offer up spiritual sacrifices acceptable to God through Jesus Christ' (1 Pet. 2: 5). And a couple of verses later: 'you are a chosen generation, a royal priesthood, a holy nation, His own special people, that you may proclaim the praises of Him who called you out of darkness into His marvellous light …' (1 Pet. 2: 9). Look across the room. We must pray for each other too. So let us do our duty. Let us pray, wherever that may take us.

Gilcomston Prayer Meeting, 23 February 2019.

Psalm 135

Psalm 135 is a jigsaw or a mosaic. Scholars use the terms when analysing it. They point out that it quotes bits of earlier scripture, and that later writers re-use chunks from it. We need not pursue that, interesting though it be. But, so what? We all do that. Between our ears we carry around this verse and that, this story and that, and the Lord brings them back to mind when we need them – sometimes when we'd rather not be reminded. Suffice it to note the point. A jigsaw. My great aunt Daisy up in Macduff loved jigsaws. She was so good at them that she sometimes did them picture side down, and get it right. A mosaic. Fifty years ago I was allowed to visit the Mosaic Workshop in the Vatican Gardens. They were making one of Leonardo da Vinci's 'Virgin/Madonna of the Rocks' for a US cathedral, and showed me the tiny pieces being used. Amazing.

So, a jigsaw, a mosaic, a collection of pieces that together make a whole. But why was our psalm written; who put it together; what is the 'whole' of this psalm? As to why, we do not know. Some say it was written for the inauguration of the Temple. Others that it was for a later event, perhaps something after the Return. But what is the 'whole' is easy. The psalm is purely and simply a call to praise. See its start and finish, vv. 1 and 21b. 'Praise the Lord' – 'Hallelu Yah'. That's difficult if you are going through the mill, but there it is in scripture.

Who put it together? We do not know. Certainly someone supremely confident in his faith. Verse 5 startles. 'For I know that the LORD is great.' That is so personal. Does the author of any other psalm confront you so directly with such assurance? Yes, there are similar statements in scripture – Job springs to mind – the 'I know that my Redeemer lives' passage (Job 19: 25–27). But this is a bit different. 'I know that the LORD is great.' 'I' and 'know', emphasised. Personal and challenging. Can we say that? Doubtless each would say 'yes'. But how do we mean it? Do we assert it, or do we merely accede to it as a statement of doctrine? We need to know the LORD as great in our own lives, whatever he brings to us. That's what our author is saying. **'I know'**. Not: 'This is an accceptable proposition'. Personal knowledge. Knowledge, not conviction. Such strength must be grounded in experience. Could it be David? Is it you?

Our author calls the servants of the LORD to praise the LORD. First, those with a specific ministry, those serving in the Temple and its courts (vv. 1–2). Beyond them the psalmist calls on the Israelites and in particular those of the house of Aaron and Levi to praise (v. 19). What has that to do with us? Well, the fact of the matter is that here we bump into the mind of a Jew of three thousand plus years ago. He identifies those that he knew the LORD had chosen – Jacob to be his own, Israel to be his treasured possession (v. 4). He calls them to praise the Lord, and spells out the great things the Lord had done for his people (vv. 8–10). I would not try to get around the fact that our author was immediately speaking of an ethnicity. It was others after him that came to see that the love of the Lord was not confined to one particular genetic constituency (Isa. 42: 6; 49: 6). And we know that more exactly. Jump to the New Testament and we have Paul's commission to bring Christ to the Gentiles (Acts 9: 15; 22: 21; Eph. 3: 8). As a result we know that our LORD is our saviour; we too are part of his people, chosen before the world began (Eph.1: 4). So we can apply this psalm to ourselves. That makes it such a comfort. Verse 14 promises: 'the LORD will vindicate his people and have compassion on his servants'. Our gathering tonight is testimony to that. It also underscores the accuracy of the immediately preceding verse: 'Your name, LORD, endures forever, your renown, LORD, through all generations'. How many generations lie between our author and us?

We praise for many reasons. Nature. The LORD is powerful: clouds rise from the ends of the earth; lightning comes with the rain; the wind blasts from his storehouses (v. 7). Aberdeenshire has recent experience – mild compared with the tornadoes that subsequently ravaged Kentucky and elsewhere. What of floods in Brazil, India and the Philippines? In short, climate change. History. The LORD's power can be seen in history (vv. 8–10). The psalmist cites the plagues, the signs that Pharaoh disregarded, the death of the Egyptian firstborn, both human and animal (vv. 8–9; Exod. 7–12). He notes the fate of Sihon of the Amorites, Og of Bashan and the kings of Canaan as the LORD brought the Jews into the Promised Land (v.10). All that was remarkable, if, of course, rather removed from us. Temporal distance can be an obstacle. Why mull over such remote events? How are they relevant to us? Well, it was through those events that centuries later Jesus was to be born in Bethlehem. But the point of history is that it is in the past. So take things forward. Each of us can look back and see the Lord at work in our own separate pasts. More generally, what about the two major wars of the last century, either of which could have seriously amended our personal histories – at the extreme, perhaps some of us would not have been born.

The LORD is great (v. 5). There are no other contenders. Some man-made silver and gold idols are lovely, sometimes they can be imposing – Japan comes to mind – but they are mute, blind, deaf, inert (vv. 15–17). But the psalm's call to praise is not based on God's overwhelming power, whether shown in nature or in history. We are not terrified into submission, praising because of threat. The psalmist nails it in v. 3a. 'Praise the LORD, for the LORD is good.' Our God is good. Supremely, for us, through Christ the Son he has taken us for and to himself, and included us among his chosen, his treasured possession (v. 4). What more do we need to know?

So as our author says, let us praise.

Gilcomston Prayer Meeting, 15 January 2022.

Psalm 137

This is a famous Psalm, well known not just to those who know their Bible. Obviously it was written at some time after the Jews were transported from Jerusalem to Babylon about 586 BC. It has been a subject for many painters – though I cannot give you a list – the biblical scenes of the Italian masters tend to blur. It has stimulated many authors, for some reason particularly after the Renaissance – though interestingly, particularly after the Renaissance rather than after the Reformation. Versions and references to it appear in Shakespeare, Spenser, Milton and others. [See Hannibal Hamlin, 'Psalm Cultures in the English Renaissance: Readings of Ps. 137 by Shakespeare, Spenser, Milton and Others' (2002) 55 *Renaissance Quart.* 224–257]. It has inspired composers. Bits of it appear in the musical *Godspell* (1971), and burrowing about on that line it seems also that the group 'Boney M' set it as a single in the 1970s when it became a major hit, Number 1 in the UK, and popular in both Europe and the US. Sacheverell Sitwell used it in his libretto for Walton's magnificent *Belshazzar's Feast* (1931). Part of the Psalm is the second section of that oratorio, and is set to exquisite music. It's tempting to try to sing it: 'By the riiiiiveeeers of Babylon'. So this is Psalm has inspired all sorts of folk. And it has layers.

The Psalm states why it is written. It is both a lament and an affirmation. Judging from verses 5 and 6 it was written by one individual. He – it would be a male in those days – puts the matter so starkly. He is a musician. He plays a stringed instrument and is a singer. So vv. 5 and 6 are very strong. If he forgets Jerusalem may his right hand forget its skill (NIV) ('forget' is replaced by 'wither' in the New American Version (NAV)). Did he play the lyre? If he does not remember Jerusalem, may his tongue cling to the roof of his mouth (NIV) or stick to his palate (NAV). A musician / singer asks to lose his treasured skills if he forgets where he came from – where his true home is.

What produced such feelings? The People are far from Zion. They have been taken from Palestine. They are in exile in Babylon. Camped beside its rivers – Tigris and Euphrates – we know not which – they hung their harps on the poplars along the water's edge. They are desolate – uprooted, aliens, captives in a foreign land. And along come their captors to ask for a few tunes – a concert perhaps, or maybe just a sing-song to pass the early hours of the night round a fire. 'Sing us one of the songs of Zion' (v. 3). In various versions it is a request for a joyful song – a song of mirth: 'sing us one of those cheerful songs we've heard you can sing'.

How could skilled songsters and harpists comply with that?

The first thing to say is that we do not know whether they did sing or not. Maybe this Psalm is evidence that they did sing – after all the singer/composer survived, and the Babylonians could be fairly drastic towards those who disobeyed commands. Perhaps, ahead of Jeremiah, they understood why they had been brought into captivity. That, as Jeremiah was to say, they should settle down and make the best of it for a while – 'serve the King of Babylon and live' (Jer. 27: 17). After all there had been all those warnings in the Old Testament, which the Jews had not heeded. They were sent into captivity because they had forgotten or ignored their God. It was good that they mourned being taken from the Land. Perhaps they did sing a song of Zion for the Babylonians. But the great thing about it was that the singing drove home to them that they had been disciplined by God. They were aliens. They were remote from the Temple – territorially the centre of their faith.

Even so, what about that ending? Verse 7 – Remember, Lord, the Edomites, standing to one side and letting the Jews be conquered and plundered – maybe indeed coming in to scavenge. This is Obadiah territory where we were in the evening service some weeks ago. Edom was always hostile to the Jews. Let the Lord take care of them.

The main bitterness is directed towards the Babylonians. The daughter of Babylon, doomed to destruction (v. 8). Happy is he who repays you for what you have done to us (v. 8). Fair enough, one might think in the abstract. But then there is the last verse – bairns dashed to death (v. 9). That gives us moderns the shudders. Yet there are so many other passages that speak of the Lord hammering those that take up arms against his people – even when the Lord has raised them up to punish the People (cf. Jer. 50–51).

We don't know exactly when this psalm was composed. Certainly there is a strong probability that it was composed in Babylonia – the last verses indicate immediacy rather than a looking back. But a slight query that rises in my mind as I read it. There is a territorial emphasis, but there seems no recognition that the loss of territory may have been due to formalism –

being more interested in Zion than in the God of Zion. After all we have evidence in Ezra and Haggai that once the Jews were back in their beloved Land, there was no hurry actually to rebuild the House of the Lord. From Malachi we can see how the priests had effectively turned from God, while continuing the form of the sacrifices. But I dare say I can be corrected on that thought.

What does come through from this exquisite Psalm, however, is that haunting feeling that you are not where you're really at home. We can learn from that layer of the Psalm. Here, in this world, ultimately, we are aliens. Our true home is with Jesus in heaven. In this life we are strangers and pilgrims, as Hebrews puts it (Heb. 11:10; 12: 22; 13: 14). Peter, the non-Roman, uses that imagery as well, speaking of being an alien here (I Pet. 1: 1). We today are also asked to sing the songs of Zion. Some do it very well. Think of the wonderful Church music of the ages. But it is astonishing how many of the composers of the most beautiful settings of Christian thought are agnostic – Gabriel Fauré, Vaughan Williams or John Rutter for example. Maybe deep down they know more than they know. It is also astonishing how many contemporary 'Christian' composers produce such second rate stuff – but that's another story.

So here we are, by the waters of Dee and Don, in the Aberdeen Babylon. Go back to the Psalmist. He would lose his skills before he forgets Jerusalem (v. 5). He will forget how to play, how to sing, if he fails to remember Jerusalem – if Jerusalem is not his highest joy (v. 6). Well, we can too sing songs of Zion in a foreign land. We can sing songs that witness to Christ, our Lord. And broaden it out. We sing in song, in speech and in our conduct, how we behave among our neighbours.

But one last note, in fact many of the Jews in exile grew cold. They just got on with life in Babylon. Some did forget, and were assimilated into Babylonian society and its ways. In Ezra 3 there is the list of those that returned many years later. It is fairly short list – some 50,000. Others returned, but had become formal and detached – those castigated in Ezra, Haggai and Malachi. But true believers like the Psalmist did not forget the real Zion. Neither should we.

Gilcomston Prayer Meeting, 31 March 2007.

Psalm 141

Some may remember that, during the vacancy, in the way that these things turn out, about every six to eight weeks I had to deal with what I came to call 'the screaming Psalms'. There David was crying to God: why was God silent? David's enemies were on the rampage, and he was in anguish. David was also savage in those psalms. His oppressors, those who defied God and wanted to trap David and sharpen their teeth on his bones, were to be destroyed – unpleasantly.

Those Psalms could be a worry. They are dreadful things to find in the Word of God. Spoken by one of God's major figures in history, they contain squeals of anguish directed at God – not behaviour that we would consider as permissible. Further, was it not uncharitable – unchristian even – for someone to wish such awful and detailed fates upon fellow human beings? Yet we found these Psalms beneficial. Although a modern editor might well not have allowed them to go into print, they are part of Scripture, and were and are part of the liturgies of the Jewish and Christian faiths.

Now? See what we have got. Somewhat different, isn't it? But I need to make three other points before we go through it.

First. The translation is difficult. If you look at different Bible versions you will find significant differences – almost to the extent you'd think you were reading a different Psalm. That's because the original Hebrew is uncertain in places. Different translations take different views as to what the actual original text is. This is notably true in v. 7. Some think the bones are the bones of those who sympathise with the Psalmist. Others that they are the bones of the 'rulers' who are to be thrown down. It is interesting to look at those different versions. But tonight we'll look at the NIV as was read.

Second, despite the heading in the NIV, the scholars say that it is not clear whether this is a psalm of David's. Some argue that it comes later in Jewish history, written by someone under pressure then. That is possible. For our purposes it makes little difference.

Third, if Psalm 141 is a Davidic psalm, I would not argue that it comes later than the screaming Psalms. You might think that it's overall tone is such an improvement on the screaming psalms that it must have been written at a stage by which David had matured and risen above the anguished lashing out. I have too much respect for what in *The Screwtape Letters* C.S. Lewis called the Principle of Undulation to argue that there is a development to be seen. We do come and go. We have all know people whom age and infirmity have affected in their reactions to adversities. I know what the effect of a minor gut infection can be on my outlook on things.

But wee what this Psalm says – and those with memories of the screaming psalms, see the difference between it and psalms written by someone whose portrait in Edvard Munch's *The Scream*.

First, this is a very personal psalm. This is someone talking with God conversationally. It is by someone who is comfortable doing that. Verses 1–2 are not rhetoric by the writer. Now, yes, it is possible for us to acquire a style, a comfortable wordiness that can be repeated without much thought – almost as jargon, as we 'say our prayers'. But see this man, coming close to the Lord (vv. 1 and 3), to the Sovereign Lord (v. 8), talking seriously, and making contact with a friend – with Him. This is not a routine. It is a conversation, albeit that we only hear one end of the exchange. He is not in a sacred place, the Temple, but asks that his prayer be like incense, and his uplifted hands like the evening sacrifice. He does not need those symbols of the temple worship. He had confidence that he can come close to his God by prayer alone. I was going to say that that is something we should aspire to – but that would be wrong. This is not a target to be attained. It is a by-product of living close to God. And as we live like that, so we can pray like this man.

But to live like that you have to live pure. The Psalmist is conscious of the dangers that surround him. Verse 3 and 4 indicate that he was among temptations. He seems to have a role that exposes him through having to inter-act with evil-doers, those who want him to take part in their schemes and take part in their feasts. He asks God to protect him.

He also asks that others will help. Telling him when he is going off the rails. I was amused when I got my hands on the current `record. You see, Mike asked me if I would take a prayer meeting after the one a fortnight ago. I said that August might be ok, but went home, read Ps. 141, and thought I'd like to tackle it. This section, about being helped by others, stuck in my mind. So on the Sunday morning I told Mike that I would be prepared to do tonight. Then that afternoon I read the Record, with the chink about being advised as to unrecognised worms and viruses. Good modern imagery!

Four points here. First, over the years I have been helped by the odd rebuke and correction. Of course, if you are living close to God you should be alerts to your own flaws, but there are times when we may need someone else to put a finger on them.

Second, I know exactly what the Psalmist means when he says in v. 6 that his head will not refuse the rebuke. Note – it is his head not his heart that will not refuse the rebuke. It's a matter of will, not emotion. It can hurt, and on the emotional level it can take some getting over.

Third, it is the Psalmist who is rebuked. The correction is not broadcast or gossiped. The problem is not identified to others first, or afterwards.

The last point is that the rebuke spoken of comes from a righteous man. It is easy to see flaws in others. The Devil will help us see them. But we need to be very sure that it is God who tells us when and how to be the answer to someone who is praying like this Psalmist. There are two dangers here, equal and opposite. One is to see nothing but good, and fatuously to praise the deficient. None of us is fully sanctified, nor will we be until heaven. The other is that seeing a fault or flaw makes us the righteous that is spoken of. My seeing a fault or flaw in someone does not prove that I am righteous. There is the parable of the mote or speck of sawdust in another's eye, and the beam or plank in your own (Matt. 7: 3–5; Luke 6: 41–42). The righteous the Psalmist is taking about will be sensitive and careful how he speaks. Too often we can damage by thoughtlessly barging in. Seeing a fault does not impose a duty to expose it. I recall reading a letter received by Mr Still. He was not sure how to respond to it, and asked me to read it. It ended: 'faithful are the wounds of a Christian friend'. The letter was accurate – as Mr Still acknowledged. It was also venomous. There are two kinds of 'righteous' men. One kind can be a devil incarnate.

But there are other kinds of evil-doers, and the Psalmist goes on to these in v. 7. The Psalmist has warned, and been ignored. He therefore prays for the overturning of evil. Here he shows signs of 'screaming', and we do not know what might lie behind it. The rulers should be thrown from cliffs. How does that square with vv. 3–4: 'set a watch on my lips …'. Given the rest of the psalm I think we can take it that this is triggered by some massive evil and opposition to God. The Psalmist prays that the schemers will fall into their own snares and traps, so there is something going on (vv. 9–10). Haman comes to mind, hanged on his own gallows (Esth. 9: 25). But the Psalmist's eyes are fixed on God. He takes refuge in the Sovereign Lord (v.

8). Yes, he prays for his safety among all the traps and snares that are set for him – he does not think that it is wrong to pray this – and that is good for us. We are Christians, not Stoics.

But what does that mean for us tonight – for prayer. I think that the news were are coming to, and the news we each already have between our ears already, fits well with this psalm. We have friends who are in situations like that of this Psalmist, friends who need help in being wise, in avoiding temptations, snares and traps. We have a God who will hear such prayers.

We will approach our Sovereign Lord, not causally but comfortably. Conversationally indeed, though with huge respect. As Mr Beaver says: 'He is not a Tame Lion'. We know him. We have seen him answer so many prayers over the years. He will show us what we should ask, even as he showed the Psalmist what to say as he lifted up his arms, and his prayer rose like incense, those many years ago. We worship the same God.

Gilcomston Prayer Meeting, 22 July 2000.

Psalm 142

This is a poem wrung from personal experience. David recalls coping with stress. Psalm 142 – 'A maskil of David. When he was in the cave. A Prayer.'

Ah, 'the cave'. Of course. We are in the cave at En Gedi. David cut off a bit of Saul's robe instead of his head. That probably already popped into your mind. As usual for these occasions I started with Calvin. He had the inestimable advantage of a legal training before defecting to theology. This is his introduction to his comment on the Psalm:

> When Saul came into the cave where David lay concealed, this saint of God might upon such an occurrence have been either thrown into consternation, or led by his alarm into some unwarrantable step, it being common for persons in despair either to be prostrated with dismay, or driven into frenzy. But it appears from this Psalm that David retained his composure, relying with assured confidence upon God, and resigning himself to vows and prayers instead of taking any unauthorized steps.

I was an academic. Maybe I still am. An academic gets a curious frisson, mixed alarm and pleasure, when concluding that a recognised authority has made a mistake. Occasionally I have recognised instances of this in the elegant eviscerations by theologs of their rivals' articles. When I read this Psalm and then that bit of Calvin I immediately thought that Calvin had got things wrong. Not that what he goes on to say in his commentary is up the creek – I use it later – but linking this Psalm to En Gedi is misconceived. It just does not fit. It was a relief later to find that others have thought along the same lines. At En Gedi David was concealed with some of his men (1 Sam. 24). Saul came in and had a wee sleep. The men encouraged David to kill Saul. Instead David sliced a bit off Saul's robe. We will get to that later. But you cannot conceive of David slipping away during all of that to compose a poem. See for yourself. These are the sentiments of someone quite alone. Verse 4: 'Look and see, there is no one at my right hand; there is no one who is concerned for me. I have no refuge; no one cares for my life.' This is isolation. This is desolation unrelieved.

So, when was it? Though the NIV version is in the present continuous tense, others including the AV translate it in the past tense. For them this psalm is memory. It was not composed during the stress it records. David wrote it down later to instruct.

Where was it? David spent a lot of time in and around caves. In 1 Sam. 23 we see him moving from place to place while fleeing from Saul (v. 13). He stayed in wilderness strongholds in the 'Desert of Ziph' (v. 11), the strongholds at Horesh on the hill of Hakilah south of Jeshimon (v. 19), and at the rock in the 'Desert of Maon' (vv. 24–25). These wilderness strongholds were fortified caves. All are possible as places where David's feelings overcame him to the eventual effusion of our Psalm. So, which cave? En Gedi?

There is a better candidate. The one other cave that is named in David's life is the Cave of Adullam of 1 Sam. 22: 1.

Go back a bit. Not long after Goliath had been disposed of Saul started to get fearful and jealous of David (1 Sam. 18: 6–9). His paranoia got out of hand. Twice Saul threw a javelin at David – cue that wonderful Rembrandt painting (1 Sam. 18: 10). By 1 Sam. 19: 1 Saul is telling Jonathan and his attendants to kill David. Things came and went thereafter, until in 1 Sam. 21 David took refuge with Achish king of Gath. Gath the home of Goliath! But he was recognised. So he feigned insanity. The tactic worked. But obviously there was always going to be a risk. So we get to 1 Sam. 22: 1: 'David left Gath and went to the cave of Adullam'.

That is the point in time that I would fix on. Yes, in 1 Sam. 22: 1b we have David's brothers and his father's household coming to him. Shortly thereafter he is the commander of four hundred, including some who had come to him in distress, as well as other debtors and discontents. But his folk came to him only once they had found out where he was, and then they had had to travel to get to him (v. 2). The others had also to find him. So, for a period between v. 1a and v. 1b David was on his own. That fits this Psalm.

David is alone. We have seen that in v. 4. He knows that Saul is looking for him with no good intentions. He has just escaped from Gath, the major city of the Philistines who were occasionally raiding into Israel. So he turns to God.

No he doesn't. Calvin points out that this is more than mildly turning to God. David poured things out – vocally. The AV makes the point most clearly: 'I cried unto the LORD with my voice: with my voice unto the LORD did I make my supplication' (v. 1). Whichever cave he was in David got things off his chest. But this is not Edvard Munch's famous painting, *The Scream*, in any of its four versions. This is not Francis Bacon's screaming Popes, nor his shrieking blue heads. David thought about, listed and poured out his actual troubles. We do not know exactly what words he used, but the psalm indicates their main lines. This is not silent prayer. This was an audible torrent. And, as Calvin says, to do that can be good. To quote Calvin's commentary again:

> To pour out one's thoughts and tell over his afflictions implies the reverse of those perplexing anxieties which men brood over inwardly to their own distress, and by which they torture themselves, and are chafed by their afflictions rather than led to God; or it implies the reverse of those frantic exclamations to which others give utterance who find no comfort in the superintending providence and care of God. In short, we are left to infer that while he [David] did not give way before men to loud and senseless lamentations, neither did he suffer himself to be tormented with inward and suppressed cares, but made known his grief's with unsuspecting confidence to the Lord.

Just screaming does nothing. Silent prayer can bottle things up, to the extent that in a kind of way it intoxicates. It is possible to wallow in misery. Instead speak aloud to God. That way you know you have someone listening – a real audience. And, by the way, an audience is also a benefit of corporate prayer.

David is not overwhelmed. He does have a complaint – his troubles (v. 2) – which he seems to have listed – but first he calls for mercy (v. 1). Through it all he recognises that when his spirit faints within him the LORD still watches over his way (v. 3a). Yes, people have laid traps for him (v. 3b), and, at that point at least, he has no refuge (v. 4b). But then he contradicts himself: he knows the LORD is his refuge (v. 5). He is in need, in need of rescue (v. 6). Wherever he was, it felt like a prison (v. 7). However he knows that when God responds the righteous will gather to him because of God's goodness to him (v. 7b).

And it happened. The family came to him (1 Sam. 21: 1b) – and there must have been others righteous within the motley crew that also gathered round him. So, when David came to set down this psalm in writing, he had seen that he could trust his LORD.

Now, see how this trust, this realisation, also fits with the events in the Cave of En Gedi of 1 Sam. 24. David did not kill Saul, though he could have. Instead he rebuked his men for their encouragement to murder a sleeping man, and he forbad them from attacking Saul. Saul was God's appointed king (1 Sam 10: 17–25). By this time David has got through the anguish, and has seen God's response to the plea of v. 7. He now has those four hundred or so. He has been protected from Saul's increasing attempts to catch him. He knew he could rely on God to control events. He knew Samuel had anointed him, and that he would eventually be king. It would have been wrong for he himself to bring about the end of Saul's kingship. So we also should not manipulate to bring about what we may think are God's plans for us. David is here saying precisely this. Are you under stress? Call on God. Do not bottle things up. Think through the troubles. List them so far as you can. Then in words let it all out – to God. He will respond. Trust him. That is what David wants us to know, and do.

Gilcomston Prayer Meeting, 14 May 2016.

Psalm 144

This is an odd one. It is like Ps. 18, but stands in contrast to it. In Ps. 18 the author is triumphant throughout. Trials are past. Things are going well. David is king; his kingdom is prospering. In Ps. 144 difficulties are present, future trials foreseen.

That is one comment. Another is this. Ps. 144 is incoherent. It does not hang together. It shifts about, from thanksgiving for victory past and martial skills, to acknowledging God's power, and then pleading for future help for which there will be further thanksgiving. Between the main sections treacherous foes worry the Psalmist (vv. 7b–8 and 11). Then comes a prayer for prosperity and peace for the people (vv. 12–14). Except for that section, the Psalm is made almost entirely of verses from other Psalms. There are also verses from Job, and perhaps from Isaiah. That gives the theologs much to mull over. It is a cut and paste job from psalms already written. It is a mish-mash. Is it by David, or has someone else put it together from David's psalms? We do not know.

So, how to tackle it? My solution comes from v. 9: 'I will sing a new song to you, O God.' That is my key. Consider it as a symphony – a symphony in several movements. The whole may be more than the sum of the parts – a flaw of Classic FM's programming of individual movements from symphonies. On that thesis it does come together. Properly to deal with it could take a while. Instead I briefly comment.

Movement 1, vv. 1–2.

> Praise be to the LORD my Rock, who trains my hands for war, my fingers for battle. He is my loving God and my fortress, my stronghold and my deliverer, my shield, in whom I take refuge, who subdues peoples under me.

How does that strike you? Yes, we cosy up to the God who loves us, who is our fortress, stronghold and deliverer, our shield, the Rock in whom we take refuge. But this God also subdues people under David, trains his hands for war and his fingers for battle. How does that fit with the world in which we live? Iraq? Afghanistan? 1914–18, 1939–45? Preparing for tonight I decided just to throw the question out, not to try to answer it. Think!

Movement 2, vv. 3–4.

LORD, what is man that you care for him, the son of man that you think of him? Man is like a breath; his days are like a fleeting shadow.

Here is a question, almost a bewilderment. Why does God bother? We are evanescent. Unless you are a blinkered creationist, the Universe is 13+ billion years old. We reside in the few vertical feet that form the crust of a small globe away out on the remoter arm of an insignificant galaxy. 'What **is** man that thou art mindful of him`, as the old translation puts it. Yet we know that this God sent Jesus to be our salvation. Think on that.

Movement 3, vv. 5–6.

Part your heavens, O LORD, and come down; touch the mountains, so that they smoke. Send forth lightning and scatter the enemy; shoot your arrows and rout them.

David calls God to his aid, to scatter the enemy. The heavens part, mountains smoke, lightning and arrows – does anyone here recall the deceiving of the Master's robot in Arthur Clarke's *The City and the Stars*, when the Old Ones pry the Universe open? Somehow I thought not. But those images resonate for me. Perhaps these verses can also conjure up the television images of the bombardment of Iraq. In terms David is contemplating the end of all things, and the appearance of his Saviour. Desperate times do conjure thoughts of apocalyptic scenarios.

Movement 4, vv. 7–8.

Reach down your hand from on high; deliver me and rescue me from the mighty waters, from the hands of foreigners whose mouths are full of lies, whose right hands are deceitful.

Problems are looming. Mighty waters were always feared. David was a shepherd, not a sailor. David turns on what someone else called 'the enemy within'. Foreigners were pressing him, seeking agreements and advantages, and lying to get them. Raising your right hand you swear an oath to give true testimony. You strike a bargain by shaking hands – see TV's 'Bargain Hunt'. Back then the right hand was used for both. But some people cannot be trusted. Maybe this is a warning for us all. Lord, defend us from such, and give us the discernment to identify them.

Movement 5, vv. 9–10a. (Paragraphing follows US NIV and Ronald Knox).

'I will sing a new song to you, O God; on the ten-stringed lyre I will make music to you, to the One who gives victory to kings, who delivers his servant David.'

I repeat my usual comment about modern hymnology. Why is it that the really magnificent modern hymn tunes are written by agnostics – John Rutter, Ralph Vaughan Williams. David will make music on the ten-stringed lyre. Would he be serene or noisily joyous, tranquil, or overwhelmingly magnificent? What would he do with a modern symphony orchestra? What would he make of devout Olivier Messiaen's *Quatuor pour la fin du temps* ('Quartet for the End of Time'), written in a Prisoner of War Camp), or his wonderful Turangalîla Symphony, particularly Movement 5, the rollicking 'Joy of the Blood of the Stars'? How would he respond to Gustav Mahler or Anton Bruckner? What of Monteverdi, Tallis or John Taverner? I despair of the rum-ti-tum gunge of much modern 'hymnology', particularly when it is underpinned by the recurrent thump of an uninteresting drum and cymbal.

'I will sing a new song'. Singing adds to the meaning of words. Music goes beyond words. We are coming up to the Proms. Hear Mahler, Bruckner, Sibelius, even Shostakovich. Music speaks in ways that words alone do not.

Movement 6, vv. 10b–11.

From the deadly sword deliver me; rescue me from the hands of foreigners whose mouths are full of lies, whose right hands are deceitful.

Amazing! Immediately after promising to sing that new song, David reprises Movement 4, vv. 7b–8. You could almost ask if he is manic. Again he asks for deliverance from the strangers that he cannot trust. See the reference in v. 11 to their right hands. But this time also there is an addition – deliverance from the deadly sword. He fears assassination. Clearly David is worried – perhaps paranoid? Things are getting on top of him and he needs God's help and protection.

Movement 7, vv. 12–14.

Suddenly, all fears disappear.

> Then our sons in their youth will be like well-nurtured plants, and our daughters will be like pillars carved to adorn a palace. Our barns will be filled with every kind of provision. Our sheep will increase by thousands, by tens of thousands in our fields; our oxen will draw heavy loads. There will be no breaching of walls, no going into captivity, no cry of distress in our streets.

When God acts, all will be well. Sturdy sons. Daughters like caryatids. Full barns. Thousands of sheep. Magnificent draught oxen to pull loaded carts. No-one will breach neighbours' walls. External threats dissolve. There will be no captivity under those who not share our beliefs. All this is an ideal. After all the Jews were to go into captivity not all that many years from David's time. But these verses outline an ideal that we can and should share. Writing these pages I find myself thinking of World War II and its sacrifices and where we are now. Sometimes freedom requires sacrifice. In two senses our freedom did.

Movement 8, the Coda, v. 15.

> Blessed are the people of whom this is true; blessed are the people whose God is the LORD.

Many symphonies end including brief reference to previous movements. Others close by affirming the fundamental key in which they have been written. This Movement does both. Think back through the verses of this

Psalm. The truth for the peoples is God, the God who loves, who is our fortress, stronghold and deliverer, our shield, the Rock in whom we take refuge – Movement 1. From Movements 1, 3, 4 and 6, he protects. From Movement 7, he is generous. And then finally the basic signature key of this symphony is affirmed. We do not know the tune, but here at least we have the theme of the new song of Movement 5, the song that was triggered by the questions of Movement 2. 'What is man that thou art mindful of him`? We are blessed that God is our Lord.

A Note of parallels, or origins.

[144: 1–2] Composed of phrases from Ps.18: 3, 35, 47–48. [144: 3] Similar to Ps. 8: 4. [144:4] Composed of phrases from Pss. 39: 6; 102: 12. [144: 5–7] Adapted in large part from Pss. 18:10, 15, 17; 104: 32. [144: 8b, 11b] Their right hands are raised in lying oaths: sc. the psalmist's enemies give false testimony. [144: 3] Job 7: 17. [144: 4] Pss. 62: 10; 90: 9–10; Job 7: 16; Eccl 6: 12; Wis 2: 5. [144:5] Is 63: 19. [144:9] Ps.33: 2–3. [144: 10] Ps. 18: 51. [144:12] Ps. 128: 3. [144: 14] Is. 65 :19. [144: 15] Ps. 33: 12.

Gilcomston Prayer Meeting, 22 June 2013.

Psalm 145

Some weeks ago I read one of those 'death experience' stories that occasionally turn up in the newspapers. This one was a bit different from the usual. The man involved was undergoing a heart operation, and he realised that he had died. His body was there below him, and he could not work out how to get back into it. Then he became conscious that there was a bright light behind him, and a voice said, 'You shouldn't be here yet. Don't turn round or you'll have to stay. But it's not your time yet.' Then it told him how to get back into his body. As he prepared to do so he said, 'I have one question before I go. What's it all about? What is the meaning of life?' 'Ah,' said the voice, with a chuckle, 'I get asked that a lot. When you come back I'll tell you.'

Obviously that man didn't know the answer to the first question of the Catechism: 'Man's chief end is to glorify God, and enjoy him forever.' Nor, perhaps, did he know this psalm. Maybe he does now, for apparently he died some years after that operation.

This psalm is a psalm of praise. It is the first of the six psalms of praise that conclude the Book of Psalms. The immediately previous ones have had elements of praise, but they also have major petitions, supplications and questions embedded in them. This one is pure praise. Psalms 146 to 150 begin and end 'Praise the Lord'. This one does not: it just pitches straight in. They are unattributed. This one is tagged as a psalm of David, and it certainly is true to what we know of David when he was functioning at his best. The subsequent psalms exhort to praise. This one is an explosion of praise. In it David extols / exalts God. You could even say he exults in God. It has the sort of joy you can find in Wassily Kandinsky, later Mondrian, Chagall or Matisse – with even a hint of Jackson Pollock.

It is an explosion. But there is a dignity to it. Read it in the King James Version. There you find grandeur, solemnity, majesty. This is Anton Bruckner, or a great building like St Paul's or one of those huge Dutch churches. The archaic cadences, the 'thee's', 'thy's', 'thou's', 'est's' and 'eth's' augment the effect.

I suggested this psalm is an explosion. It is. But it is a controlled explosion

– a better comparison might be to a fire-works display. This is one of the seven alphabetic acrostic psalms in the Bible. The others are Pss. 25, 34, 37, 111, 112, and 119. 'Acrostic' means that this psalm has been carefully constructed. Each verse starts with subsequent letters of the Hebrew alphabet. In fact this one is imperfect, because a verse for the letter 'n' is missing in the older Hebrew texts. There is a hole in the sequence. Perhaps an early copyist made a mistake. After all there were no verse numbers to keep you right in those days. Don't think that, all of a sudden I am a Hebrew expert, but I can read the entry for Psalm 145 in Wikipedia. The second part of v. 13 in the NIV reads: 'The Lord is trustworthy in all he promises and faithful in all he does', but that is not found in the Hebrew text. Some think that the Seventy who translated the Old Testament into Greek in the third century BC noticed the hole and stitched in the extra words. At any rate they first appear in the Septuagint. They are not in the KJV.

So what? Two things. First, we cannot see David's linguistic artistry. Only the Ronald Knox translation (Ps.144, conform to the Catholic Bible numbering) follows the acrostic requirement, but it adds nothing – indeed the Knox version is clumsy. Second, knowing about the acrostic element reassures. Well-thought-out form can reveal. Think of the joy of later Mondrian – the 'Broadway Boogie Woogie', and the 'Victory Boogie Woogie' come to mind. Careful construction does not diminish the psalm's impact. The mind is a wonderful tool. It's a gift we need to use.

The psalm begins: 'I will exalt you, my Lord, the King.' This is not a statement of intention. Rather it is a statement of fact. Occasionally we do have to keep ourselves on track by exhorting ourselves to praise. But there are occasions when praise just bursts out in joy. In v. 2 David says he will extol the Lord every day. At that my forensic streak wakes up and asks 'Did he?'. The rest of the psalm gives plenty of reasons to celebrate God, but we do have the Bible narrative, and all those other Davidic psalms that reflect a floundering spirit. Maybe one message for tonight is that we're not going to be in peak spiritual condition all the time. There can be dark nights of the soul. But it is at these times we should turn to psalms like this one, and think of God, think of our Saviour. A daily effort keeps us on track. But sometimes joy will burst out, if we let it.

In this psalm sometimes David is addressing the LORD, and sometimes he is chronicling the wonderfulness of God for those who are going to be singing his words – remember this psalm was written to be used for public worship. Early he identifies a logical difficulty. The LORD is great, and his greatness cannot be fathomed (v. 3). But that doesn't mean we cannot try to fathom it, for God has revealed so much – more than we appreciate. And the generations of believers know that. Vv. 4–7: 'One generation commends your works to another; they tell of your mighty acts. They will speak of the glorious splendour of your majesty, and I will meditate on your wonderful works. They tell of the power of your awesome works, and I will proclaim your great deeds. They celebrate your abundant goodness and joyfully sing of your righteousness.' The point is repeated in similar terms in vv. 10–13.

However, the unqualified righteousness of God could be daunting. Can sinners sing joyfully about it? After all towards the end of the psalm David notes that God will destroy the wicked (v. 20b). But David points to another fundamental, God's love. Vv. 8–9: 'The LORD is gracious and compassionate, slow to anger and rich in love. The LORD is good to all; he has compassion on all he has made.' He 'upholds all those who fall and lifts up all who are bowed down' (v. 14). He 'is near to all who call on him, to all who call on him in truth. He fulfils the desires of those who fear him; he hears their cry and saves them. The LORD watches over all who love him' (vv. 18–20a). David, of all the people we know in the Old Testament, knew that from experience. That is why David will 'speak in praise of the LORD' and calls on 'every creature [to] praise his holy name for ever and ever' (v. 21). But others know that as well. They too are saved and their needs are met (vv. 15–16). With our knowledge of Jesus, sent to save us, meeting our needs in full by dying for us, we can join the generations of v. 7 celebrating God's abundant goodness. We can joyfully sing of His righteousness.

So, let us do that. Let's sing the 'Old Hundredth', Ps. 100.

Gilcomston Prayer Meeting, 11 May 2019.

Cf. Daily Express, 15 April 2019.
https://www.express.co.uk/news/weird/1114104/afterlife-man-died-surgery-god-meaning-of-life-spt

Psalm 147

We are getting to the end of the Book of Psalms. Its last six, psalms 145–150, are a sequence each praising God. Of them Ps 145 may be a personal statement by David: its rubric does say 'A psalm of praise. Of David.' The others have no such heading and all begin and end 'Praise the LORD'. But there is difference among them. Last week's psalm, Ps 146, is very personal: 'I will praise; I will sing'. Psalms 147–150 are more inclusive. They are for everyone to make their own, if I can put it like that. This psalm's internal references are to Jerusalem (vv. 2, 12) and Zion (v. 12), and it also speaks of the LORD gathering the exiles of Israel (v. 2). Nowadays these mean the Church. Peter, for example, writes to God's elect, to his chosen (1 Pet. 1: 1; 2: 9), to a holy nation, God's special possession, the people of God (1 Pet. 2: 9–10). All can take the teaching of this psalm and digest it. Praise will result.

But for some there is a sneaking inhibition that can amount to a cognitive dissonance or intermodulation. Does or will science make God irrelevant? That question is an example of the Devil's propaganda, intended to obfuscate and paralyze. This psalm is the antidote. Let me take a wee detour.

Has anyone else been watching the commissioning of the James Webb space telescope? Launched last Christmas Day it's now in halo orbit at Lagrange point 2, one million miles further from the Sun than we are. The eighteen hexagonal segments are being adjusted to focus the mirror. A fascinating process.

So, what has that to do with Ps. 147? Well, one of the things the Webb will do is capture light from very close to the beginning of the universe. We may see some of the first galaxies forming, even the first stars. That will help us better to understand how the universe works. I do wonder what the writers of the psalms would make of that. Such an advance will feed agnostic tendencies – to know more about the processes of the universe can make God seem remote, if not improbable. Certainly the atheists will be pleased. For them scientific findings are incompatible with belief in God.

We must pray about that. The point is that science does reveal the 'how' side of 'why'. But for some it also masquerades as answering the fundamental 'why' question. It does not. When there is a clear sky get somewhere really dark and look up. Science does not explain the sense of wonder you feel when contemplating the universe. Again, science does not explain our innate sense of 'right'. Adapting his phrasing for tonight, Paul writes in Rom. 1: 19: what may be known about God is plain. In *Hogfather* (Terry Pratchett: London: Gollancz, 1996), Death says to his granddaughter Susan, you can 'grind up the whole Universe, and sieve it oh so thoroughly, analyse it oh so carefully, and you will never find a single atom of truth, or justice, or mercy, of beauty or loveliness'. But the writer of tonight's psalm knew all about that. This psalm speaks of wonder, beauty and loveliness, and also of truth, justice and mercy.

Begin with nature and that sense of wonder. God's power and authority are there. The psalmist goes celestial in v. 4. The LORD determines the number of the stars and names them, but I have to say our author is more interested in the earth and its weather. He did not know the wonders of deep space. We have that privilege. For him the Lord 'covers the sky with clouds; he supplies the earth with rain and makes grass grow on the hills. He provides food for the cattle and for the young ravens when they call' (vv. 8–9). There is snow spread like wool and frost like ashes. There is golf-ball hail, and icy winds. But they are turned down into breeze and snow – hail and frost become flowing waters – water, always an acute concern in a parched land (vv. 16–18). And implicitly in all these are the elements of beauty and loveliness. There is the strength of the horse, not to mention the legs of the warrior (v. 10), though the delight of the Lord lies elsewhere.

That leads us to truth, justice and mercy. The psalmist does not expressly identify them, but they are there. And if you think about it they are innate in us all – blunted and spoiled, yes, but still there. Look at the news. Why do people complain 'it's nae fair' or 'there's no justice' unless there is an idea of fairness and justice. Yes, there is a doctrine of total depravity, but every one of us still has some recognition of what is right. Remember that the Devil himself in effect complained twice that it was unfair that God protected Job (Job 1: 8–11; 2: 3–6). But there is the obverse of right. There is also an innate sense of what is wrong, a sense through which the LORD can provoke a sense of sin and thereby lead the sinner to himself.

However, the psalmist goes beyond that. There is mercy in action. Look at vv. 2–3: 'The LORD builds up Jerusalem; he gathers the exiles of Israel. He heals the broken-hearted and binds up their wounds.' Or the latter halves of vv. 13, 14. He '… blesses your people within you. He '… satisfies you with the finest of wheat'. Down through the centuries that has been true of the Lord's protection and care of his Church, his people.

But also down through the centuries for some those phrases must echo bizarrely and feel false. Today we can look at history and we look at current affairs. What about the first halves of those verses; 'He strengthens the bars of your gates …' and 'He grants peace to your borders . . .' ??

Well, we don't know when this psalm was written, but we cannot think that the writer was ignorant of history, or indeed of the current affairs of his time in the neighbouring areas and kingdoms, not to mention domestically. And yet this is a psalm of praise. Despite any contra-indications there are grounds to trust the LORD. The essence is this. Although men can see the wonders and blessings of nature, and although there is still an innate recognition of right and wrong, the LORD has gone further. I turn to the end of the psalm, vv. 19–20: 'He has revealed his word to Jacob, his laws and decrees to Israel. He has done this for no other nation; they do not know his laws.' God has revealed himself in his word, and, centuries later than this psalm, in his Son, Jesus.

That is why, like our author, we turn to praise the Lord, for it is good 'to sing praises to our God, how pleasant and fitting to praise him!' (v. 1).

Let us praise.

Gilcomston Prayer Meeting, 9 April 2022.

Psalm 148

To everything there is a season, says the Preacher (Eccles. 3: 1–8). Included in his list are times to laugh, to dance and to love. This is one of those times, for this psalm is a rejoicing. It is a sensual psalm, where love of God, evoked through knowledge of his creation, overflows. It is a jewel, a moss agate with swirling depths or a fire opal coruscating. It is the Hope Diamond, its glorious facets flashing as you move and see green and blue, red and yellow. Or to go another way it is a bonsai Bruckner, with immense visions opening to left and to right as you progress.

This psalm talks in wide terms, which we could glide over as generalities and intellectual polysyllables. But, if you let its magic work, if you really let it get to you, the writer is someone who knows about Creation, about the wonders of the world, of the Universe. He has let that wonder course through the very frame of his being. In preparing for tonight – in preparing tonight's text – I have done likewise. I have dredged my memory and let the wonder flow. I have gone to my Space Law, whatever that is. I have gone to my travels. Mum took me to London in 1946 just after the war and that infected me. As some of you know I collect places and things. Thirty countries not counting airspace at the last round, and Brazil to come in three weeks.

I think that is why it's me and not someone else that is here tonight to deal with Ps. 148. I hope therefore that if any is tempted to dismiss what follows as a Lyall ego trip you will repress that thought. This psalm is not so much for the mind as for the feelings evoked as you wallow in it. I will wallow. You replace my thoughts with your own.

For me this psalm rings so many bells because it draws up so many memories. Indeed for any with a really good memory let me remind you of the study I did on this psalm here in Gilcomston back in 1969, with slides, after our first trip around the world. I tried then to show the wonder of this world and thereby the glory of God. I know what this Psalmist was feeling. I mentioned the Hope Diamond. The psalm is a similar marvel. But let's get into it.

Verses 1–6. I think of the starry nights we used to know before sodium lighting obscured their glory. I think of the Northern Lights of Old

Aberdeen that we use to see from the Torry Battery when I had just got LRS 29. I remember leaving the hospital after Frankie was born – they gave him to me first. I came round the corner of the Matty and there was Orion glittering high over Beechgrove Church, confronting Taurus the Bull, with Sirius the Dog Star and Procyon – Canis Maior and Canis Minor – scurrying behind him. I think of a couple of evenings on the road from Fennimore to La Crosse in Wisconsin in the middle of the USA when I stopped the car, turned off the lights, got out and just stood and enjoyed it. I was in what elsewhere I have called Simak Country, high on the bluffs above the Wisconsin River. It is an old unglaciated land and you would think that you could see the very curve of the Earth. Above, there are the stars. The glory of the northern Milky Way and the constellations, Auriga, Lyra, the Bears – Ursa Major and Ursa Minor. To the west Cygnus, and rising to the east Gemini and Leo. There is a brief meteor and a couple of satellites going north-west to south-east. I think of the heavens seen from the roof of the Hilton Hotel in Tibet in Lhasa where the altitude makes everything so clear. It was glorious. Or there is the southern Milky Way seen from Fiji, New Zealand or Australia, clearer and more glorious that the Northern, with Fomalhaut and the Southern Cross riding high

I think also of the pictures that have come to us by the wonders of technology from the Hubble space telescope – the marvels of the Eskimo Nebula or the Great Nebula in Orion with the Crab Nebula at its core. I think of the tornadoes between the stars, of twisters light years long and of the Lagoon Nebula – the Pillars of Creation. I could give you a huge list, or the website address if you want to see it for yourself. I think of the meteorite collections in New York and Washington. In the Museum of Natural History in New York is the Woman and The Dog that Peary brought back from Greenland, and other lumps of rock that once were wheeling far out in space, possibly way beyond Pluto. You can touch them and feel their age and remoteness. I think of the Moon in her phases, the craters, the lunar maria, the mountains, and the bit of the Moon we touched in Washington. I think of the nuclear furnace that is our Sun.

And what about this earth that we sit on? Before passing to vv. 7–12 I remind you of this. The elements that our Earth and we ourselves are made of are star stuff created in those immense cauldrons in space. The carbon, hydrogen, oxygen, iron, iodine and other elements that go to make the bodies of each of us were formed in those immense fires we call stars.

So what about this Earth? Again my mind darts about. V. 7: the great sea creatures and ocean depths. My mind crowds. Images of snorkeling on the Great Barrier Reef. Whales flipping their tails as they dive off South Island, New Zealand, at Kaikoura. Porpoises in front of the boat at Milford. Fish in so many aquaria. Hawaii – a three storey aquarium was one wall of the hotel dining room, Sentosa in Singapore, Deep Sea World at the Forth Bridge. The seals at Blakeney in Norfolk. Salmon leaping at the Brig of Feugh.

Next there is the weather. V. 8: think of the storms. We in this part of the world know little of the great and terrible storms. But some of us have been around elsewhere where storms play skittles with the mountains, and we now have television and can see the hugenesses of what we call the forces of nature. Note the end of v. 8. These do the Lord's bidding. That is a difficult when you see floods in Mozambique, or the effects of Caribbean hurricanes, the tornadoes of America's 'storm alley', or the sea surges that go along with those weather patterns. They can raise questions in our minds. Let us acknowledge that. But the questioning itself shows that we are human. That God has allowed us to wonder about things right and wrong, and even to apply or misapply that to what God permits. We are human. When last did a dog think about such things?

Mountains and hills, v. 9a. I cannot but first connect that with the storms of v. 8. I think of the plate volcanoes in Hawaii's Big Island – evidence that we sit on but a thin skin on the surface of our Earth. At the Volcano House Hotel you go down the passage between the cafeteria and the gift shop, and suddenly you are on the balcony on the very edge of the crater, a mile and a half wide and 500 feet deep. I think of fields of Aaa Aaa lava like cooked plowed fields – or the surface of Mars if you recall those pictures. I think also of the viscous toffee-like Puhoehoe lava, of which I have a wee bit in our stone bowl at home, and the sky-lights in the crust of lava tubes that let you see rivers of molten rock. I think of the hot springs of Rotorua, the bubbling mud pools of Whakarewarewa, the sinter beds, and the Pohutu geyser. The steaming cliffs of Wairaki that used to be the Red and Pink Terraces. That takes me a village close by Rotorua that was buried when Mount Tarawera blew up twenty-miles away. Think of Mount St Helens exploding. The convulsions of earthquakes, including the very mild one I was in in North Vancouver in August 1964. In short, think of the TV series 'Savage Earth' and its imitations, all dealing with the magnificences of Wild Nature.

That was how mountains came to be, but what else fills the mind when you read of the mountains and hills of v. 9. If I say 'mountains' what comes to mind? The Highlands? The view down Loch Maree? I see the grandeur of the Rockies, with Mount Aberdeen at the back of Lake Louise, or Castle Mountain at Banff. New Zealand, the Southern Alps, the Remarkables hemming Lake Wakatipu at Queenstown, the Southern Alps and Mount Cook, the approach to Milford Sound and its immensities with Mitre Peak rising 9000 feet straight from the waters of the Sound, and the rain that poured down on us a couple of years ago. I think of the glaciers of South Island New Zealand, the poise and control of the Fox and Franz Josef between their high jagged side-valleys. The strange mountains at either side of the Li River east of Guilin in China, or the Himalayas and the mountains hemming the valley where Lhasa sits in Tibet. Chunks of rock, so I think of Uluru – Ayer's Rock as it used to be called – and the Oglas some thirty miles away. I think of Yosemite Valley, of El Capitan and the Half Dome in California. I think of the Alps especially Mont Blanc, and that whole area with its pinnacles and glaciers, and the Aguille du Midi 12000 stark feet above Chamonix.

What about the fruit trees and cedars of v. 9b? I have seen the Grizzly Giant of the Mariposa Grove of California. If one accepts Bishop Ussher's dates it must have been a stripling of some 80 feet when Abram was getting the message to get out of Ur. The Grizzly Giant throws its first branch at about 140 feet, which is about the height of the Gilcomston steeple, and its base is as large again as our tower's. There are the solid greynesses of huge kauri pines north of Auckland and the rednesses of the Scots Pine. On the other end of the scale there are orchids, begonias, fuschias, daffodils and tulips. There are the dandelions and daisies, if you ever take the time to really look at them. There are glorious of the Duthie Park hothouse, and the wonder of the roses on what used to be the old flagstaff hill down there. There's the beauties of the sweet pea, of the lupin, dahlias and so many other. I think of Hungary, and fields of sunflowers all turned to the sun, and of Fiona aged two running through a wild flower meadow over near Miscolz.

What about the animals and all cattle of v. 10? Dogs, cats, the cows the Psalmist mentions. I have not been on safari but of more exotic thingies I think of many and varied zoos – panda in Chengdu in China, wolverines and the bears in Ranua in Finland, walruses in Harderwick, hippos munching cabbages in Auckland, crocodiles snapping up chickens in Orlando, the Primate House in Cologne – they have families of chimps, gorillas and orangutan. And the elephants and giraffes of the zoos there and in Berlin or London. The huskies and reindeer pulling Heather and me on a sledge through the darkening Finnish winter evening.

Small creatures and flying birds, v. 10. I think of the eagles of the Mississippi Valley seen first from an outlook point high above the river in the late evening as I went down to Simak Country on my first visit. I think of the flurry of the birds when I was grouse beating up at Granton-on-Spey, or a couple of years later down at Glen Lethnot. I think of the Humming Bird House that used to be in Edinburgh zoo, aviaries all around the world and the wonders of butterfly houses here and there.

And so at last we come to v. 12. To man, to the kings, all nations, princes young men and maidens, old men and children. This is not 'What is man that you are mindful of him', though that should be somewhere in our minds. This is man as the crown of creation, the highest that the Lord has created. Think of man as something good, as God created him. Not the faults, not our awful history, not the fallen creature. But think briefly at the least of what God has wrought through man, that man should be aware of the glory of God and the three Creation that He has put him into. I think of Copernicus on the Frankenberg Castle battlements beside the Baltic. I think of Paris last November. I went to the Pompidou Centre and stumbled into an exhibition on Time. There, just beside the entrance was a glass case and inside was Galileo's notebook recording his sighting of the moons of Jupiter over a month of evenings in whenever – the circle for the planet and those rough crosses as night by night he observed and recorded and laid the basis of modern astronomy.

I come back to matters of space. I think on those nights in Wisconsin, in Auckland, in Australia, in Tibet, when I saw the smooth progress of satellites across the starry heaven. I think the Hubble, the Chandra and the Compton space telescopes, revealing the wonders of the universe. I think all the various remote sensing satellites probing this, our world. I think of the medical advances not known to our Psalmist. I could have died in Auckland in 1968 but was saved by surgery of which the Psalmist knew nothing. I think of the philosophers that I studied and others those names I know – men who thought long and deep, though not always well, about the nature of man, of society and indeed of God himself. Is it not marvellous that our Lord, the maker of heaven and earth, of the universe and of the virus – incidentally have you noticed that the word virus is buried in the word 'universe' – that the Lord of all this should have created something that could contemplate, be it ever so inadequately, what God has done? That man should seek to understand the workings of the sun and of the human genome.

Verse 11. 'Let them praise the name of the Lord for his name alone is exalted: his splendour is above the earth and the heavens'. God is wonderful beyond all these things that crowd into my mind when I read this psalm.

But then we come to the point of the psalm. Given all the glories of creation the fundamental point is the relationship with God. Verse 14: 'He has raised up for his people a horn' – and the footnote indicates that 'horn' symbolizes a strong one, a king. And that 'Horn' is the praise of all his saints, of Israel, of 'the people close to his heart'. We are in that close relationship with the Person who gave us Jesus and who made and maintains all the glory we see in nature. The realization that that Person was his God, and his friend, drove the Psalmist to praise the Lord. I hope it drives us too.

We are here at God's calling. Maybe we have come reluctantly. Perhaps earlier this evening we thought of better ways of spending it. But we came, out of habit, out of curiosity, or for some other reason.

Whatever God has used to get us here, into this room, we are here. I hope that by letting you see what this psalm has triggered in my mind you also will have been fired up. If so, like the Psalmist draw on your experience and the wonders of television – draw on that to fill out the words we have looked at. God's creation has called to us. It is wonderful. So, to the last words of the psalm, let us praise him.

Gilcomston Prayer Meeting, 9 September 2000.

Psalm 148

Did anyone hear Monteverdi's Vespers of 1610 on Radio 3 last Tuesday evening? This massive Psalm is an equivalent as it passes its refrain from choir to choir and voice to voice calling on the whole of creation to praise its Maker. It starts far out, then closes down to focus on the Earth, and then comes on to humanity, before it ends with exhortation once again. It stretches the mind and makes you think what is really real.

'Praise the LORD. Praise the LORD from the heavens; praise him in the heights'.

Praise who? The typography of the NIV shows us that the praise is of Jehovah. Those block capitals are used to put the name Jehovah into English print. So this call is to praise God at his most majestic. The angels and his host (his armies) are to praise him (v. 2), which seems obvious, but it extends beyond that. Does Kim Jong Un know that?

Praise him from the heavens, in the heights (v. 1), the sun and moon, the shining stars (v. 3), the highest heavens and the waters above the heavens (whatever that may mean) (v. 4). Sun and Moon are to praise (v. 3) and we can appreciate that easily enough. What about the shining stars? It is difficult for us now in a modern city to appreciate the glories of the heavens – the immensity. Street lighting, especially that orange type which is so good for seeing with, makes it impossible to see the stars. But whoever wrote this Psalm did not have that problem. There were no street lights in Old Testament times. I can recall the days of the gas lamps, when you could see the stars from almost any side-street in Aberdeen. But even now we can escape the modern lights. Get away somewhere, and on a clear night you can see the glories of the Milky Way.

However, in a way we have it better than the Psalmist. We have modern technology, which has so expanded our knowledge and our sight of the glories of the astronomical world. One of my memories is of rather reluctantly going into an exhibition in the Pompidou Centre in Paris, that odd building that carries its plumbing on the outside. I really was there to see exhibits in the floor below, but having paid for general admission I was, as an Aberdonian, going to get my money's worth so I went to the top floor first. There was a special exhibition, and its poster said it was about Time. It was. Just to the left inside the door was a glass case with a couple of old books in it. I almost walked past it, but stopped. I'm glad I did. The books were Galileo's notebooks, and one was open showing his notes on successive evenings when, using the newfangled telescope, he was the first to see the four major moons of Jupiter, Io, Europa, Ganymede and Callisto. His sketches marked each speck of light with a small 'x' relative to Jupiter, and over those evenings he charted them as they moved. Imagine his puzzlement. Stars that moved and yet were not shooting stars; stars that seemed to be linked with Jupiter. From those observations Galileo was to understand there were moons round other planets – and so much else was to follow. Imagine his excitement, seeing things no-one else had ever seen. Additions to the praisers of God. I remember the first time I identified the Andromeda Nebula, that misty patch 2.5 million light years away under the right leg of Andromeda's 'W' shape. Did Galileo see it as well? I don't know. He did have that telescope. But certainly he would not have realised it was so far away. It too is called to praise by this psalm.

Come right up to date. Go to hubblesite.org and other google-able websites carrying pictures from the astronomy satellites, and see the glories of the Universe. The results from Hubble, Chandra and Spitzer are beautiful. Those nebulae: the Pillars of Creation in the Lagoon Nebula – a star nursery indeed. The distances and the scales involved can be daunting, but see vv. 5-6. 'Let them praise the name of the Lord, for he commanded and they were created. He established them forever and ever: he fixed their bounds which cannot be passed.' Established forever and ever. Imagine yourself down at the church spire corner on Union Street. Look west towards Holburn Junction. Would you be able to see a tennis ball? Nearly fifteen years ago over a ten day period in December 1995 the Hubble took images of a tiny area in Ursa Major, the 'Plough', 'Great Bear' or 'Saucepan'. The area looked at was 2.5 arc minutes – the same that would be subtended by a tennis ball a hundred and ten yards away. The area looked blank. But when the images were processed they revealed more than three thousand galaxies with unknown millions of stars in each of them. Our God made them. 'In reason's ear they all rejoice and utter forth a glorious voice' as Joseph Addison (1672–1719) put it three hundred years before the Hubble.

In the next section, vv. 7–10, our attention comes to the Earth and its contents. Here we are in the *Blue Planet* series, and again with technology we have the chance to appreciate even more than the Psalmist could. Sea monsters and all deeps (v. 7) – whales, schools of fish, and deep sea critters including those wormy things that grow on the deep sea volcano vents, and the crabs and other crustaceans that crawl over them, not to mention the other weird entities of the abysses. Then there are the wild animals and all cattle, creeping things and flying birds (v. 10). What's your favourite? So I thought, but then I thought of another question. When did you last take time just to stand and stare at a bird, or listen to bird-song. Just now every evening we have a blackbird that sits on a TV aerial across the road, and he sings and sings. When I whistle to him (it is a male) he whistles back. I am not so good in blackbird so I may be saying the most outrageous things, but we sing together. When last did you take time to stand and listen to the birds? Or try a duet?

Beyond that there are all the inanimate things of the earth, mountains and all hills, fruit trees and all cedars (v. 9). Mountains first: have you a memorable mountain or two in your memory? Mountains – Everest or Mont Blanc. Hills – Clach-na-ben or Craigendarroch. Cliffs south of Greyhope Ness, covered in seabirds at this time, with maybe a puffin strutting about – you'd need the binoculars for that. Then there's the trees. For me there are so many, the Grizzly Giant in California, a hundred or so years old when Abraham was starting to move out from Ur, or the gracefulness of the Sliver Birches now overrunning Dinnet Moor. And as for cedars – we don't have so many in Aberdeen, but there's a beauty in the park at Hazlehead, but if you go there look also at the Monkey Puzzle tree (Auracaria auracaria) just west of the restaurant – a living fossil. Size is not everything. You can go the other way. Take a magnifying glass and look at some moss growing on a wall – a wee world of marvels.

Then there's the fire and hail, snow and frost, and the stormy wind fulfilling his command (v. 9). Perhaps that's more difficult for us to appreciate, given last winter, or the Iceland eruption. But all are called on to praise God, their maker.

And so finally we home in on people. The closing Magnificat of the Vespers begins. Kings and rulers, all peoples, young men and women, old and young together (v. 12). That's us. Not just us. It is everyone. For at the last all will bow the knee to him, even if some will do so unwillingly.

Let them all praise the name of the Lord, for his name alone is exalted, his glory is above earth and heaven (v. 13). It is the call to the whole of creation, to the glories of the *Blue Planet,* to the wonders revealed by space telescopes, remote probes or microscopy. But, as I contemplate marvels, a wee warning thought goes off in my mind. It is possible to enjoy the wonders of nature on earth, or creation in the further Universe, and leave it at that. The Sense of Wonder – 'Gosh! Wow!' as some put it – can be addictive, but it can stop at that sensation. We are called to see past it to the Creator. And Christians have an additional element to help us take that step, to trigger our praise. This is the final Gloria of the Monteverdi Vespers as soloists and choirs come together in majestic polyphony. 'He has raised up a horn for his people' (v. 14). The word 'horn' means a leader, a strong protector. We do not worship Olaf Stapledon's dispassionate, impassive *Star Maker* (first pub., 1937). This 'horn' is sent by the loving God. We, whose leader is the Christ, our Saviour, we have the fullest reason to join in a praise of God that goes beyond the glories of nature. '[P]raise for all his faithful, for the people of Israel who are close to him. Praise the Lord' (v. 14).

Praise him now.

Gilcomston Prayer Meeting, 5 June 2010.